SACRE CORDON BLEU

Michael Booth is a travel writer and journalist who writes regularly for a variety of newspapers and magazines including the *Independent on Sunday*, Condé Nast *Traveller* and *Mo...* His first book, *Just As Well I'm Leaving: to the Orient with Hans Christian Andersen* was published in 2005 and he is currently working on a book about his family's food adventures in Japan. He lives and cooks in Paris with his wife, Lissen, and two children, Asger and Emil.

By the same author

*Just as Well I'm Leaving: To the Orient with
Hans Christian Andersen*

SACRE CORDON BLEU

What the French know about cooking

Michael Booth

JONATHAN CAPE
LONDON

Published by Jonathan Cape 2008

2 4 6 8 10 9 7 5 3

First published in Great Britain in 2008 by
Jonathan Cape
Random House, 20 Vauxhall Bridge Road,
London SW1V 2SA

www.rbooks.co.uk

Addresses for companies within The Random House Group Limited can be found at:
www.randomhouse.co.uk/offices.htm

The Random House Group Limited Reg. No. 954009

A CIP catalogue record for this book
is available from the British Library

ISBN 9780224077965

The Random House Group Limited makes every effort to ensure that the papers used in its
books are made from trees that have been legally sourced from well-managed and credibly
certified forests. Our paper procurement policy can be found at:
www.rbooks.co.uk/environment

Mixed Sources
Product group from well-managed
forests and other controlled sources
www.fsc.org Cert no. TT-COC-2139
FSC   © 1996 Forest Stewardship Council

Typeset by Palimpsest Book Production Limited, Grangemouth, Stirlingshire
Printed and bound in Great Britain by CPI Mackays, Chatham ME5 8TD

To Lissen

What! perhaps someone will say, another work on cooking? For the past few years the public has been deluged with writings of this sort. I agree. But it is precisely all these works that give birth to this one.

from the preface of Menon's
Le Manuel des Officiers de Bouche (1759)

Chapter 1

Delia Smith was on fire. The flames licked her face but she remained passive, gazing into the middle distance. Even as she began to boil and blister, the familiar, wan smile remained stoically fixed. But soon she was aflame: St Joan of Norwich, blazing, burning, burnt and then ashes. Nearby, Nigella was roaring too, her saucy wit no defence against the orange tongues that tickled her décolletage. Within seconds she was charred beyond recognition.

Jamie Oliver had not quite caught fire. I gave him a poke and sprinkled him with lighter fuel. He flambéed like a crêpe Suzette, and I watched the familiar, fleshy grin curl into a manic leer.

Someone threw Sophie Grigson onto the burning pile and I winced. It was all I could do to stop myself jumping into the flames to save her but my wife, Lissen, sensing my resolve was weakening, put her arm around my shoulders and squeezed tightly. She knew what these people had meant to me; she knew how much pleasure they had given me, how they had enriched my life and kept me occupied. These celebrity chefs had inspired my love of cooking for over a decade, but now they were fuelling the evening's pyrotechnics. Even Sophie must burn.

I lingered for a moment over Rick Stein, recalling some expensive and elaborate seafood experiments as his face bathed in the dancing flames. 'Michael, what is *that*?' asked my sister, pointing at the book in my hands. Lissen followed her gaze: 'Come on, this was your idea. If we are going to do this, we're going to do it properly.' I threw Rick, limply, in the direction of the bonfire: 'On you go!' He only made it to the edge. Lissen picked him up and threw him into the heart of the flames where he ignited briefly, then vanished.

It's true, it had been my idea to end the evening with a cookbook bonfire in the garden. But I had also had two gins and several glasses of wine, so hardly expected anyone to take me seriously. Surely it is at times like this that one's loved ones are supposed to intervene to protect one, not let one set fire to hundreds of pounds' worth of cookery books.

It seems some people have an aversion to television chefs. Several of my friends and family assembled for our farewell dinner that night had thrown themselves into the task with a gusto not seen since Goebbels's book bonfires in Berlin's Opernplatz. I, on the other hand, do not. In fact, over the last decade I have been in thrall to just about every single one of them, from Ken Hom to Keith Floyd, from Delia's *One is Fun*, to the *Two Fat Ladies*. I have watched their shows, caught the repeats on cable, bought the books that accompanied the series and, slowly, methodically, *slavishly* attempted to make just about every recipe. I genuinely believe Jamie Oliver to be some kind of autistic savant genius, for instance, while Delia is single-handedly responsible for weaning the British off soggy greens and Bisto. Rick Stein is the Codfather; and Nigel Slater writes like an angel. I wouldn't be surprised if Nigella really did turn out to be some kind of goddess.

So why the bonfire?

It's a long story. For a full explanation we need to go back to 1981. No, let's do this properly and return to 1972, around about the time I began to eat solids . . .

To say that I was a fussy eater as a child is misleading only in the sense that I didn't actually eat anything much for the first ten or so years of my life, apart from chips and Tunnocks' tea cakes.

Dinnertimes were traumatic, a dark cloud glowering over every day. The meal would usually begin with my mother presenting some beautifully prepared dish, which she had crafted with great love from the best produce she could afford – pedantic care having been taken to remove anything green, or that had bones, or a texture that might conceivably provoke histrionic, repulsed gurning. The rest of the family would then take pains to express their delight, downing fork-fuls with loud praise while I sat there with a gargoyle grimace, claiming either not to be hungry, to feel unwell or, when faced with a dish containing cooked carrots, threatening to hold my breath until I died.

Usually they would go through the ritual of a few well-intentioned attempts to persuade, cajole or, finally, bribe me into eating before we reached the inevitable climax of a full-blown, hair-tearing connip-tion fit on the floor, followed by the inevitable plate of tea cakes in front of *Dallas*, and then bed.

Other than that I survived, like some kind of pre-teen air plant, on bread (white, pre-sliced, un-buttered) and orange squash. But I could not avoid food altogether, particularly away from home. Visits to elderly relatives for Sunday lunch were an especially troubling prospect and invitations to friends' houses for meals took on the air of a royal visit to Tonga as my mother had to pre-approve the menu or forward a long list of 'Michael doesn't likes'. I can recall to this day the throat-tightening horror of being presented with a plate of gammon and cabbage at the home of one schoolfriend, and the hot shame of a half-hour spent pushing it around my plate as the rest of the family wolfed theirs down. If only they'd had a dog.

I didn't have any eating disorders; I wasn't anorexic, I wasn't bulimic, I was simply an insufferable fusspot. I am sure many chil-dren are like this; I just didn't know any of them. My brother and sister both had healthy, normal appetites and more often than not they would hoover up my leftovers, making me feel even more feeble. I gave up going to birthday parties out of mortal fear of shrivelled sausages on sticks and over-buttered cucumber sandwiches. On more than one occasion my mother received a call to come and retrieve her child who was, at that moment, thrashing around on the floor like a stricken octopus having been offered a well-intentioned plate of baked beans. I rarely made it to Pin the Tail on the Donkey, let alone the party bag.

So how does one go from truculent, pre-teen mealtime refusenik, to a food-obsessed, thirty-something glutton (let's not tiptoe around this with terms like gourmet and *gourmand*), who will cross a county after a fresh-caught Dover sole tip-off, and re-mortgage his house for a white truffle?

The year, as I said, was 1981. We were motoring through France on a family holiday with two other families, aiming for a camp site in the Jura. We stopped overnight at a small *auberge* two hours south of Paris and, once precarious roof racks had been secured for the night, headed for the dining room – in my case, resigned to another night of famine.

My sister had spent the weeks leading up to the holiday – my first trip abroad – goading me about French eating habits. They ate frogs, she claimed, and had slugs for breakfast. There were cooked carrots in everything and horse was a speciality. French children ate yoghurt – which, if I understood correctly, was *alive* – for breakfast, and the more a cheese smelt of pensioner's feet, the more highly they esteemed it.

Pre-trip research had revealed that they did not sell tea cakes in France and so I had packed as many boxes in my cardboard suit-case as I could, but, on lifting the lid in my room a little earlier, a devastating scene of marshmallowy carnage had been revealed. Starvation, which I had somehow kept at bay for all these years, now seemed a very real possibility. But then, as we entered the *auberge*'s dining room and were shown to our table, something peculiar began to happen. An alien sensation began in my nostrils, then filtered down to my palate and stomach where it started to stir previously dormant gastric juices. I was actively looking forward to food.

It was unusual enough that our party of six adults and eight children, aged from two to eighteen, was being welcomed so warmly and accommodated by a hurried rearranging of tables and chairs – children were frowned upon in English restaurants in those days, hence, I suppose, the otherwise perplexing rise of the Wimpey Bar – but the notion that I was beginning to salivate at the prospect of slugs' brains and horse doings was perplexing. Had my parents slipped me some new wonder drug as I slept in the car, perhaps the same thing they laced Mr T's milk with in *The A-Team* to get him to fly? Or was I simply dreaming?

We sat down. There was no menu, no choice. I was in the hands of fate, but I felt strangely relaxed, as if in the state of pre-slaughter resignation that becalms cattle at the abattoir. There was sorcery in the air, not just the siren smells of sticky reductions and roasting meats from the kitchen, but a bewitching feeling that I had never experienced in the context of a dining room before. For me, the smell of cooking usually invoked dread and nausea but here in France, in the epicurean epicentre of my gustatory nightmares, my nostrils were atwitch in anticipation, my mouth a Niagara of saliva.

The meal passed in a blur of transcendental sensual ecstasy. There were langoustines to start, unbelievably sweet in a white wine broth; then an entire roasted quail, juicy and tender with a creamy potato gratin and crisp mange tout, followed by runny, ripe cheeses and a crème brûlée that was the very essence of eggy excess. All washed down with bottle after bottle of Orangina (with *real* orange bits floating in the bottom!), and rounded off with a puff on my Uncle Arthur's cigar and a sip of my dad's cognac.

Had I looked up from my plate I would have seen those who knew me staring in dumb disbelief. But I did not look up. I simply ploughed through whatever the waiters put in front of me. This was an unremarkable menu, these were – are – all staples of a good provincial French restaurant, but twenty-five years on, I can still remember every bite.

It would be misleading of me to claim that from that day on I became some kind of teenage Master Chef, to be found pressing my nose up against the windows of Michelin-starred restaurants and reading my mother's Elizabeth David by torchlight under the covers. However, once back home I did at least begin to eat green things. And, as I grew older, more memorable meals out followed, most of them in France, but some in the kind of lacy, provincial French restaurants you used to find in Britain but which are now all estate agents. When I left home and went to university, I had to cook for myself. It dawned on me that, with the help of a cookery book or two, I could do better than the spaghetti and ketchup my friends lived on. I borrowed a Delia from my mother and embarked on a voyage of culinary self-discovery, further encouraged by the revelation that girls liked to eat too.

After university came a couple of abortive careers, until I wound up as a travel writer with a sideline editing guidebooks on foreign cities. My interest in food had by then become an all-consuming passion with hours spent creating the daily evening meal, days spent preparing elaborate dinner parties, and fortunes spent in local butchers and fishmongers, interspersed with occasional rucksack raids on Books for Cooks and bankrupting weekends in the restaurants of Paris. When condensing a city into an 'Insider' guide, an 'Essential' whatever or '48 hours in . . .', I always made sure I bagged the restaurant section and, so, over six years or so I got to eat in some wonderful restaurants.

This further fuelled my obsession but it also rendered unavoidably apparent the gulf between the stuff – rough approximations of the photographs in TV chefs' cookbooks – that emerged from my kitchen and the food that I enjoyed in the restaurants I wrote about. It didn't take too many Michelin-starred experiences for me to realise that following a Delia recipe and knowing how to cook were two very different things. For starters, I grew to realise that recipes are doomed from the start. Supposedly any fool can follow one (unless it's one of Heston Blumenthal's, in which case I need about three days and the patience of a hermit) but the simple, unavoidable truth is RECIPES DON'T WORK. There. I have said it. Someone had to. I realise this places me at odds with a multi-million-pound branch of the publishing industry, but it's true. I would say that around three-quarters of all the recipes I have ever followed in my life have had one or more flaws, whether it's been oven temperatures; missing steps;

cooking times; the order in which ingredients are incorporated; quantities; or even the ingredients themselves. Even when I follow Jamie Oliver recipes to the letter I seem to end up with burnt garlic before I have even begun. My mum has condemned Nigel Slater out of hand on the grounds of a chocolate brownie recipe that refused to work twice. Alistair Little's *Keep it Simple* should, in my view, be outlawed under the Trade Descriptions Act. I've tried Jean-Georges Vongerichten's recipe for spaetzle twice and both times ended up with something that looked like a by-product from the construction industry. And you don't need to spend too much time in foodie Internet chat rooms to discover that many find Nigella's recipes somewhat 'vague'. I will probably find myself battered to death with a spatula in a dark restaurant back alley for saying this, but have you ever tried to follow an Elizabeth David recipe? I find them infuriating! And all of this goes double for books about baking, which is a discipline notorious for requiring precise measurements and instructions, and is far more susceptible to the environment you are working in. Following a recipe is like building a house without adequate foundations, architectural plans or professional builders. In the dark.

When you think about it, the failings of recipe books are inevitable. It is not the writers' fault. In fact, I do believe that most cookbooks are written with the best intentions at heart (and in all of the above cases, I am sure they are), usually by highly skilled cooks, and their recipes are properly tested, but how can Delia or Jamie or Heston possibly know the exact condition, size, ripeness, tenderness or colour of the ingredients you will be using? How can they know how efficient your oven is or how cold your fridge is? How can they know how thick your frying pan is, or the quality of meat you are using? How does Delia know that you should leave tomatoes in boiling water for a minute, as she suggests, to shed their skins – what if they are particularly ripe? You'll be left with a mush. How do they know the temperature of your kitchen, or whether you like to cook with a window open, that your Kenwood has seen better days and doesn't quite whisk with the gusto it once had, or that your grill is so caked in grime that it can barely muster half the heat it ought to?

And these are merely the issues that plague the well-written, thoroughly tested recipe books. What about all those hastily cobbled together recipes in the back of women's magazines and the Sunday supplements, or all those dodgy postings on the Internet, on blogs and notice boards that many home cooks have started to use more and more? You really have to have your wits about you if you venture into cyberspace for cooking instructions.

Some times recipes do work, of course, but those occasions are, I suspect, more to do with a blessed alignment of the culinary planets than any rigorous intent on the part of the cookbook writer. But even when recipes do work, cookbooks rarely, if ever, *empower* you to cook. It took me years of harrowing kitchen failures to realise this, but a *proper* cook knows techniques rather than formulas; a proper cook can look at a plate of raw ingredients and conjure an infinite repertoire of dishes. A proper cook, I eventually convinced myself, needs just one cookery book: Auguste Escoffier's *Ma Cuisine*.

Though he died in 1935, Escoffier is still remembered as the 'king of chefs and the chef of kings', and chefs regard him as the culinary oracle. I bought a copy of *Ma Cuisine*, the bible of classical French cooking, and had a look at some of the recipes. A short while later, disorientated and confused, I carefully placed the book on the shelf in the kitchen, next to my copy of *Pukka Tukka*. I would return periodically to *Ma Cuisine*, cautiously, as if it were an unexploded bomb, open it at a random page and within minutes feel a piercing migraine coming on. It was one thing, it seemed, to be able to whip up monkfish wrapped in prosciutto *à la* Jamie or even one of Delia's twice-baked soufflés, but quite another to assemble even the simplest of Escoffier's dishes. Take *foie de veau sauté à la bordelaise*: for this 'simple' calves' liver with tomato sauce there are no fewer than nine cross references to other recipes that make up its constituent parts, many with their own cross references to other constituent recipes, and all involving roasting bones, reducing stocks, trussing, *demi-glace* this, *timbales* of that and quite possibly *suédoise* of the other. Maddening, daunting and, to my eyes, impossible. They were recipes, but not as I understood the concept.

For a while I simply lived with this new found insight into my culinary ignorance, assimilating it together with all the rest of my limitations, like being rubbish at DIY and anagrams. But food is so much more important than shelving and my amateurishness gnawed away at me every time I reached for Delia. The praise of dinner guests, who genuinely believed I was a decent cook, rang hollow. I wasn't a decent cook, I was a worthless fraud. A foodie-by-numbers, join-the-dots chef merely able to follow a few simple instructions to produce dishes that were probably being served at middle-class dinner tables from Oslo to Oxford to Ohio, and everywhere else that had fallen under the tyrannical yoke of the TV chef.

Like many foodies weaned on TV chefs, I had grown bored with their insistence that food be fast, easy and cheap to make. I wanted more from my cooking – I didn't want simple and quick, I wanted complex and slow. I was tired of throwing a tray of hastily tossed fish and herbs in the oven for fifteen minutes; tired of salads that took ten minutes to prepare; tired of couscous and pasta; bored with 'tear it up and bung it in' cooking. It seemed to me that all the TV food shows were aimed at people who didn't like to cook. But what about those of us who were willing to put in the hours?

A couple more years passed with many more epiphanies in great restaurants. What were the secrets of this alchemy that had me happily handing out wads of notes for the briefest of sensations? Why couldn't I do these things at home? Why did my wine reductions always taste of vinegar no matter how hard I stared at them while they were simmering, and why did my foie gras disintegrate if I so much as let it glimpse a frying pan? How could I possibly pass judgement on the work of top chefs from a position of such indefensible ignorance?

The word 'indefensible' is a clue. It's all very well for Gordon Ramsay to lambast another chef's cauliflower soup, or for Ian

McKellen to pour scorn on someone else's Iago, but how could I summon the gall to pronounce upon the technique of a professional chef working in a Michelin-starred kitchen?

By learning to become a professional chef myself, and then by going to work in a Michelin-starred kitchen, that's how.

Over a period of a couple of months a plan began to form. I would quit my non-existent job; we would cash in our savings; sell the car, the house and my set of Jamie Oliver non-stick frying pans (which always seemed to boil rather than fry my food); and move to Paris where I would learn to cook like a professional. As plans go it was reckless, short-sighted, high risk and virtually guaranteed to end in catastrophe. Thinking about it, perhaps 'plan' was too strong a word. I did some research, talked to some chefs and food writers I knew, and found out that the best place to do this was the *Cordon Bleu* cookery school, the world-renowned bastion of classical French cooking. The school had developed from a cookery magazine founded in Paris in 1895 and is named after the blue ribbon from which the sixteenth-century knights of the Order of the Holy Spirit suspended the distinctive cross that symbolised their order. More potent, as far as I was concerned, was the fact that the school has a direct link with Escoffier, via Henri-Paul Pellaprat, the author of *L'Art Culinaire Moderne*, who taught there for thirty-two years and worked with Escoffier to codify French cuisine in a form that remains relevant to this day. One could even say that Le Cordon Bleu invented the TV cookery format we know and love with chefs demonstrating techniques and dishes to an audience of enthusiasts: the first demo being held in rooms close to the Palais Royal in January 1896. Other claims to fame include teaching American food icons Julia Child and Dione Lucas to cook, not to mention Jacques Chirac and Dustin Hoffman. The school also invented Coronation Chicken for the banquet to mark the coronation of Queen Elizabeth II.

There are now twenty-five *Cordon Bleu* schools around the world, but the Culinary Arts Programme at the Paris school on *rue Léon Delhomme* in the fifteenth arrondissement remains the flagship course. The *Cuisine Diplôme Le Cordon Bleu* would be my goal. Over nine months, in exchange for a sum of money about which I am still in denial, the school promises to turn students into classical French chefs, fully versed in the various techniques of French cookery and able to create dishes from scratch, and to present them to a professional standard.

This was only the first part of my master plan. Other than being able to prepare impressively complex dinners for friends, there seemed little point in going to all the trouble and expense of learning how to cook to a professional standard without at least a trial run of my skills. My aim, after graduating (should I make it that far), was to go to work in a top Parisian restaurant – ideally one with a Michelin star which, though a flawed way to judge a restaurant, is still a fair indication of a quality kitchen. This, and only this, would offer a true test of my skills, and banish my critic's guilt for ever. And, of course, there was always the possibility that it might lead me to an entirely new career . . .

Though you wouldn't guess it from her appearance, my wife Lissen can eat and drink me under the table. I suspect this has something to do with her Viking genes (she is Danish). Her hearty appetite, as well as her love of Paris would, I hoped, persuade her to go along with this reckless plan. And I was right. She said yes in a heartbeat.

I hurled Gary Rhodes into the fire and Lissen threw on the last of the hundreds of recipes I had torn from the pages of the Sunday supplements over the years. Only one book, *Ma Cuisine*, remained and, back inside the house, as the others began to clean up the mess from the dinner I had made earlier, I placed it in the last of the removal boxes.

Tomorrow we would leave for Paris and a new home, lifestyle and perhaps even career. My plans included not just learning to cook, but also improving my French and exploring the culinary temptations of

Paris – finding the best restaurants and markets, the finest bakers, butchers and *chocolatiers*. It was as noble a way of jeopardising the security and well-being of my family as I could think of.

Chapter 2

In Paris one is always reminded of being a foreigner.

Roman Polanski

Having cleared away the last flakes of singed cookery book from the patio, packed the last cuddly toy in the last straining suitcase and bidden an anxious farewell to the final boxes for storage, Lissen, Asger, aged four, and Emil, sixteen months, and I set off for France. Asger would be starting at a new school with a new language; Lissen would be adjusting to a life away from her friends and network; and Emil would have a whole host of new, well-meaning elderly ladies to alarm with his tiger impression while out shopping.

A couple of months earlier, Lissen and I had spent two days in Paris trying to find a new home and a school for Asger. The former had turned out to be a classic chicken and egg situation in which the chickens were required to offer evidence of nationality, marriage, regular income and grandparents' debt profiles, while the eggs kept losing all the paperwork. In short, to get an apartment, we needed to have a resident's bank account and to get a resident's bank account . . . you're ahead of me. Other people's bureaucratic nightmares are never terribly interesting, so I will spare you the details of what became a protracted campaign, except to say that, if my life depended on it, given the chance, I would have chosen to solve the Gordian knot blindfolded, using a barge pole held between my teeth, rather than deal with the demands of the BNP Paribas.

Happily, Lissen has an extraordinary knack of finding choice apartments. Wherever we have moved, within a few days she has been able to source — by sheer willpower, I think — a spacious, quiet, practical place with the view everyone wants, for a peppercorn rent. Despite having seen her do this on four separate occasions during our time together, I still wasn't taking anything for granted. I'd heard about the virtual impossibility of finding a place to live in Paris, with all those stories of queues of prospective tenants in their best suits with bulging files containing a lifetime's paperwork beneath their arms, picketing apartments barely fit for cattle. So I had arranged for us to see fifteen apartments in five different arrondissements within forty-eight hours, planning our schedule down to the minute, including lengthy lunch breaks, breaks for snacks and dinner reservations. Lissen, meanwhile, flicked casually through *Le Figaro*, found an ad that sounded interesting, and left a message on the estate agent's answerphone.

Fifteen stables later we were heading back to our hotel room prior to flying home early the next morning, when Lissen's phone rang. It was the agent, a Madame Raffarin, responding to her message. Were we interested in viewing the apartment on Avenue Marceau? The only other remotely habitable apartment we had seen had been one overlooking the railway lines behind Gare Saint-Lazare with an overpowering fragrance of rancid fat, traumatic stains in the bath and a transvestite hooker stationed outside the front door. So, interested we were, particularly when we discovered that Avenue Marceau is one of the spokes that radiate from the Arc de Triomphe – the next one, clockwise, from the Champs-Elysées in fact.

It turned out to be a classic, broad, Hausmannian avenue leading down to the river, the camouflaged trunks of its serried plane trees screening dignified *fin de siècle*, six-storey apartment blocks. It makes up one side of the so-called 'golden triangle' of Paris, which together with the Champs-Elysées and Avenue Montaigne corrals most of France's top fashion houses. As with much of central Paris, these apartments were built in the late-nineteenth century from that soft, warm, white limestone which ranges in subtle shades from 'uncooked dough' to 'well-cooked biscuit' – a magical masonry that seems to

14

soak up light during the day, suffusing the city with an bewitching glow at dawn and dusk.

I knew that a handful of the world's finest restaurants lay within walking distance; restaurants whose kitchens were run, if not under the constant supervision, then at least under the periodic monitoring eye of some of the most accomplished and esteemed chefs of the past half century – such as Alain Ducasse, the first man ever to have three triple Michelin-starred restaurants to his name; Joël Robuchon, one of the pioneers of nouvelle cuisine and widely considered the greatest of all French chefs; and the molecular magician, Pierre Gagnaire. There was the small matter of an average bill of two hundred euro per person for the privilege of eating their food, but I would worry about that another day.

As we strode up the avenue to our appointment I caught tanta-lising glimpses of *chocolatiers*, *boucheries* and *boulangers* in side streets, as well as another brief, equally auspicious sighting: Roman Polanski's impressively thick, greying, coiffed hair disappearing into a doorway (he lives on nearby Avenue Montaigne – the street with the highest density of trout-pout plastic surgery victims and perfumed Pekinese in the world).

Excitement turned to embarrassing levels of fawning desperation on my part – Lissen, being more used to this kind of thing, kept relatively cool – as Madame Raffarin, tall, grey-haired and trussed tight in a gold-buttoned Chanel jacket, showed us in through the front door of the apartment block and into a lavish marble entrance hall. Passing a statue of Aphrodite in an alcove just in front of the concierge's ground-floor residence (a concierge!), we crammed into a three-person lift for a clanking ride to the third floor. There, the lift opened onto a deep, wine-red carpet, before wide, wooden doors (actually metal, painted to look like wood) filleted with metal lattice grills. Madame Raffarin unlocked the doors and stood aside.

It required just a glance at the dark, aged parquet flooring, gilded mirrors, high, stuccoed ceilings, and antique furniture for us to realise that this was the fantasy Parisian apartment we had never dared imagine we might find. Lissen's shamanistic real-estate mojo had provided for us again.

We were told the apartment belonged to a Madame de Laurent (the 'de' prefix being a telltale of the French nobility). Many of her family's *objets* and paintings remained. The dining room was lined with shelves of dusty antique books. In the living room hung a vast oil painting of a sun-dappled country estate, with a bay-windowed chateau in the background and, presumably, de Laurent's ancestors – the women dressed in voluminous crinolines, the men in top hats – frolicking in the foreground. Opposite was a print, dated 1783, of a fruity, bewigged gentleman – the Comte de Saint-Germain, a *Célèbre Alchimiste*, according to the inscription below. Each room had a marble fireplace. The Persian rugs and velvet curtains were faded and threadbare in parts and the place clearly hadn't seen a lick of paint since de Gaulle was in office, but this only served to make it less of a museum and more of a potential family home.

Slightly less impressive was the kitchen which, typically of apartments like this, was stark and stuck at the end of a corridor. That said, given the general standard of French domestic kitchens this one was a veritable showroom. Most kitchens I've seen in France have been museum pieces, with Formica worktops, *Abigail's Party*-era decor and patterned linoleum floors. I'd seen better equipped kitchens in camper vans. Based on this discovery I had developed a theory about the state of a nation's kitchens being inversely related to the quality of their cuisine. America and Britain have among the least enviable culinary traditions in the world, despite, or perhaps as a result of, lavishing extraordinary amounts of money and attention on their kitchens. Meanwhile, the domestic kitchens I have seen in, say, Thailand, Italy and France, have often been little more than makeshift galleys. Nevertheless, in these unprepossessing environments have flourished three of the world's greatest cuisines. There are exceptions – Eskimos have both dire cooking facilities and a particularly unappealing cuisine (including, as I understand it, one dish in which they bury a dead seal and leave it to fester before eating it) – but I still hold it to be broadly true that, while we coo over the ice-making function of our Smeg fridges and our matching lipstick-red Kitchenaid mixer, the French just get on with making really good food.

At least this kitchen was reasonably well equipped. The day before, we had seen one with just a two-ring hob, no oven and two heavily tarnished SNCF mugs. Evidence that a previous resident had been a keen cook included a ricer – an implement resembling a makeshift hurdy gurdy – and a mandolin, for the thin slicing of fingertips. A definite sign, I felt, that the apartment should be ours.

But it was not our apartment quite yet.

Lissen and I walked around in silence, passing surreptitious, wide-eyed glances, and trying not to look in any way deviant. To calm down I walked over to the living-room window to check out the view. I could clearly see the top half of the Eiffel Tower to the left; to the right was the Arc de Triomphe; while more significantly, across the street below I spied a grand-looking *boulangerie* and *chocolatier*. I squeaked involuntarily and beckoned Lissen over. She followed the direction of my furious nodding, raised her eyebrows slightly, and then turned back to Madame Raffarin who was asking us something about the rent and the terms.

Were we smokers? What? *Us?* Did we play any musical instruments? Never! We of course had documentary evidence of regular income totalling three times the rent? Um. And references from previous landlords, as well as a letter from our employers and bank verifying we were who we said we were? Erm. And we had no problem blocking out a year's rent in advance as a *caution* (a uniquely Draconian form of housing deposit locked into an independent bank account for the duration of the lease)? Ah, that. *Well* . . .

We, of course, had none of this.

But my mind was already racing ahead to visions of warm croissants for breakfast, fresh cream cakes at teatime and intermittent *flans nature* (addictive vanilla custard tarts, served in slices so thick and heavy you can literally feel them bringing your metabolism to a grinding halt as you digest them) throughout the day. I saw glamorous, candle-lit soirées where I offered witty bon mots and elaborate canapés to sophisticated Parisian women in slinky cocktail dresses while their husbands scowled jealously. Then I thought a bit more about the cakes.

I wandered out into the hallway connecting to the bedrooms and bathroom where, hanging on the wall, was a series of fourteen sombre prints depicting the death and funeral of Napoleon. As an omen for a prospective English tenant did this cancel out the ricer? In the master bedroom there was a nineteenth-century oil painting of a North African man, replete with fez and gold brocade tunic, fighting to control a rearing, white stallion beneath a stormy sky. The horse's nostrils were flared in rage as its front legs pawed the air. I imagined a similar reaction from Madame Raffarin once she discovered we were hopelessly out of our depth, but returned to the living room to find Lissen explaining our situation and pledging to have the necessary paperwork on her desk within three days.

The demands, not to mention the rent, were so beyond our means that they entered the realm of the ridiculous (though, the truth was, by Paris standards it was a fair price). Perhaps I could sell some stories while I was in Paris; Lissen, who is a singer, might get some more gigs; or, failing that, we could send Asger and Emil down to the corner of the Champs-Elysées to perform their – actually quite accomplished – rendition of the 'Me Ol' Bamboo' routine, from *Chitty Chitty Bang Bang.*

The next two weeks were especially tense as we struggled to negotiate our way through a quagmire of paperwork and juggle our finances. But then, suddenly, the lines of communication went dead. Madame Raffarin stopped replying to emails, every time we phoned we got her voicemail; faxes remained unanswered. We feared the worst, discussed those scenarios in detail (maybe the transvestite prostitute would be up for a bit of babysitting?), and did a great deal of deep sighing while gazing into the middle distance. We were due to move to Paris within two weeks.

Then, as if emerging from a long tunnel, Madame Raffarin's mobile came back into service. She had been on holiday but neglected to tell anyone. Yes, everything with the apartment was fine; she would send the contracts the same day. A week later we were in, our few possessions unpacked and distributed where their presence would cause the least offence to the rest of the furniture.

We hit the streets of Paris early the next bright, hot August day, intent on acquainting ourselves with our neighbourhood and neighbours . . . only to discover that there were no neighbours, and the neighbourhood was closed for business. The only signs of life were the police guards outside the Spanish embassy next door. The whole of Paris, particularly those who live in the eighth and sixteenth arrondissements on whose borders we lived, were on holiday for the entire month, as is the case every August in Paris. It was as if we had turned up early for a party only to find that the hosts hadn't even returned from shopping for Pringles and plastic beakers.

Our apartment building was empty, too, but for the concierge, Madame Bauvais, a short, smiley, dark haired woman in her early fifties with a penchant for floral print blouses, A-line skirts and with her hair permanently in curlers. She took an instant liking to Asger and Emil's chubby cheeks and, in a lengthy speech of which we understood but a fraction, welcomed us to Paris.

Chapter 3

The gourmand has only a belly, whereas the gastronome has a brain.

Pierre Larousse

In the first couple of weeks we revisited Paris' greatest hits: the Louvre, the Rodin Museum, the Sacré Coeur, Notre-Dame and so on. Unfortunately these sightseeing trips followed a pattern determined more by child wrangling requirements than gourmet exploration. While Lissen prepared the kids to go out, I would bury myself in guidebooks trying to find a good restaurant for lunch. Once at the museum, or wherever, we would spend about half an hour looking at stuff before I would start to get fidgety, worrying that, as we hadn't made a reservation, the restaurant would be full. Something else would then catch Lissen's eye and we would spend another half an hour looking at more stuff before I finally persuaded her to leave. But then, more torment, as the kids would need to run around and let off steam which meant that when we finally arrived at the cosy-looking bistro it would be packed with greedy, smug locals. I would stand grimacing anxiously in the open doorway just long enough to catch a whiff of roasting meats and simmering sauces and glimpse a dessert cabinet resplendent with glossy chocolate tarts and float-away peach soufflés. We would usually end up seated on a torn vinyl banquette, beneath plastic plants, in some smoky, sparsely populated brasserie choosing from a menu that would, over the next couple of weeks, become drearily familiar — *salad niçoise, confit de canard* or *steak au poivre* and *tarte tatin* — while a row of paint-stained workmen stood eyeing us suspiciously from the bar. Worst of all, it usually ended up costing virtually the same as the end-of-the rainbow bistro.

21

This was not a good start. It was, it seemed, remarkably easy to eat badly in Paris. The first lesson, then, was this: good food required good planning.

At least the markets were open to all. Our local turned out to be the Wednesday and Saturday morning market on Avenue President Wilson at the bottom of Avenue Marceau. Large supermarkets are banned from central Paris, which can be infuriating if you are in a hurry. But for me a good French market is Disneyland, the Louvre, a Caribbean beach and a bungee jump all wrapped up in one: pleasure, art, relaxation and stimulation. From the first stall, Lorenzo's, the best fish stall in Paris, its icy scree resplendent with writhing crabs, hillocks of crusty oysters and alien sea urchins; on past the bounteous fruit and vegetable stalls; the compelling viscera of the butchers' glass cabinets; acres of cheeses, flowers and breads; until I eventually emerged back into daylight an hour later, the outside world was banished. I was transported. This, I thought to myself, reflecting on years of shopping in English and Danish supermarkets, must be how early-eighteenth-century explorers felt when they finally arrived at some south Pacific island after months at sea with nothing but maggoty ship's biscuits and their own urine for sustenance.

But a good French market can be overwhelming the first few times you visit. Why are there crowds by one vegetable stall, yet another is deserted? Which fish stall is the freshest, and can their fish really be this expensive? And what on earth is that grey, spongy stuff in the butcher's cabinet? Slowly, through experience and, later, the tutoring of experts, I began to learn a few of the tricks of a successful trip. The first rule I figured out for myself early on, which was, to get the best service, to get the personal recommendations about which pâté to taste or what cheese is in season, or the odd bunch of complimentary parsley (or on one occasion a whole, ghostly white calf's foot), I had to patronise no more than a handful of stall-holders – one from each category of fish, fowl, meat, veg, fruit and dairy, plus the Lebanese stall that sold a terrific sharp, fresh white bean salsa. (I soon learned never to buy bread from the market as it was not as fresh as the *boulanger*'s). It was no good skipping from one stall to another picking up a head of broccoli here, a punnet of strawberries there, as if in the opening titles of a Mary Tyler Moore sitcom. If you want to be treated with any respect you need to demonstrate your loyalty to specific stallholders, dropping ten or twenty euro every week with the same people.

A good place to start was Jöel Thiebault's vegetable stall, also reputedly the best in Paris, where they sell ancient varieties of carrots in various, non-orange colours; gnarled, chunky tomatoes as big as grapefruit; rainbow-coloured turnips; and purple broccoli. Thiebault's family has sold vegetables grown on its farm in Carrières-sur-Seine here since 1873 and its staff, each of whom has the looks of a movie star, have perfected the art of ignoring customers, confident that Thiebault's vegetables are so renowned – he is named on the menus of many of the restaurants he supplies – that they will endure an eternity to buy them.

It took time for the stallholders to get to know me. In fact, it was about a month before they acknowledged my existence at all and several times I petulantly walked away from stalls that ignored me (spiting only myself – French stallholders, like the shopkeepers, aren't overly troubled by mundane rituals of commerce such as the exchange of money). The first few times I attempted to buy something I would stand in line; be ignored as regulars were dealt with before me; until, finally the stallholder allowed me to catch his eye for a moment. I would launch into a carefully rehearsed request, in French, closing my eyes in order to concentrate better, only to open them and find the stallholder had been distracted by a passing acquaintance. When he returned I was forced to repeat my request. This was my first encounter with the red-faced man with the spectacular comb-over and gruesomely stained apron, whom I now like to think of as 'my chicken man'.

Peeved at not having been taken for a serious shopper, instead of pointing at his cheapest chickens, I pointed to the ones from Bresse. Bresse chickens are generally held to be the finest in France, quite possibly the world. These elegant, white-feathered, blue-legged birds are the only fowl to carry the French food quality mark, the *Appellation d'Origine Controlée* (AOC). They are raised under strict quality controls – corn fed, and free to roam the lush local grass-land in Bourg-en-Bresse close to the Jura Mountains in eastern France. Most supermarket chickens are killed at around six weeks but Bresse chickens are allowed to roam free for sixteen weeks before being dispatched. As a result, their meat, though tougher than a battery chicken's, is firm and dark and much more tasty. The nineteenth-century French gastronome Jean-Anthelme Brillat-Savarin called them 'the queen of poultry and the poultry of kings'. Like Thiebault's vegetables, Bresse chickens are mentioned by name on some of the finest menus in the world; they are the divas of the chicken world. Needless to say, they cost a packet. Right, I thought, this'll show him I'm not some fly-by-night tourist (though what a tourist would be doing with a raw chicken is a moot point). Rather satisfyingly Chicken Man actually did a double take, raising his chin slightly in the air and narrowing his eyes doubtfully. Was I sure I wanted this one? Yes, quite sure, thank you.

It was over twenty euro. That'll teach him! I marched triumphantly up Avenue Marceau with my prize; ruined it in the oven that evening (Bresse chickens are better gently poached, I later discovered); and had to promise never, *ever* to spend that much money on a chicken again.

Blowing the cost of a decent bistro lunch on a bird is just one of numerous rash purchases I felt compelled to make to gain the respect of the Avenue President Wilson stallholders. Others included an entire, fresh, vacuum-packed duck liver that, at the time, I hadn't the faintest clue what to do with; a cheese that was borderline toxic and necessi-tated a full-blown fridge clear-out after it had gone; and a root vegetable that I still have yet to identify. But gradually I perceived a change. At my fruit stall, when I chose a melon and passed it to the stallholder, he asked me when I planned to eat it. 'The weekend,' I replied. He sniffed the melon, squeezed it, shook his head and swapped it for another. I knew that, likewise, there were degrees of ripeness for Camembert, but I was still taken aback by the cheese woman's careful selection of one 'for next week'. She must have inspected about half a dozen before deciding on the optimum example, not just squeezing them, but kneading them with the serious intent of a reflexologist probing for a wonky metatarsal. The acceptance of the President Wilson stallholders, signalled by a smile, or even a jokey admonishment when I walked past without buying something, felt like a personal endorsement of my shopping discernment.

I appreciate the cheek of adding recipes in something trumpeting itself as an antidote to the tyranny of cookery books but these are all very free-form recipes, more suggestions really – and you are of course free to add or subtract ingredients. In many later instances the recipes in this book are a good way of demonstrating a technique I've learned that you might find interesting (though not in this case, as it requires no technique at all).

Between arriving in Paris and the start of my education I had no culinary guidance whatsoever. I grew desperate and invented this vegetable bake after one of my early scattergun market splurges. I think I was in a stage of Jamie Oliver withdrawal or something, so it is a bit of a mess (the chefs at Le Cordon Bleu would be appalled), but it's a great lunch or weekday supper to have when no one's looking.

Marceau Market Melange

Ingredients (Serves 4)

Some oil – olive, peanut, sunflower, doesn't really matter

1 aubergine, cut into slices about the same thickness as a paperback of *The Old Man and the Sea*

1 fennel bulb, sliced about a bit. You're supposed to peel the stringy bits, but I never do

Some garlic cloves (optional)

1 or 2 onions (or a few shallots), each sliced into bite-sized wedges

Thyme and rosemary (dried is as good, if not better in this instance, than fresh)

About 6 tomatoes. First remove their cores with a paring knife, then remove the skin by scoring a cross on their underside, placing them in boiling water, counting to ten or so (longer if they are less ripe – watch for the skins to start to peel), cooling them immediately in cold – preferably iced – water, and then peeling. You then de-seed them simply by halving the tomatoes horizontally (not to be pedantic, but I later learned that it doesn't work if you halve them top to bottom as some of the seed cells will remain intact), and then squeeze them as you would lemon halves. Then quarter into 'petals

Some slices of Bayonne or Parma or any thin-sliced, air-dried ham

Some crumbly goat's cheese and/or mozzarella

Brush the oil over the bottom and sides of a baking dish. Place the aubergine slices over the bottom, stuffing the fennel, whole garlic cloves still in their paper shirts and onion wedges in between, drizzle over a little more oil, toss and season. Place in a preheated oven at about 180°C and cook for about twenty-five minutes or so, until the aubergines begin to soften. Next sprinkle over the herbs – if fresh the rosemary chopped as finely as you can be bothered – and layer on the tomato pieces. Cook for another ten minutes or so, until the tomatoes relax. Their juices will soak down through the herbs, infusing nicely into the vegetables. Then, tear the ham into pieces and layer it over the tomato petals and crumble the goat's cheese over the top (or slice and layer on the mozzarella, or both if you like), then place the dish back in the oven for a few minutes. Some guests suggested that I sprinkle some grated parmesan over the top at this point, but I think that's too much – the ham is salty enough. The lucky ones with the garlic cloves get to press their sweet pulp out with a fork and mix it in with the rest of the dish. Serve with crusty bread and a hearty Côtes du Rhone – or anything alcoholic you might have in the house.

Knowing that Paris was now our home somehow changed how we felt about it. This was not the smug snobbery of, 'actually, we live here' – our lamentable French undermined any claims to native airs – it was more that we didn't have to retreat to a hotel room at dusk like all the other visitors, but returned to our own place. We may not have had a trouser press and chocolates on our pillows at night, but we could bring takeaway food home without having to smuggle it past reception and no one was going to rifle through our smalls when we were out. Despite the grandeur and the gilding, Madame de Laurent's apartment soon felt like our home; all it took were a few toys scattered about the place, some coats in the hall and, of course, the smell of cooking.

Or rather burning as, bereft of instruction from my beloved cookery books, I was way off piste, out of control and hurtling, skis wide apart, for the nearest tree stump. An attempted roast leg of lamb ended up looking like a caveman's weapon of choice; several key ingredients forgotten from a stew rendered it fit only for land-fill; and a Thai curry was so spicy it made our eyes water at twenty paces. Without Nigella to guide me, I could barely boil an egg. It was clear that, instead of the capable cook I held myself to be, prime material for Le Cordon Bleu to burnish into a new culinary star, I would be starting almost entirely from scratch.

The thirty-first of August, my first day at school, could not come soon enough.

Chapter 4

Listen to me with attention, then, and learn, so that you will have
no more reason to blush for your creations.

Brillat-Savarin

Before leaving for school that first morning there were a couple of
boxes to take down to the street in time for the daily refuse collec-
tion. These were the last of our packing boxes and, as they wouldn't
fit in the communal wheelie bin, I left them on the pavement. By
the time I had returned to the apartment Lissen was standing by the
living-room window. 'Come and look at this!' she said. Down below,
the armed police who stood twenty-four hour guard over the diplo-
mats next door had walked over to the boxes. One was talking into
his walkie-talkie. They looked agitated. 'My god, they think it's a
bomb!' I cried, unsure whether to run downstairs and explain, or
just sit tight and pretend it would all go away, which often helps.

Five minutes later, another vanload of police arrived, threw a
cordon around the boxes and began photographing them. As I
left the building a little later – my face fixed in an expression of
mildly bemused concern – they were poking the top box with a long,
telescopic stick.

Though the fifteenth arrondissement is one of Paris' larger districts
it is also its dullest by quite a margin; there are no landmarks, no
museums and no interesting shopping streets of any note here. The
Eiffel Tower looms majestically from its home in the glamorous
neighbouring seventh, but few tourists venture this far south other
than to stay in its cheap hotels or pass through on their way to an

exhibition at the halls of the Porte de Versailles. The fifteenth is where Parisians come to breed. But, it is here, in rue Leon Delhomme – a quiet, residential side street – that the flame of one of France's most cherished and revered traditions is lovingly tended.

I arrived for my first day at the premises of Le Cordon Bleu just after eight in the morning to find a lengthy queue of new students standing on the pavement in front of a rather plain, modern concrete building. A couple of smaller groups of students in chef's whites, dogtooth check trousers and sling-back clogs stood to one side, smoking and eyeing us with disdain. I tagged on the end of the line.

As I waited I couldn't help overhearing the man behind me talking about his cheffing experience. 'Yeah, I don't really know why I'm coming here,' he was saying to two Asian girls also in the queue. 'I've been working in a restaurant where I live for half a year. They put me on the service line after a day. I think I probably know a lot of this stuff, but, you know . . .' He shrugged as if to say, 'What the hey, it's only a few thousand euro, maybe they can teach me *some-thing*'. I turned round to face them. 'Hi, I'm Michael. Where are you from?' I asked. The man was shorter then me, podgy, with a long, black ponytail; a goatee beard and a gold earstud in his left ear. He was dressed in black. I didn't know it then, of course, but this man would become my nemesis.

'Texas,' the man – his name was Paul – replied and, saying nothing more, turned to face his female companions and continued talking to them. My first attempt at forging a new friendship was firmly rebuffed, but I was determined not to give up. I turned to the woman in front of me with the cascading, Pre-Raphaelite hair. I introduced myself and this time the greeting was as warm as Paul's had been frosty: 'Hi, I'm Tessa!'

I'd defy anyone not to like Tessa who, as we stood waiting, explained that she was a former cheese steward from one of New York's top bistros. Tessa was bubbling with enthusiasm and had the ceaseless curiosity that characterises the true foodie. Why was I here? What did I want to do after I was finished? she asked. Tessa had not long graduated from university where her thesis for her International Studies degree had been in food and its role in international politics. She had a dream of becoming a food journalist and had saved for five years to come to Le Cordon Bleu. She had cashed in her life savings, loaned herself up to the max on credit cards to pay for the course, and was looking for part-time jobs to pay her way – bar work, babysitting, tutoring, anything – during her time in Paris.

We chatted some more before being greeted by the school's PR director. As Tessa signed in, a fishmonger's van pulled up. You and I are the same, I thought to myself as I watched the driver unloading trays of fresh flat fish. We are both raw material submitting ourselves – you, admittedly, against your will, I, following significant financial outlay – to the guiding hand of the world's greatest culinary educators. It is rare that I empathise with dead flounder, and clearly a little weird, so I stopped and went inside.

The school hasn't always been here on rue Leon Delhomme. In fact, Le Cordon Bleu hasn't always been a school. It began, as I've said, in 1895 as a weekly food magazine, *La Cuisiniére Cordon Bleu*, run by journalist Martha Distel. For a time it was the periodical of record for the greatest cuisine in the world, helping to define techniques, recipes and conventions that are still followed today. The most renowned chefs of the time wrote for *La Cuisiniére Cordon Bleu* and, within a year of it starting, the magazine had begun organising practical demonstrations. The Cordon Bleu magazine folded in the 1960s, but the school continued, growing steadily in stature and reputation. By 1905 the name of Le Cordon Bleu had spread around the world. It welcomed its first Japanese student that year and was already the preferred choice for would-be chefs from across Europe. The school survived both wars, spawned a sister school, *L'Ecole du Petit Cordon Bleu*, in London, and went on to launch a host of star chefs upon the world.

The current building was purpose built for Le Cordon Bleu, opening in 1985 after the school had been bought by André J. Cointreau, head of the Cointreau liqueur family (which also owns

Remy Martin cognac). Cointreau dragged the school out of the 1950s and into the modern era, not just moving it to new premises, but by hiring respected and experienced cuisine and patisserie chefs, and expanding the business globally. During the seventies the school gained a reputation as the kind of place posh girls came to during the year between finishing school and being married off to some landed inbred in order to continue the inbreeding programme upon which the British and French aristocracy depends. They were often joined by their mothers, who had nothing else better to do or, since the divorce and loss of staff following their own inbred husband's philandering, had been forced to learn a little more about what went on 'below stairs'.

Cointreau swept through with a professional broom. He introduced a range of Cordon Bleu tableware, kitchen equipment and cookery books, and turned the brand into a corporate operation. The school began offering short courses – named 'Sabrina' courses after the 1954 Audrey Hepburn film, in which she learns to make an omelette at the school – as well as wine and even flower arranging courses. He bought the London Cordon Bleu school in Marylebone, which up until then had operated independently, and, during the 1990s, opened schools in Japan, Canada and Australia. Today Le Cordon Bleu is a globally recognised brand, with twelve schools in ten countries – Australia, Mexico, the US, France, the UK, Brazil, South Korea, Japan, Canada and Peru. It has almost single-handedly created and defined the phenomenon of cooking schools which straddle the worlds of the professional and the amateur kitchen.

Naturally, the Paris school is the mother lode, the custodian of a 500-year-old culinary tradition. Students from over fifty countries travel here to learn the mysterious and often arcane techniques of haute cuisine – many of them, like Tessa, making huge sacrifices in order to do so. Some of them could have attended a school in their own country but choose to learn how to cook in France. For them the Paris Cordon Bleu is the no-compromise option to an all-or-nothing dedication to food. Having decided to drink from the fountain of French culinary knowledge, they chose to drink at the source.

In all there were fifty-five new students starting with me on the Basic Cuisine course that day. Others would be beginning Basic Patisserie or, in some instances, both. We would be joining around a hundred existing students who had already progressed to the Intermediate or Superior levels of Cuisine and Patisserie (some of whom I'd already seen smoking on the pavement).

I had been in two minds about taking the patisserie course myself – one of the minds couldn't shake the image of an unlimited supply of homemade *flans nature*, *millefeuilles*, chocolate *fondants* and *croissants armandes*; the other saw the eight-thousand-euro enrolment fee, the dull technical aspect of baking and the kind of anally retentive madmen who become bakers. To try to help make up my mind, earlier in August I had attended a patisserie demonstration.

Chef Cotte, who gave the demonstration, was a handsome, barrel-chested wise guy with a hint of the young Gerard Depardieu about him and an engaging line in smirks and grimaces. He was a former pastry chef at *La Tour Argent*, one of the grand old restaurants of Paris, and his delicacy with a rolling pin belied his bulldog's physique as he showed us how to make various different kinds of *petit four* with a balletic grace. Three hours whizzed by; it was mesmerising watching a chef at the top of his game assemble several different cakes at once, all the time explaining what he was doing, cracking 'jokes' ('Since I am French, I am a great drinker . . .' heavy pause, 'of water!'), fielding questions with dismissive shrugs and grunts or – in the case of what he felt to be especially stupid questions – a exaggerated, down-turned mouth and raised eyebrows. But at the end of the day, it was still just biscuits he was making. It was all a little too meticulous, measured, obsessive and mechanical. It was chemistry, not cooking.

Ultimately patisserie would be a distraction from my prime purpose in coming to Le Cordon Bleu: to become as close to being a professional chef as I could and, eventually, to see if I could survive in a professional Parisian kitchen. In a restaurant kitchen the patisserie and cuisine sections are entirely separate, one tribe eyeing the other with suspicion or, occasionally, disdain. Cuisine chefs think pastry chefs are nerdy, and a bit gay, 'They make one course, while we make seven!' one cuisine chef told me; another claimed that the pastry chef on the *Titanic* survived only because he was drunk and had ample fat reserves. Meanwhile pastry chefs consider cuisine chefs messy and undisciplined. You took either one route or the other. So, though the idea of being able to knock up one's own rum babas had a definite appeal, I knew in my heart it was a self-indulgence too far.

And, besides, we would learn plenty of cake and dessert recipes on the cuisine course.

Chapter 5

It is impossible to begin to learn that which one thinks one already knows.

Epicetus

At the end of my first day at school I stood frozen, hunched in horror over the sink in the corner of kitchen 2PS, the centre of the eye of a culinary storm. Around me in this cramped, low-ceilinged, windowless, second-floor kitchen variously buzzed, panicked and flailed my fellow students of Basic Cuisine Group E, each scrambling to assemble a simple *potage cultivateur*, a thin vegetable soup, the first dish that we would ever make at Le Cordon Bleu.

I had just scored a deep gash all the way across the pad of my left palm while trying to wash my nine-inch, precision-forged, single-piece, high-carbon stainless steel cook's knife. In that moment – the split second when your heart holds its breath and the blood almost ceases to pump – I hoped against better evidence that the cut was not deep; that pain and, in this case, ensuing humiliation might somehow have been avoided.

Making vegetable soup had never been so exhilarating.

You realise that Le Cordon Bleu is a proper school, as opposed to some kind of culinary holiday camp, or one of those corporate team-building centres, the moment you step through the doors and into the small, open-plan reception. It is painted in the same cheap, institutional pastel colours of every school the world over; as with any school we were warned that people will (and do) steal things if you leave them lying around; and administrative offices fill every broom closet. This is a non-stop production line for chefs and so the décor is rather frayed, the staff a little jaded. And then there were the smells, not all of them fragrant (the meaty smell of simmering stocks mingled with industrial cleaning products and fried fish), that filled the air.

The small atrium, or 'Winter Garden' as it was rather grandly called, lay just around the corner from reception and was packed with students milling like marathon runners at the start of a race. I stood for a moment looking at the noticeboard which listed the previous term's top five students by name and nationality, along with the next couple of weeks' timetables, and several job vacancies – one seeking a private chef for a yacht touring the Mediterranean; another for a *commis chef* position in a two-star Paris restaurant. I tried to imagine how it would feel to see my name on the list of best students, but even with my gift for self-delusion this was a stretch. I noticed some other first-day students begin to make a move and followed them past a makeshift sign directing us to the ground-floor demonstration kitchen.

My stomach was aflutter with long dormant pangs of school days' anxiety mixed with the giddy thrill of embarking on a new education. I loathed school, detested virtually all of my teachers, and my greatest phobia is a room full of strangers. My encounter with Paul, the self-proclaimed semi-professional chef, hadn't helped much. The night before I had dreamt that I had arrived at the school naked; I had grabbed an apron, which I thought did a good job of preserving my modesty, only to catch sight of my exposed posterior in a mirror. I ended up running nowhere in particular, which is how most of my dreams seem to end.

Fortunately, this morning I had something to pretend to be engrossed in while surreptitiously eyeing the other students: a thick A4 binder handed to each student as we entered the demo room. Along with several pages of rules and other basic information including brief biographies of the eleven chefs who taught at the school, a description of the knife kit we would be given, and a glossary of French culinary terms, this was the recipe book for the Basic Cuisine course. It would be my bible for the next nine weeks of Basic Cuisine, the first of three levels I must complete in order to be able to call myself a Cordon Bleu chef.

The demo kitchen was windowless with banked seating for about sixty students. It, too, was frayed at the edges, with chipped tiles and flaky paint and a ragbag assortment of plastic stacking chairs. We sat facing a large work station topped with thick brown marble. Built into the work surface were two rows of three electric hot plates. Ovens of various description – some with glass doors, some with steel doors – filled the wall behind the worktop, while to our right was the assistants' work area, where Superior students helped the chefs with demonstrations. Above it all hung a giant mirror, angled towards the students to give a perfect view of the chef's varying degrees of male pattern baldness.

I looked around at my fellow students – a disparate bunch of races, genders and ages – from late teens to early fifties. I was surprised to see the gender mix was close to 50:50, with perhaps the women shading the majority. For some reason I had expected a greater female bias. 'I'd expected more women,' I said to the woman sitting next to me, a Korean called – I could see from the photo ID badge we had been given – Kim. She smiled nervously, got up from her seat and went to sit somewhere else. Strike II.

The school administrator commenced a lengthy introduction to life at Le Cordon Bleu. This is how it would work: each level of the course would consist of thirty cookery demonstrations which would take place in this auditorium, and thirty practical sessions in one of three kitchens elsewhere in the school. Each of the demos would last about three hours during which the chef would show us how to make three or more different dishes – usually a starter, main and dessert (roughly two hundred and seventy dishes in all). Each demo would be followed, if not immediately, then usually the next day, by a practical session in one of the kitchens – the *grande salle*, which was spacious and had windows overlooking the street, or one of two *petites salles*, somewhat smaller and less inviting (one of them being the windowless kitchen on the second floor). For the practical sessions we would be divided into five groups of between nine and twelve students, and attempt to make one of the dishes we had seen in the demo, alone with the chefs – who spoke only French – to supervise us. As well as the demonstrations and practical sessions there would also be weekly demonstrations by visiting guest chefs from some of Paris's top restaurants; a market visit with a chef; and a couple of student parties to look forward to.

Then came the rules, of which there were many. Discipline, appearance and, particularly, punctuality are taken very seriously at Le Cordon Bleu, we were told. There would be a roll call on the dot at the start of all demos and practicals, which could start at 8.30 a.m., 12.30 p.m., 3.30 p.m. or 6.30 p.m. If we arrived late we would not be allowed to enter. Arrive late on more than four occasions and you would fail the Basic Course and not be allowed to progress to Intermediate (cue the sound of a toilet flushing and money spiralling drainwards). The stern administrator also informed us that the thirtieth and final practical session of Basic Cuisine – which seemed an awfully long way off – would be the final exam which, again, we needed to pass in order to progress to the next level. It didn't really register with me at the time, but to achieve a pass we would have to learn ten recipes by heart and, on the day, choose one from a hat. We would then have to make the dish without any notes, instructions or assistance from the chef.

Each week two students from each practical class would act as kitchen assistants, collecting the ingredients for the entire class from the basement, where the preparation kitchen and storerooms were located and where, I later discovered, the chefs convened for raucous lunches in the back room. The kitchen assistants were responsible for checking that the practical class had everything it needed for the day. They then had to load it into a dumb waiter and send it up to the correct kitchen, chase up the stairs to collect it when it arrived, and distribute it to the students. If they forgot something they would have to race down two or three flights of steps in the middle of the session to retrieve it or risk invoking the wrath of the chef and their fellow students. The assistants were rotated alphabetically, 'If your name is Aaron Aardvark, you can be sure you will be on duty this week,' explained the administrator. A quick look down the list of students indicated that I was my practical group's Aaron Aardvark.

As she spoke a chef arrived and began pacing behind the work station, carefully placing various implements on the countertop. He was a bulky, bespectacled man in his early fifties, dressed in chef's whites, with a blue neckerchief and a tall chef's hat, or *toque*. He had a kind, jowly face, with small, brown eyes heavy with bags, and a rough, pink complexion. His name was Chef Bruno Stril.

We broke for coffee and croissants and I chatted to a tall, thin, amiable New Yorker called Stephen. Stephen, in T-shirt and jeans, was a gourmet food buyer. It was his job to scour the globe for delicacies to sell in the States. 'I'm looking to branch out,' he told me. 'Maybe into catering when I get back home. If not that, then I really think this is going to give me a solid basis for work in the future.' Stephen had tended to gravitate towards Europe for his work and, as I got to know him over the next few months, he became a good source of tips and information about weird and wonderful foodstuffs.

This was the first real chance students had had to get to know each other. There were three main questions: 'Have you found somewhere to live?'; 'How good is your French?; and 'Do you want to be a chef?' We were interrupted by Chef Bruno slamming a large plastic chopping board down on the marble.

'Okay!' he said, clapping and rubbing his hands. 'I want to get a lot in now because you are new and fresh and paying attention. Let's start!'

We returned to our seats. The South Korean and Japanese students had bagged the front row, placing their digital cameras on each chair in the manner of holidaying Germans with their towels on hotel deckchairs, as they would for the duration of the course.

This was Basic Cuisine, so naturally we would begin with the basics, the chef continued, and proceeded to show us how to wash our hands. Happily this would be the first and last time any express reference was made to me regarding hygiene during my time at Le Cordon Bleu. I was clear from the start that we were all adults and all responsible for our own bacteria. It is a cliché – but in my experience sometimes true – that the French, and French chefs in particular, do take a view of certain hygiene practices which elsewhere might cause distress. I'm thinking of the routine tasting of things with fingers; mixing with bare hands; using a chopping board for meat, washing it, then using it for fish, washing it again, and using it for vegetables and so on; eating raw meat and eggs – all of which I would witness during my time at the school and personally wasn't bothered about.

Next up was the peeling of a carrot. 'Always peel towards you,' said the chef. 'Only amateurs peel away.' I breathed a sigh of relief: my carrot peeling technique, at least, was up to scratch, but it was clear there would be a good deal of explaining of unfamiliar raw materials to the Asian students. This seemed fair enough. If I were to take a cooking course in, say, Kyoto, my ignorance would be absolute. Thus we were introduced to celery, aubergines and broccoli. Chef Bruno had to explain the difference between cider and champagne to a Taiwanese girl and, more usefully, told us to always remove the cores from late season garlic cloves for dishes that were cooked relatively quickly, as they are hard to digest and you won't smell too great the day after you've eaten them (advice which should be posted in every Metro train in Paris next to that cartoon of the rabbit catching his fingers in the train doors).

From underneath the worktop the chef brought out a black oblong case – about the length of a violin case. He undid two plastic clasps on the front, and unrolled what looked like a kinky assassin's toolkit. If it is possible for a hush to fall over a group of people who are already silent, then such a hush fell over us now. We were a room of 007s, to Chef Bruno's Q. This was our *trousse*, or knife case,

packed with the finest quality German-made Wüsthof utensils –
not just knives for cutting, filleting, paring, peeling, turning,
channelling, cleaving, boning and zesting, but pastry bags with
various sizes of both plastic and steel nozzles; heavy duty scissors;
a steel trussing needle; a pastry brush; a pair of tweezers (for de-
boning fish and prettifying pastry); an exoglass spatula (to cope with
high temperature liquids); a whisk; a meat fork; dessertspoons and
teaspoons; and a table fork. There was a *fusil*, or sharpening steel;
a double-ended melon baller; an apple corer; and a triangular shaped
tube of ironmongery that turned out to be a sugar thermometer.
This comprehensive chef's inventory was included in the price of
the course, as was a set of electronic weighing scales and various
sizes of Tupperware boxes for carrying home the food we would
make, all of which we were advised to mark with our initials using
nail varnish or coloured tape. I couldn't wait to get my hands on
the knife case but, from a couple of rows behind me I could hear
Paul's withering verdict, 'Nah, I've got my own knives – Japanese.
German ones suck.'

For this first demo the chef would be showing us how to make
a simple *potage cultivateur*, or rustic vegetable soup. It was a useful
way of demonstrating knife skills and various classic French vegetable
cuts. There was a precise method for preparing each vegetable. With
Chef Bruno there was a precise method for everything: I'd wager
he's the type of man who irons his Y-fronts. He was obsessive about
washing the leaves of the cabbage, for instance, filling a large bowl
with water, rinsing each leaf individually at least twice so that the
detritus fell to the bottom of the bowl, then, rather than holding on
to the leaves while he poured the water out, carefully removing them
from the water so that the dirt didn't get stirred up and cover them
again (he would later show us the same technique for salad leaves
and – most finicky of all – spinach), before removing the white stalk
from each leaf individually. The outer leaves of the cabbage were
discarded entirely. Never mind that they are rich in flavour and,
generally, the deeper coloured a vegetable, the more healthy it is,

haute cuisine values appearance as much as taste and, certainly, both of those qualities rank above any health benefits. These tough, corrugated leaves looked like a spinster's rubber swimming cap and had no place in a *Cordon Bleu* preparation.

Each end of each *haricot vert*, meanwhile, was to be snapped individually by hand at its natural breaking point, never chopped with a knife, before each bean was then chopped into three-millimetre-thick rounds. The celery was denuded of its outer stringy veins with a few passes of a potato peeler, and then sliced into short, wafer-thin oboe reeds. These were than cut into small triangles, or *paisan*, as were the leeks which were halved lengthways, their core leaves removed, and then the outer leaves flattened out on the chopping board before being cut.

Stril showed us how to hold the chef's knife – the largest in our kit – by pinching the top edge of the blade closest to the handle between our thumb and index finger and wrapping our other three fingers under the handle. His chopping action was actually more of a sawing movement, as he cut down and away from himself, making virtually no noise. Apparently the flashy karate chop favoured by some chefs blunts the knife and results in less clean cuts.

'You must curl the fingers of your other hand into a fist,' continued the chef, 'otherwise you will end up with fingers all the same length.' He stood with his non-chopping arm laid on the chopping board at a right angle to the chopping arm. 'Your non-chopping arm should form a perfect ninety-degree angle to the blade in order to allow maximum control, to give precise, uniform cuts,' he explained. As with bad driving habits, if you have been doing it one way for a lifetime, it takes some practice to re-programme yourself, but it is worth it in the long run.

Next, we were given a master class in how to chop an onion. Chef Bruno always began preparing onions in his hand rather than on the chopping board as there was a risk of contamination from soil. He never used his fingers to peel onions or garlic. 'When I go home I don't want my hands to smell, the juice gets under your nails.' Instead he used a short paring knife to cut the sprout from the top of the onion and the hairy root from the bottom, before peeling away the brown paper skin and the first layer of the onion. Only then did he place the naked onion on the board, first cutting it in half through the root, then slicing each half very finely from its root to the tip leaving a small piece of the root uncut to hold the fronds of the onion together, before slicing it again, this time horizontally, parallel to the board at half-centimetre increments from the bottom up. He was now left with a kind of onion hula skirt and which he then chopped crossways to produce perfectly regular, teeny tiny cubes. The cuts are known as *ciselé*, or *brunoise* for slightly larger cubes. You get better results from chopping an onion this way, as opposed to randomly chopping backwards and forwards through a pile of onion as you might do with herbs, he said, because it minimises the bruising of the onion and prevents its juice from seeping out.

He showed us how to make a bouquet garni. This is a standard aromatic flavouring parcel, used in countless dishes and stocks. A bouquet garni is made by taking the green part of the leek leaf, washing it, and using it to envelop a sprig of thyme, two bay leaves and either some parsley stalks or leafy celery tops, and tying it up with string. Chef Bruno wrapped his in seconds with a few swift movements producing a neat, fat spliff. Finally, he produced a block of *poitrine de porc* – salted bacon – which looked like something you might give the dog to chew on to keep him quiet, and chopped it into *lardons*, or short, fat matchsticks.

And all of this was before he had yet to cook a thing.

The method for making the soup itself was simple enough: he sweated the vegetables in butter and oil – in a specific order – with the bacon, before adding water, bringing to a boil and simmering for twenty minutes or so. Stephen, the gourmet food buyer, asked a question about cooking with tap water, versus using bottled water. I too had heard that some chefs, like Paul Bocuse, use mineral water because it doesn't contain chlorine and other additives, but Chef Bruno dismissed the idea altogether: 'If it's potable, it's good,' he said. Towards the end he added thin, translucent potato *paisan* – rinsed of their excess starch – to the water along with the other, faster-cooking vegetables, checked the seasoning throughout and skimmed the scum that floated to the surface with a clean, caressing sweep of his ladle. This would turn out to be a chief preoccupation of the Cordon Bleu chefs, who would attentively skim any stocks, sauces or soups every five minutes or so to rid them of any excess fats or impurities that surfaced during their cooking: it was virtually an automatic reflex for them to stop what they were doing, pick up a ladle and waft it over the pot (this is not so important in most restaurants where they usually have time for stocks to cool, allowing for undesirable substances rise to the surface and congeal naturally).

The resulting soup, which was divided into plastic cups for us to taste at the end of the class – as would be the case with everything the chefs prepared in demonstrations – was clear, with a kaleidoscope of colourful vegetables. As no stock had been used it had a faint but refreshing flavour. Chef Bruno served it with croutons, made from thin, toasted slices of baguette fried in clarified butter and topped with grated gruyère (ready-grated from a plastic bag – I was more than a little shocked to see), and toasted for a few seconds under the grill. The crouton was served separately, he was at pains to point out, *not* floating on top of the soup. It was about as far removed from the slap-dash of the modern television chef as a Fragonard is from a Jackson Pollock.

Other essential tips that we learned in that first, epic demonstration? There were many. With knives as sharp as razor blades, a slipping chopping board could cost you a fingertip. To keep our boards in place the chef recommended we place a couple of lightly dampened sheets of kitchen paper underneath – a brilliant tip. We should always keep a bowl on our worktop for scraps and waste material, both to save repeated trips to the bin and to prevent a mountainous build-up of peelings and discarded packaging from contaminating whatever you are preparing (the plastic top from an empty bottle of olive oil I once left in a Lancashire hotpot sprang to mind here). Before we started cooking, we were to gather all the equipment we were likely to need on a tray and keep it near to hand – for this reason, among many others that were to become apparent over the coming months, a good shelf above the cooker would become a crucial design criterion of my dream kitchen.

Though a certain amount of what Chef Bruno was telling us fell into the category of 'stating the bleedin' obvious', even during this very first lesson of Basic Cuisine I learned more of a practical nature than I had ever learned from any cookery book. This was not just the hows and the whys of food preparation, but the how-to-do-betters as well. Before the demo had even commenced Chef Bruno had said that Basic Cuisine was the most important course at Le Cordon Bleu. 'He would say that,' I'd thought to myself at the time, but by the end of those first three hours I knew it was true. Whatever other extraordinary techniques and dishes, and however elaborate the later menus would become, the simple, patient wisdom of Chef Bruno over the next two and a half months would give us the most thorough grounding we could hope for. If we listened well and applied what we heard we would have the foundations upon which careers might be built.

The blood began to gush, silent and relentless. I stood paralysed by the sink in the second-floor kitchen at the end of our first practical session, making the soup Bruno had shown us. Was that a smirk I saw on Paul's face as he looked up from his own swift, precise, *professional* chopping? I looked down dumbly, weighing up whether or not to panic as the soap suds started to turn tomato red in the sink beneath me. Chef Bruno hurried over, having instinctively realised something was wrong from my posture. Digital mutilation is obviously a routine occurrence in a professional kitchen, particularly one full with first-day rookies. He hustled me out of the kitchen to the first-aid cabinet mounted on the wall in the hallway, helping me clean and bandage the wound. '*Ce n'est pas grave*,' he said, with a consoling pat on the back, guiding me back to my stove.

We had received our knife kits and uniform just before the session and this, I suppose, was a kind of baptism for mine. That, and the knowledge that the best chefs' hands are a web of scars and burns, was some consolation. It wouldn't be my last cut, that was for sure, but hopefully it would be the deepest.

As I left school on that first day I stopped at the *tabac* beside Vaugirard Metro station to buy a pack of cigarettes. I winced as I creased my palm to take the change from my pocket but managed to light the cigarette and smoked it with my other hand, standing for a few moments in quiet contemplation of a momentous day. My head was a-hive with the mass of information it had been bombarded with – not just the cookery lesson, but the people I'd met and the mysterious etiquette of chef relations (is it Chef 'Christian Name', or Chef 'Surname'?). Much of it we students would have to figure out as we went along. Deep in thought, I tossed my lit cigarette into an open wheelie bin outside the neighbouring café. It was some minutes later while I was still waiting on the platform that I realised what I had done and immediately ran back up the stairs. As I emerged into daylight I could see a crowd of people around the bin, now crowned with white foam from a fire extinguisher and looking like a large, green Baked Alaska. At the end of the street I caught a glimpse of blue lights announcing the imminent arrival of the *Sapeurs Pompiers*.

Two emergency services in one day was an irresponsible tally (and with that cut it could so easily have been three) but the damage was done. Nothing would be gained from presenting myself as the guilty party for disrupting their afternoon of table tennis and baked potatoes, or whatever it is firemen get up to in their down time. So, with my, by now well-practised, look of innocent concern in place, I hurried back down the station stairs and home.

Chapter 6

There is no calamity greater than lavish desires and there is no greater disaster than greed.

Lao-Tzu, Chinese philosopher

It would be nice to think that Lao-Tzu quote was in my thoughts as I watched my first ever soufflé slowly, poignantly implode on the marble top in one of the Cordon Bleu kitchens, but ancient Chinese wisdom rarely springs to mind in the midst of kitchen catastrophes. Instead, I was desperately hunting round for some way to revive this sorry, eggy deflation which was now slowly seeping from its ramekin across the work surface like some mutant life form.

I realise my soufflé misadventures might perhaps seem of little importance, particularly in the context of the news that winter. The Paris suburbs were aflame with racial tension, and it seemed avian flu was about to wipe out half of Europe. But, though we were just a few miles from the race riots in Paris's *banlieux*, we might as well have been on another continent – the only indication that anything was awry was the occasional urgent, then dying siren outside our apartment and the apocalyptic headlines in the newspapers. The long dormant news journalist in me occasionally nudged the proto-chef, whispering in his ear, 'Shouldn't you be out there, feeling the pulse of contemporary urban France? British Journalist Race Riot Scoop! Hold the front page!' and other lines from Spencer Tracy movies, to which the proto-chef would usually respond with a nascent Gallic shrug.

As for the bird flu, although France's foie gras farmers were afluster, rounding up their birds to cosset them away indoors for the winter (one Perigord producer, it was reported, moved his family out of their house to accommodate his geese, the family taking up residence in an old Citroën van), I found it hard to take it seriously at all. Bird flu? Come off it. Why do coal miners use canaries to check for gas leaks? Because birds are feeble hypochondriacs. If shire horses were keeling over I might be worried. That didn't stop some of the American students taking precautionary measures of their own: 'I'm not touching any birds unless I'm wearing plastic gloves,' one of them told me a few days after the crisis had begun and, sure enough, when we came to prepare a roast chicken the following week, she was wearing surgeon's gloves and prodding the offending bird as if she had just heard it ticking.

Being the Aaron Aardvark of the class, during the first week of Basic Cuisine I was charged with being the kitchen assistant for the group, gathering the raw ingredients from the walk-in fridge in the basement and portioning them in the practical kitchen for the eight other students in my class. It was like being the milk monitor at primary school, but without the prestige. For that first, calamitous soup-making lesson the chef himself had done this, but for the second practical session it was my responsibility.

I was late. My excuse was a fairly shameful one: I had loitered in our local *boulangerie* after noticing that the American movie star Johnny Depp had come in after me (he is married to the French actress/singer Vanessa Paradis and I assume they have a place in Paris). I had already bought my elevenses *flan nature*, but seeing Depp I pretended to be fascinated by the chocolate display in order to spend a few brief moments in his presence. This is pathetic for a man of my age, I appreciate. Despite having interviewed a few famous people (good taste forbids name-dropping of course, but if I were to say the names 'Lionel' and 'Blair' you would have some idea of the echelons in which I mingled), I am a sucker for celebrity. Even more pitiful is the overpowering urge I get to try to become their best friend. So, I had sidled up to Depp in the queue. He was wearing his usual Keith Richards dressing-up box garb – an obviously very expensive leather jacket, battered trilby hat and artfully distressed jeans. He smelled lovely.

'I love those,' I said pointing to the *flans nature*, and grinning, 'I eat two a day sometimes.' Hardly a Wildean bon mot, but it was all I could think of at that moment. Depp looked at me with concern, perhaps even a hint of fear, forced some kind of acknowledging grunt, grabbed his baguette and fled. Madame behind the counter, who already held me in some contempt following an incident in which I had coughed over her croissants, scowled at me.

All of this meant that, by the time I arrived at school that day, the men's changing room was packed. The changing facilities at Le Cordon Bleu are impossibly cramped. On average, each student has about as much space to change from civvies into the standard issue check trousers, double-breasted chef's whites, open-heeled clogs, white neckerchief and cloth hat, as a prisoner has inside an iron maiden. By the time I had dressed, grabbed my recipe book and slung my knife kit over my shoulder, I knew that my fellow students would already be waiting in the kitchen for their ingredients, yet still I paused by the mirror in the winter garden.

For the first week or so catching sight of myself in my chef's get-up would always prompt a double take. Le Cordon Bleu takes its uniforms very seriously and students are marked on their presentation and cleanliness. I had attended our second demonstration with my trousers on back-to-front (always a risk with an elasticated waistband), and that the same day I had been reprimanded by a chef in front of the entire Basic Cuisine group of fifty-five students for not wearing a neckerchief and having my top button undone. The *next* day a different chef told me off for wearing my watch, another kitchen felony, apparently.

Though it provided yet another unpleasant schooldays' flashback, I realised that the school's obsession with uniform was merely an extension of one of the fundamental principles of haute cuisine, that if something looks good, it is halfway to tasting good. If we looked like chefs, perhaps we stood a chance of becoming chefs. All uniforms have the power to transform – that is the idea of course – but I did not recognise myself as I stood staring in the mirror. I looked younger for a start, and a good deal tidier than usual. But I felt a fraud, particularly the first time I went out on the street wearing it to get some lunch in a nearby *boulangerie*. It felt like I was on my way to a fancy-dress party but the ladies serving in the shop had assumed I was a real chef and treated me with great reverence, giggling coquettishly as they handed me my change. But Johnny Depp does not become a great guitar player by dressing like a Rolling Stone, and neither did I become a chef just because I had the uniform – the Swedish chef from the Muppets, perhaps, but nothing more. Shaking these thoughts from my head and hurrying with as much dignity as I could (and hurrying in an apron is a whole new skill), I went to collect the ingredients from the basement.

If I had thought the kitchen on the second floor was a harsh food preparation environment, the *sous sol* prep room, or *garde manger*, at Le Cordon Bleu was even worse. Here in the basement, starved of daylight, toiled several Superior Cuisine students alongside the full-time kitchen staff, making stock in giant metal vats, preparing buckets of vegetables and filleting fish for the chef's demonstrations and the regular functions held at the school. That said, it was a model of good hygienic practice compared to George Orwell's description, in *Down and Out in Paris and London,* of the kitchen of an unnamed grand hotel close to the Place de la Concorde where he worked for a while in the late 1920s.

'The kitchen was like nothing I had ever seen or imagined,' writes Orwell. 'A stifling, low-ceilinged inferno of a cellar, red-lit from the fires, and deafening with oaths and the clanging of pots and pans.' He concluded that 'the more one pays for food, the more sweat and spittle one is obliged to eat with it.' Which I fear is probably as true today as ever.

Once again I felt like the squitty little new boy as I asked one of the Superior students, a strikingly fat young man from Venezuela, where I could find the ingredients for Basic Cuisine Group E. He jerked his head towards the far end of the kitchen, not bothering to look up from the meat he was portioning. I hesitated, torn between causing further annoyance and arriving even later for class. 'I'm sorry, do you mean those shelves, or in the cupboard?' I asked. He sighed exaggeratedly, 'It's not a cupboard, it's a fridge,' and continued to saw at the red flesh.

By the time I finally made it up to the kitchen, having in the meantime sent the tray of ingredients to the wrong kitchen via the dumb waiter, I was confronted by a glowering Chef Chalopin.

As would become apparent over the coming weeks, Marc Chalopin was not an easy man to like: shortish and pent-up, he wore sinister, bottle-bottomed, frameless glasses through which he would squint sceptically at students like a parade sergeant inspecting new recruits. His face remained emotionless unless he was particularly offended by something a student had done, in which case he would grimace – a look once memorably described by one student as 'like a man who can't pee'. Though he was one of the youngest chefs, he was no more sympathetic towards students' frailties. He moved slowly but economically and with purpose in the kitchen, and was one of the most impressive chefs at the school in terms of his technique. A former protégé of Joël Robuchon and Alain Ducasse, he had joined Le Cordon Bleu in 2001 and had been sent soon after to South Korea where he was appointed executive chef at Le Cordon Bleu-Sookmyung Academy. He had only just returned to the Paris school to take up a post as a slightly more humble chef de cuisine: as a clearly prodigiously talented chef now in charge of the culinary Keystone Cops that was Basic Cuisine Group E, it didn't require a great leap of imagination to wonder if he might be a bit miffed.

'You are the assistant?' he asked me as I arrived, drenched with sweat (it was an unseasonably hot September), and flushed with embarrassment.

'Yes, so sorry I am late.'

'If you are the assistant, you should assist, no?'

'Yes, I am really, really sorry, you see I . . .'

'This is not assisting. I will take marks if it happens again.'

He turned on his heels and strode off across the kitchen.

The first practical sessions were edgy, anxious times for all the students. In my own kitchen, though I often panicked, made mistakes, and occasionally had tantrums when things went wrong, I never felt nervous. But here it felt as if we were performing – for the chef and for each other. Though I took meticulous notes during the demonstrations, the moment I began to cook I would start dropping, breaking and mangling anything that fell within reach. I found myself checking and double checking every ingredient and every step of the recipe, peering at my notes Mr Magoo-style, as if someone had transcribed them into Sanskrit while I hadn't been looking, and constantly glancing at what the other students were doing out of the corner of my eye . . . only to find they were looking at me out of the corner of theirs. I had regressed from a reasonably competent home cook to a bungling novice who couldn't be trusted to open a tub of mustard (literally as, while making a rabbit and mustard casserole in week two, I left the plastic tub of mustard on a warm hot plate. The result was an *Amoco Cadiz*-style environmental catastrophe with noxious plastic fumes filling the air and molten mustard everywhere).

Then there was that soufflé which we made in our third practical session and which, in truth, never did rise in the first place. According to the renowned French molecular gastronomist Hervé This (pronounced Teess), the secret of making a soufflé rise is to 'heat it from beneath, use very firmly whipped egg whites and seal the surface in order to prevent the release of bubbles formed inside'. He suggests one does this by lightly grilling the surface of the soufflé before cooking. I did none of this and ended up with runny omelette.

I fared little better with simple vegetable preparation. Though I would always begin chopping vegetables with meticulous precision in the manner of Chef Bruno, I would usually catch sight of other students moving on to the next stages of the recipe, panic, and end up with an indiscriminately mutilated pile. Our fourth practical session required us to make an *estouffade de boeuf bourguignon* (essentially a beef stew). I botched an onion beyond repair and had to ask the chef for another. The trouble was, in my fevered state, I couldn't for the life of me remember the French word for onion. I had to ask another student. Often by the end of those first practical sessions I was doing well if I could recall my own name. I would travel home on the Metro in a kind of bewildered trance, trying to understand what had gone wrong each day, mulling over my mistakes again and again until I went to bed that night.

I ascribed my kitchen anxiety partly to the presence – usually hovering over our shoulders – of the chefs. Like Gandalf entering a hobbit house, the chefs increased in stature in the kitchens. I had been impressed by their wisdom and skill during their demonstrations, during which they would make three or more courses simultaneously without breaking sweat, all the while giving constant running commentary, and with only an occasional 'Here's one I made earlier.' But here in their natural environment they moved with the grace and assuredness of accomplished sportsmen, swiftly whisking an emulsion that had separated, adjusting seasoning or, when nothing could be done, putting a sauce out of its misery by dispatching the pan to the *plongeur*, or washer-upper. I so desperately wanted to impress them, but there were two obstacles to this. The first was that, because I had been quite successful in learning, parrot fashion, a few sentences in French, the chefs assumed I was fluent and would jabber away at length in the mistake belief that I had a clue what they were saying. The other problem was that every time I spoke to them I became as tongue-tied as a hormonal fourteen-year-old on his first date. My first proper conversation with Chef Bruno went like this:

Chef Bruno: 'Where are you from?'

Me: 'Hmm? Ha-ha!'

Chef Bruno: 'No, where do you come from?'

Me: [long pause] 'Oh, ah, England! Ha-ha!'

Chef Bruno: 'You like le rugby?'

Me: 'Brighton!'

Chef Bruno: [miming throwing an egg-shaped ball] 'No, le *rugby*'.

Me: 'Oh, no, *le cricket*!'

The chef looked puzzled and walked off. If the ovens had been gas, I would have baked my head. I have only ever played cricket once in my life but, confused and panicking at the prospect of a Frenchman being nice to me, I had fashioned some bizarre autobiographical cliché of Englishness. Here was a prime bonding opportunity and I had screwed it up. I vowed to prepare better rugby small talk before the next practical.

Chapter 7

It is to the production of perfect stocks that the sauce cook should devote himself.

Auguste Escoffier

I was not the only student to undergo an unfortunate transformation upon entering the kitchen. There was also Soon Yuk. This unassuming young man from South Korea, whom I never heard speak outside of the kitchen, became a culinary showman within it. Clearly well versed in the moves of the macho TV chefs, he imitated them to perfection – sprinkling salt from above head height, crashing pans about the place, and tossing utensils across the marble work surface once he was finished with them, as if a team of assistants was on hand to clean up after him. His sautéing technique was particularly theatrical, involving exaggerated, wristy pan flicks, which would usually send the contents bucking all over the floor. I once overheard him give a running commentary to an imaginary camera crew. His food was appalling.

Of course, there was no TV crew or team of assistants, but what we did have, and were eternally grateful for, were the *plongeurs*, or washer-uppers. They were friendly, patient men – usually African – who spent the entire day up to their elbows in cruddy suds and earned the students' undying gratitude on a daily basis. Often the younger students would carefully wrap the food they had cooked in tin foil and present it to their *plongeur* at the end of the session, by way of a thank you. I had a family to feed on an ever-shrinking budget so this wasn't an option for me; instead I tried my best to keep the number of pans and sieves I used to a minimum, offering a guilty wince every time I added to the towering pyramid of soiled kitchenware that beside the jacuzzi-sized sinks.

We took responsibility for washing our knives and other kitchen equipment that required special treatment – like the thick, black-bottomed frying pans which we were only supposed to wipe clean with kitchen roll. It took a while for Soon Yuk to realise this, however, which led to a sarcastic dressing down from Chef Chalopin during our fifth practical session, making a roast chicken and *jus*. Soon Yuk had left a mucky whisk in front of the chef. 'What is this? A present for me?' he asked. Soon Yuk, whose French was even worse than mine, looked dumbfounded. 'Uh?' he replied. 'You have given me a present, oh thank you,' said Chalopin, waggling the whisk in Soon Yuk's face. Someone nudged him and the penny dropped. He took the whisk, looked down at it as if it were the most confounding object he had ever seen, and slowly walked over to one of the sinks, where he stood for a while contemplating his next move. I was closest and so showed him how to take washing up liquid and place it on a sponge and then wash his whisk. He looked back at me like a quizzical but grateful Labrador; slowly, over the coming weeks, he learned to take responsibility for his equipment. He never did stop the salt thing though.

I had been looking forward to the demonstration on how to make stocks, which came in the second week. Stocks are the foundation of classic haute cuisine (the French name for stock is *fond*, meaning foundation). What fascinated me about stock was that, though it may taste of very little and even that need not necessarily be a pleasant flavour, in combination with other ingredients – the juices from meat, sweated vegetables, alcohol, cream and butter – it could become something transcendently delicious. In the same way that with a great suit you should never notice the clothes, only the man who is wearing them, a great stock should never dominate a sauce but complement and enhance it.

As I would discover, to make a truly great *fond de veau* – veal stock

– requires a similar amount of expertise and experience as a Savile Row tailor. Part of what made my Escoffier recipe book so frustrating was the fact that, invariably, halfway down the list of ingredients would be the apparently innocuous listing of 'veal stock' – in reality an enormous bother, both to buy the ingredients for, and to make in a domestic kitchen. But now, at last, I would learn how to make my own.

Chef Bruno began the demonstration in a sombre mood: 'You will be the last generation to learn to cook with bones. Legislation is slowly stopping us from using bones. You can still get them from butchers in Paris, but for how long . . . ?' He shrugged as if a ban was inevitable. With veal stock in particular such a key component of many classic French dishes, Bruno was effectively sounding the death knell for haute cuisine, but he didn't seem too concerned. Then again, the French have a boundless capacity for generating crises and then ignoring them. They have long been convinced that virtually every aspect of their way of life is under threat from Brussels bureaucrats. And it is true that, from the force-feeding of geese and ducks to produce foie gras, to veal transportation, to horse butchery, to the terrible fate that befalls their frogs, their cuisine could almost have been designed solely to goad thumb-twiddling bureaucrats and Paul McCartney. Historically they have always managed to circumvent any rules imposed from without; when it looked as if foie gras was under threat, for instance, the French parliament promptly declared it a national institution. But though the simpler *jus*, made by recuperating meat brownings from the pan with water, has negated the need for stocks in many contemporary kitchens, they are still a long way off finding an alternative to veal stock.

There are two types of stock, the chef explained. The first are white stocks, which are made from the bones of birds, veal, or fish, which you gently simmer in water with some aromatic vegetables and herbs. White stocks tend to be lighter and less strongly flavoured than brown stocks, the second type, in which you fry or roast the bones – and sometimes the vegetables as well – before simmering. You can use poultry, beef, veal, lamb, pork, game or even the shells of shellfish to make a brown stock, just as long as you get them nice and brown before simmering. After making a stock you can use it to make soup, in casseroles or to braise meat and vegetables, or you can reduce it to about a third to make a super-intense stock called a *demi-glace,* or reduce it even further to as little as a tenth of its original volume, to make a *glace* – a sticky, dense reduction that can add wonderful richness and flavour to sauces.

Alternatively the stock can be clarified to make a consommé. Entire treatises have been written about the art of making this clear, amber beef broth which uses a mixture of minced beef, tomato and egg whites to self-filter the particles from the stock. As you heat the stock from cold the beef mix forms an unappetising crust on the surface which you then baste with the stock through a hole in its surface. (We did this just the once at school in order to make an aspic from the consommé, which we then used to decorate a plate for a pâté we had made. I had hoped to gloss over the entire sorry episode as, for some reason, I got it into my head to create an undersea scene on my plate using blanched leeks to represent seaweed and carrots cleverly cut into the shape of goldfish, which I fixed in place using the meat jelly. As the chef pointed when marking it, this would have been very nice had the terrine been made from fish, but as it was a pork-based terrine it didn't seem entirely appropriate.)

The key to a good veal stock – any stock – is good bones; the fresher the better. Any good butcher should be able to supply bones cut into small pieces. Similarly, you shouldn't be tempted to use knackered old, rubbery carrots and limp leeks in your stock. Alice Walters, owner of the famous Californian restaurant Chez Panisse, once said that 'A stock made with garbage will taste like garbage,' and Chef Bruno seemed to concur.

Veal Stock

Ingredients

1.5-2kg veal bones, cut into pieces by your butcher

Mirepoix – this is the standard aromatic vegetable base (the Italians call it *soffrito*) for many dishes, usually comprised of carrots, onion, shallot, garlic and celery. It is named after Field Marshal Duc du Lévis-Mirepoix, although, in fact, it was his cook who invented it. A *mirepoix* should never dominate a dish, so usually plan to use about twenty per cent the weight of *mirepoix* to bones. To make a *mirepoix*, peel, rinse and roughly chop the vegetables. The size you cut your *mirepoix* depends on how long you will be simmering the stock. Fish stocks, which simmer for a much shorter time, need more finely chopped vegetables than a veal stock, for example

Peanut or sunflower oil

3 tomatoes, peeled (by coring, scoring, then blanching for a few seconds in boiling water until the skins begin to withdraw, then immediately chilling in cold water), de-seeded and roughly chopped, although, in truth, I am not sure it matters if you just roughly chop them – pips, skin and all

Tomato paste – a good squeeze

Bouquet garni

Cold water to cover well

1 clove

15 peppercorns

Parsley stems and mushroom trimmings are great if you have them

Better still, if you have an ox tail or a veal foot, you are on course for something truly miraculous.

Everyone should make a veal stock at least once in their life although it can seem a bit of a kerfuffle. Though perhaps not as flavoursome, veal bones are better than beef bones because they produce more gelatine when cooked which makes for a more glossy, better-looking sauce.

First, rinse the bones in cold water and dry well. If you want to make a brown stock, heat some neutral-flavoured oil – nut or sunflower, not olive – in a good, thick-bottomed roasting pan, add the bones, roll them around in the oil a bit, and place the pan in the oven at 220°C for forty to fifty minutes, turning them occasionally and keeping an eye on them so they brown but don't burn. For a lighter stock, blanche the bones – bringing them to the boil from cold, then remove from the water – and simply simmer them in fresh water with all the other ingredients; although, frankly, if you are going to all this trouble, you might as well roast the bones and make a stock with some proper gumption. Alternatively, you can fry the bones in batches in the pan on the hob until they are dark brown.

The bones will render some fat as they roast. Once they are finished remove them and use the same pan with the fat from the bones still in it to fry the *mirepoix*, half the tomatoes and the tomato paste for a couple of minutes to get them up to a good heat, then put the pan back in the oven for twenty minutes. When the vegetables are nicely caramelised, remove the pan from the oven and drain off as much of the fat as possible, using a sieve to catch the precious brown bits and vegetables. Deglaze the pan with some water, and scrape any brownings that have gathered on its surface. Pour this flavourful *jus* into the stockpot, which needs to be narrow and high-sided to minimise evaporation during simmering. Add the bones, the *mirepoix* and brownings from the sieve along with the rest of the ingredients, cover with cold water (always start off with cold water because the fat will rise more rapidly to the surface than with water that is already boiling), up to around two inches above the bones, and bring to the boil. Reduce to the barest of simmers – the French call this *frémir*, 'to tremble' – for about three hours. It doesn't matter if it's two and a half, but you will need at least two – and many chefs say double that – to extract the full flavour from the bones. Simmer it gently because this doesn't stir up impurities in the way that a rolling boil would and keeps the stock as clear as possible. This way it will also stay fresher longer.

Using a ladle, skim the surface of the stock from time to time as it simmers to remove the 'impurities' (an ugly grey-brown foam – fat mostly) which will rise to the top, rinsing the ladle in a bowl of water in between skims. Alternatively, if you are in no hurry to use the stock, forget about skimming it, and, when it is finished, strained and cooled, just remove the fat that will congeal naturally on the surface.

Parsley stalks or mushroom trimmings are valuable flavours for a good brown stock. Chefs guard these with their lives, Bruno told us, so if you have any, chuck them in with the vegetables. Bruno also tossed in a white veal foot which he said contained lots of gelatine to make the final sauce glossy. After you feel the stock has cooked long enough, leave it to settle so that all the detritus falls to the bottom, then strain it through a *chinois*, taking care to leave the impurities on the bottom of the pot, and finally refrigerate it.

In some kitchens the chef will either take that stock and then use it as if it were water to make a new batch of 'double stock' with new bones and garnish, or reboil the old bones and then use that liquid to start a new stock. I go all funny just thinking about how great the sauces made from those stocks taste.

One of the students asked if there were different ways of making veal stock. Yes, the chef said, as many different ways as there are chefs. Most have their little tricks, some dust the bones with flour before roasting, others prefer not to roast the vegetables, or to deglaze with red or white wine after the bones have been roasted and then reduce the wine before adding water. Some prefer to add the vegetables about one hour before the end of the cooking because they feel it keeps their flavour fresher. Some even add a little commercial stock powder to their own stocks for added oomph. Of course, learning when to add the vegetables, judging precisely when a stock is ready, identifying the moment a stock has extracted all the flavour from the bones but hasn't yet turned dull through over-simmering, all this takes years of experience. You need to be aware of not just the flavour, but the smell, the colour and clarity; I suspect it is one of those innate intuitive things that French people are born with, but the rest of us have to learn through years of trial and error.

Chicken stock, which the chef moved on to next, is easier to produce in a domestic kitchen than veal stock, though there are still pitfalls. You use the carcass and bones left over from a roast chicken, removing two bitter-tasting glands secreted beneath the parson's nose, and taking off as much of the bird's skin and fatty deposits as you can. It is good – though not strictly necessary – to blanche the chicken carcass (which requires that you bring it to the boil in just enough water to cover, and then change the water before adding the vegetables), which helps to keep the stock nice and clear. Again, you shouldn't add too many vegetables. 'Only ten per cent of the weight of the carcass should be vegetables,' Chef Bruno said, adding a few extra chicken wings – their excess, fatty skin removed – into the pot for a little flavour boost. 'You're not making vegetable stock. And it is important to simmer gently. Those nice smells you get when you are cooking food? It's the flavour disappearing into space. Not good.'

This gentle approach applied to any kind of reduction. 'Don't boil it like washing!' Chalopin once shouted at me as I reduced a sauce on full blast, 'Start with as little liquid as possible and reduce gently.' Interestingly, Chinese cooking takes a more robust attitude towards making stock – Chinese chefs advocate boiling stocks at full blast. Similarly, I once read that Marco Pierre White advises the same – cooking stocks at a higher heat for a shorter time keeps them tasting fresher, he says.

As with the veal stock, the final key to a good chicken stock was to skim the scum that forms on the surface at regular intervals, an act I came to find deeply satisfying – like cleaning a dirty window.

Making fish stock, or fish *fumé* (the next day's lesson) is a similar process to making chicken stock. Fresh fish should not smell of anything much, the chef explained, holding up his glittering, silver bream as evidence; their eyes should be clear and not sunken, their gills bright red and their flesh firm. The less you wash a fish, the better it keeps its freshness and flavour. Usually when the chefs demonstrated anything mildly brutal involving dead animals, there would be sharp gasps from the Asian ladies in the front row. This time they were prompted by Chef Bruno showing how to gouge out the eyes of the bream with a potato peeler, then rip the gills out – both of which ruin the clarity and flavour of a stock, as does the skin, which turns it grey. He snipped the fins off with a pair of stout kitchen scissors, and pulled the guts out, making sure to remove the swim bladder and any pockets of blood remaining inside. Blood is the enemy of a clear stock, which is why the next step after removing the fillets – leaving the roughly chopped fish bones and head to degorge in icy water for a minimum of ten minutes – was so important.

Carrots are a no-no in fish stock, apparently, as they are too sweet. As with all stocks, the chef cautioned against using salt early on in the process unless you could be absolutely sure that the stock was not to be reduced for a sauce at a later time, which would intensify the salt. Oily fish such as salmon, trout or mackerel are not suitable for making stock, which is why they are rarely served with a sauce.

Finally, Cordon Bleu chefs were always reluctant to advise on freezing food but Chef Bruno did concede that a good way to store stock was to reduce it before freezing to intensify the flavour and save space, and then add water when you defrosted.

One of the most impressive things about the way our chefs worked was their scrupulous avoidance of waste. They would find a use for virtually every morsel of meat, fish, vegetable and fruit that crossed their work surfaces. Apple cores and peel were stewed to extract their natural pectin for use as a thickener for desserts; the flavour-some stalks of herbs were kept to blend in vinaigrettes or, in the case of parsley stalks, to be wrapped in the bouquet garni to bring an extra subtle aroma to stocks or sauces; and, as I have said, mush-room trimmings were especially prized, being thrown in the stockpot or added to sauces. Nothing was wasted (on one occasion a chef actually picked out a morsel of lobster meat I had thrown into my waste bowl, and added it to my sauce). 'Save the fat from duck breasts,' one of the chefs told us. 'It costs the same as the meat.' Another gave us an excellent recipe for iced tomato and strawberry gazpacho: 'If you've got some crappy old tomatoes left over . . . ,' he made a whistling sound to imply, 'Bob's your uncle.' My mother, who lived through post-war rationing and has given me so much sound cooking advice over the years, instilled something of the same 'waste not want not' creed in me, so I had an especial appreciation of dishes that incorporated the things we usually throw away, like the fish dishes we were shown that were served with a sauce made from the fish's bones.

After that first fish practical in week three I found myself in the changing room getting dressed next to Hermann, an Austrian with a shaved, polished head and handlebar moustache. Hermann was originally from the Tyrol, he told me, but now lived in Uruguay – which explained his deep, almost ebony tan. He was a merchant seaman who often spent months at a time at sea on gas tankers. He loved to cook, particularly Asian food, and continued to tell me about his life over a beer in the bar round the corner from the school.

'I get five or six months off every year and I thought I would come here and learn to cook properly,' he told me in a depth-charge baritone so resonant I felt it as much as heard it. 'I've done courses in Thailand but wanted to do something a bit more serious.' Though he was an intimidating presence, Hermann turned out to be a softy, gently helping other students during the practicals and lending his equipment when we forgot ours. As he was staying alone in Paris, he used to give the food he made to the beggars on the corner of rue Vaugirard. In fact, I only ever saw him close to losing his temper once. With me.

This was at the end of the same week; we were making *feuilleté de poireaux et oeufs Pochés, avec sauce Albufera* (puff pastry with leeks and poached eggs with Albufera sauce made from cream, butter and stock). The challenge here was making our own puff pastry but I was struggling with the interminable origami of enveloping butter with dough. Up until this point I had assumed puff pastry was something that grew only in the freezer departments of supermarkets, like raspberry ripple ice cream, but we were shown how to make it from scratch by using dough to wrap a block of so-called 'dry butter' – a special pastry butter with much of its liquid content removed. You then rolled out the parcel as thinly as possible, folding the top and bottom thirds up to meet each other in the middle, turning it ninety degrees and rolling again, repeating the procedure up to six times (this precise layering is the reason why you can't simply roll unused puff pastry into a ball for use later on, you must place the scraps in layers on top of each other, otherwise the pastry won't puff). It is crucial that the parcel remains as cold as possible otherwise it will burst, the butter will leak, and the pastry won't puff, but at the same time it must also be warm enough to remain elastic for rolling. Leaking butter turned out to be the least of my troubles.

At the same time as making puff pastry we were also making a shortcrust pastry. Not for the last time in a Cordon Bleu kitchen I felt like a contestant on *The Generation Game* and I managed to mix up my ingredients for the two pastries, using 150ml of water for the puff pastry when only two tablespoons were required. Chef Thivet, more used to teaching Intermediate students than beginners like us, was on duty that day; he took one look at what I was doing, rolled his eyes and ordered me to start again. Seeing that everyone else around me was now well on their way to finishing their dishes, I started to panic but I began again and carefully placed my new dough in the fridge beside Hermann's, who was working beside me. After turning away to check my, by now, burnt leeks, I went back to the fridge to retrieve my shortcrust pastry, and began hastily rolling it out onto a flan tin. Except it wasn't my shortcrust pastry; it was Hermann's half-prepared puff pastry.

Thivet, who must have been wondering if I had strayed from some kind of remedial group no one had told him about, noticed the mistake first. I followed his raised eyebrows to the flan tin in front of me and realised my error. At this moment Chef Chalopin entered. 'What shall I do?' I whispered to him. 'Go to church, light a candle, pray,' he said. I considered simply walking out of the school and never returning, but we were going to be making raspberry *clafoutis* the next day and I couldn't possibly miss that. I rolled Hermann's puff pastry back into a ball and stuffed it into the fridge, grabbing what I thought was my shortcrust and began stuffing it into the tin. But it wasn't my shortcrust, it was Hermann's. Hermann, suspecting something was amiss, exploded with a volley of Bavarian insults which I was happy not to understand, and took the pastry from me. But both pastries were by now beyond repair. He would have to start all over again.

He didn't speak to me for the rest of the session and I had to be guided like a lobotomy patient through the rest of the recipe. At the end Chef Thivet shook my hand as if offering condolences at a funeral.

From this experience I learned two crucial rules: the first is that, when making two different types of pastry, do not measure out all the ingredients at the same time, as you will never remember which goes with which recipe and, rule two, never touch a Tyrolean's shortcrust.

Chapter 8

France will never be a country like others; France has a duty to excel before the world.

Dominic de Villepin

Though all the students had paid a significant sum to attend Le Cordon Bleu, any idea that we were paying customers, or that the chefs were subservient to us, was soon forgotten. Their naturally autocratic air and our appreciation of what they were showing us made us feel more like privileged inductees into a sacred sect than employers. We didn't bat an eye when, for instance, a chef threw a tantrum or indeed a whisk across the kitchen – as happened when Chef Patrick Terrien, head of Intermediate Cuisine, caught me using one to blend choux pastry after he had *specifically* told us we must use a spatula. Nor did we question them when they insisted that we use pre-grated gruyère on a potato gratin, even though pre-grated cheese is clearly against God. No, the chefs were very much in charge and, though some of the students might in their civilian professions have earned more money than they did, they commanded our unquestioning obeisance. To us they were benevolent, occasionally wrathful and often tetchy gods.

It soon became clear that Le Cordon Bleu is not one of those places where middle-aged singletons come for a few days to watch someone knock up a quiche Lorraine, drink themselves silly and get off with each other. It is a working school, which means that, as well as the erratic mood swings of the chefs, the equipment and facilities could sometimes be a little tired and emotional. One day in week four, for instance, I opened a fridge in a practical kitchen to find an old John Dory gaping back at me. Sinks became blocked on a daily basis, largely because students failed to scrape out dirty pans before rinsing them. One day, as we chopped onions, we realised that we could barely see for the tears streaming down our faces: the air conditioning had broken down. Occasionally one would turn on a hot tap and only cold water would flow. For a few weeks until the cleaner finally spotted it, I could recognise my locker in the changing room from the dismembered corpse of a cockroach which lay before it.

The kitchen equipment and facilities were surprisingly rudimentary too. We cooked over hot plates, rather than a gas flame, even though electric plates take eons to warm up and cool down, and gas is far more controllable. There was only one broiler – or grill – between three practical kitchens. Instead of copper pots and pans, which Chef Bruno admitted were superior, we had battered stainless steel ones which, though five or six times cheaper, looked as if they had been formerly used in silent movie-era comedy sketches. The *chinois* (fine, conical sieves, essential for straining sauces) were battered and misshapen, and, as for the rest of the kitchen equipment, apart from a few whisks, ladles, measuring jugs and slotted spoons, there was none.

This was not the case during demonstrations when the chefs would wheel out all manner of fascinating devices to help them prepare dishes. During the demonstration on how to make a potato *gratin* the chef had shown us how to use a mandolin to slice potatoes quickly and evenly claiming that it was 'like having an extra member of staff in the kitchen', but I hardly ever saw a mandolin in the practical kitchens, and spent ages patiently trying to slice potatoes finely and evenly by hand. Then there was the seemingly mythical 'Paco Jet' machine, one of the great secret contraptions of the professional kitchen which could process frozen food into sorbets or frozen purées in an instant. The trouble was, Paco Jets cost around four thousand euro each. I never got a sniff of one. Meanwhile, I had always believed that professional kitchens employed different-coloured chopping boards for fish, meat and vegetables. I asked one of the chefs why we only used gigantic, white Perspex boards for everything. 'It's true we should use different-coloured boards,' he admitted. 'But we just don't have the space to store them.'

And then, in early October, the mice started to invade. I saw my first one in an upstairs kitchen during a practical session. He glanced at me with rodential disdain, approached, picked a piece of debris from the floor in front of me, turned and disappeared behind an oven. I thought I ought to mention my encounter to the chef on duty that day, Chef Jean-Claude Boucheret, one of the older teachers at the school. Chef Boucheret, a grey-haired, moustachioed native of the Auvergne, was a multiple prizewinner. A former member of the French Culinary Olympic team, he had been a finalist in the prestigious *Meilleur Ouvrier de France* (Best craftsmen in France) competition and named a *Chevalier de l'Ordre du Mérite Agricole* by the French government. And the response of this titan of French cuisine to the news of our visitor? He broke into song – the theme tune to Disney's Mickey Mouse show – accompanied by a little jig.

I have a theory about chefs, which seems to apply particularly to French chefs. Why, one wonders, do they all, ultimately, seem to go mad? Why are ranting and raving, tantrums and sometimes tears – to which we must now add dancing – an accepted part of the job? What lies at the root of the aggressive behaviour of top chefs like Marco Pierre White, who begat Gordon Ramsay, who begat Tom Aiken (who allegedly 'branded' one of his chefs with a hot spatula)? This intrigued me for many years until I started to cook for other people, and then I understood perfectly. The problem begins, I believe, when a man is required to share kitchen space with another living human. As a man, the notion of performing two tasks at once is unthinkable, like patting your head while learning how to line dance. If I am cooking, particularly if it is something ambitious for guests, I simply can not cope with having anyone else in the kitchen. The radio, yes, Radio 4 even (though obviously not anything involving Melvyn Bragg), but no one who will require an engaged response to their latest house valuation or the new Harry Potter. So, imagine if a dozen people invaded your kitchen and didn't just try to talk to you about their concerns over their children's school, but started actually *interfering* with your food – taking it away from you, adding ingredients or seasoning and generally mucking about with it. Then, imagine that you have paying guests beyond the kitchen door upon whose pleasure and satisfaction your entire reputation and financial future rests. Instead, then, of condemning their outré behaviour, we ought to ask ourselves, is it any wonder that chefs are a bunch of neurotic-hysteric control freaks?

As for French chefs, they have the added challenge of having been brought up as French people. The problems start, I believe, when they go to school. Most French schools work on a similar principle to foie gras farms, with pupils being force-fed facts by relentless authoritarians (indeed, I've heard that in some rural French schools teachers actually hold students between their legs while doing this). French pupils are not taught to question or interpret, create or play, they are programmed to regurgitate facts, unquestioningly. They learn heaps, of course, and if you compare, say, the geographical, political or literary knowledge of the average sixteen-year-old French child with that of his American peer, you might begin think the American a little backward. But ask a French child their own opinion on something or tell them something funny it will often result in a blank look.

This Gradgrindish education is, I believe, responsible for what the outside world perceives as French arrogance. They're not arrogant, they are simply insecure – arrogance being the first refuge of the threatened. Confront a Frenchman with something beyond his ken – and therefore, crucially, beyond his control – and they go to pieces, at least internally. Externally they will probably be looking down their nose at you or, if pushed into a corner, puffing out their chests and flying off the handle into a molten rage. So here we have the two essential characteristics of your classic French chef – condescension and anger – both of which are compounded by the fact that most

70

chefs leave school early to enter the apprentice system and so don't even have the impressive erudition of their compatriots to fall back on. France's chefs are, if you like, *über* Frenchmen – which, I think also explains their underdeveloped and often politically incorrect sense of humour. When a Japanese student missed a practical session, one of the chefs, forgetting her name, simply pulled the corners of his eyes upwards to indicate 'where's the Japanese one?' I looked aghast. 'What?' he asked, genuinely confused (I am not for a moment suggesting the chef harboured racist sentiments towards Asians – quite the opposite). Then, as if offering a defence, he said: 'French eyes!' and pulled his downwards.

It should hardly come as a surprise, then, that French chefs are also profoundly chauvinistic. At Le Cordon Bleu this manifested itself in two ways: one sexist, the other racist. In terms of the former, the chefs would buzz around the younger female students like post-card salesmen around the tourists at the *Sacré Coeur*. Many of the chefs had worked in Cordon Bleu schools in South America and used their limited knowledge of Spanish to flirt shamelessly with the younger Colombian and Mexican female students, who in turn would giggle and flutter their eyelids and doubtless boost their grades, as I silently seethed like an ageing wife displaced from her husband's bed by fresher flesh (although, I would like to stress, we are very firmly in the realm of the metaphor here).

'Cooking is like a woman,' one of the chefs told us during a demonstration one day in early October, 'It needs to be pretty, and good for you.' Another told us that soufflés were also like a young lady, in that you 'need to treat them very delicately'. Meanwhile, according to Chef Terrien, 'Cuisine is like a tango with your lover' (I never did figure that one out).

As for the racism, this was aimed at two clear targets. The first was a by-product of the ancient and tedious enmity between France and England, a barely perceptible undercurrent which surfaced usually on those rare occasions when one of the chefs would be forced into offering a grudging approval of something I had cooked (*'Pff! Pas mal pour un Anglais'*), but most memorably during one of Chef Chalopin's demos in week five. Chalopin suddenly broke off from showing us how to make *soupe de moules légèrement safranée*, and turned to the blackboard behind him. Here he drew three circles of diminishing size. They were brains, he explained, before proceeding to label the largest 'Male' the second largest 'Ape' and the smallest 'Englishman'. Saying nothing further by way of explanation, he returned to the demonstration.

Chalopin happened to be supervising my practical session later that day and I decided to confront him as, being the only Englishman in the room at the time, I had taken this ever so slightly personally.

'Ah!' I said as he entered the kitchen that afternoon. 'Here comes the friend of every Englishman!'

Chalopin looked puzzled.

'Eh?' he said.

'The brains,' I said, 'that you drew today.'

'Oh', his face fell, and he began to look furtive. 'You are English?'

'Yes.'

'I thought you were American.' To see Chalopin embarrassed was a novel prospect, and by now several students had cocked their ears in our direction. Fumbling for an exit, Chalopin paused, coughed and, trying desperately to change the subject, dredged up some English-themed small talk.

'What is Mrs Thatcher doing these days?'

I thought for a moment and made a 'drinking a tumblerful of scotch' mime. He looked a little shocked, then laughed. Diplomatic incident averted.

Chapter 9

No high-spiced sauces, no dark brown gravies, no flavour of cayenne and allspice, no tincture of catsup and walnut pickle, no visible agency of those vulgar elements of cooking, of the good old times, fire and water ... every meat presented in its own natural aroma, every vegetable its own shade of verdure.

Antonin Carême

The second, perhaps more surprising target for the chef's prejudice were the Italians. French chefs, particularly those of a classical bent, are airily dismissive of Italian cooking and can be withering about even the most innocent, common or garden Italian ingredients. 'Italian cuisine is basically French cuisine but with pasta,' one chef claimed when a student asked him why we were never shown any Italian recipes. When asked if he was using olive oil to fry onions for a rice pilaf, Chef Bruno could barely suppress his horror: 'Olive oil and rice is too weird! There are some things written in the Bible.' The chefs of Le Cordon Bleu mostly cooked with sunflower or peanut oil, using olive oil only under extreme duress, such as in the making of an unavoidably Provençal dish like braised fennel. And, as usual, they were right. We have been conditioned by TV chefs to use olive oil in everything but actually it has a too dominant flavour for many dishes and, more importantly, can't reach temperatures that are high enough for frying meat properly. As for the health issues, as far as I understand it (or have convinced myself out of convenience), as soon as you heat olive oil the advantages diminish.

As for pasta, this was dismissed in all its forms under the blanket term 'noodles'. 'We don't do al dente here,' commented Chef Bruno one day as he tasted my slightly-too-crunchy braised carrots. In other cases, if an Italian dish or ingredient simply could not be avoided, they would simply give it a French name (I have since discovered that the French have done this with a long list of dishes they have managed to convince the world were their own invention). When we came to make that quintessential Italian comfort food, *gnocchi*, for example, many of us were surprised to find the dish had been appropriated by the French as *gnocchi à la parisienne*.

Again, I think the explanation for this lies in a deep-seated insecurity. You need only venture back a few centuries to discover that it was, in fact, the Italians, and not the French, who led the way in culinary matters – something few Frenchmen would care to concede today, I suspect. During the Renaissance, Italy's obsession with classical Antiquity encompassed not just the visual but the edible arts. A revival of interest in ancient texts, such as Pliny the Younger's letters (which also contain the famous account of the eruption of Vesuvius), and Apicius' *De re coquinaria*, with its elaborate recipes for, among other delicacies, dormouse, led to a reappraisal of ingredients such as truffles, wild mushrooms, artichokes, offal, oysters and caviar among late fifteenth-century Italians. Pork and sausages grew more popular, onions were more frequently used, and cooks turned away from the highly prized spices of the Middle Ages to locally grown herbs such as rosemary and thyme. Bowels, tripe, tongue, noses and eyes were all back on the menu. The Italians were ahead of the French in the production of ceramics too; they invented the dining room; were the first to fall for chocolate; and were early adopters of the white tablecloth and starched napkins. It is to the Italians that we owe the gratitude – or perhaps blame – for developing the vocabulary of wine appreciation. Unable to countenance the thought of using their fingers to eat with, they took up the fork almost a century before the French, at a time when a new breed of specialist emerged in the grand houses of Florence and Rome: the gastronome. Their spiritual leader was the King of Naples, who did much to define the choreography of banquets and dining rituals for the next century and a half.

From Naples the baton of culinary indulgence was passed to the Popes, who turned lavish dining into an Olympic sport Sir Roy Strong's history of grand eating, *Feast*, details one notable Papal feast, given in 1583 by Clement VII in honour of the sons of the Duke of Bavaria:

[The] second course had a *poussin* for each guest accompanied by a pastry shell stuffed with cockscombs, testicles and gooseberries, large pies filled with kids' eyes, ears and testicles, and boned and stuffed calves' head. The fourth course boasted a dish of capons' testicles and a salad of goat's feet . . . The most spectacular display pieces included 'white peacocks in their feathers, adorned with perfume in their beaks', a marzipan Hercules wielding his club against a pastry Hydra stuffed with chopped veal, hard-boiled egg yolks and pine nuts, and 'lions constituted from hares in large pies'. The finale was a model of the Castle of St Angelo [the site of the dinner], out of which came 'red-billed partridges, harnessed with gold and silver cloth, little hares and white rabbits with collars of little bells round their necks and corals in their perfumed paws'. There was a blackamoor king riding an elephant with a castle on its back full of live birds, a hydra which disgorged red moles and dormice, a horse out of whose mouth flew goldfinches on silken threads, a flower-bedecked bull which was an automaton and walked up and down the table, and a fully-rigged ship filled with sweetmeats from Bergamo. There were Pisan biscuits, English pies, meat cooked in the Florentine and French manner, tortellini stuffed with cheese and ham in the German style and quince paste from Portugal.

With the Popes giving the all clear, the creation of gut-busting dinners became an acceptable pastime for Italy's educated classes. Refinement in the kitchen was an extension of the glorification of God's work – after all, who had created the raw ingredients?

Meanwhile, the Humanists embraced the notion that eating offered something that stimulated all the senses, gave the body fuel and offered food for thought. The description of Pope Clement's monumental blowout reveals the Italians' obsession with the showier aspects of grand dining, perhaps ahead of concerns about the food itself, but for the next century the most significant books on food were still published not by Frenchman, but by Italians.

Meanwhile the French, distracted by endless internecine political bickering, lagged way behind not only the Italians but both the Germans and even the English. It used to be believed that the French finally began to catch up when Catherine de Medici married the French king Henry II in 1533 and brought Italian chefs to Paris, but the truth is that, though the Romans had long ago introduced the Parisians to the practice of roasting stray cats alive (which took place on the Place de Grève well into the seventeenth century), it took another half century or so for the more refined advances of Italian cuisine to cross the Alps.

So much for noodles. So how, then, did the French come to rule the culinary world, with Paris at its centre?

The global supremacy of French cuisine, so dominant during the nineteenth and most of the twentieth centuries, was founded upon the gluttony of its kings. The appetites of Le Roi Soleil, Louis XIV, for both food and women were insatiable and brazen. At the start of his reign the king dined in public in an orgy not just of food, but fashion, politics and lust. But as his reign progressed, Louis became more private, his dining less formal and more simplified. His successors ate in public only once a week, albeit still managing to consume enough to feed a small town in one sitting. 'I have seen the King eat, and very often eat, four bowls of different soups, a whole pheasant, a partridge, a big plate full of salad, chopped mutton in its juice with garlic, two good pieces of ham, a plate full of pastries, fruits and preserves,' Madame Palatine, sister-in-law to Louis XIV, once wrote. (The most famous victim – albeit unintended – of Louis' gluttony was, of course, the Prince de Condé's honourable steward-chef François Vatel, who committed suicide when he ran out of fish for a royal banquet. The more pragmatic Escoffier later said that he would simply have served them chicken breast – 'They would have been none the wiser.')

Slowly France was moving away from the ritualised, show banquets of the Italian Renaissance and shifting its focus to the food on the plate and, as Italy descended into pre-unification meltdown, it left the door open for the new French Republic to commandeer the stoves of Europe. 'The umbilical cord with Italy was thus cut', is how Sorbonne professor Jean-Robert Pitt puts it in his history of French cuisine. In fact, France had begun to wrestle the culinary initiative from Italy's grasp a century earlier with an explosion in the publication of French cookery books. Over two hundred were published within a century, the most important being La Varennes' *Le Cuisinier François* (1651), which explained, among other chefs' secrets, how to make stocks and then thicken them with a roux made from flour cooked in melted butter. Indeed, by 1746 there had been a back-to-basics revolt epitomised by a book, *La Cuisinière Bourgeoise*, which advocated a more simple style of home cooking. But whatever style they were promoting, these books were above all *French* cookery books, not Italian or German, and they paved the way for the rampant mythologizing of French cuisine – asserting its regional roots, the superiority of French chefs and creating the first food superstars. The books tapped into a market among the growing middle class of Europe who aspired to dine as the royals did and wanted to mimic their grand '*service à la francaise*' dinner parties, in which meals were served in silver tureens and bowls at the table (essentially a kind of buffet, albeit with waiters), which was eventually replaced in the nineteenth century by '*service à la Russe*' (in which each course was arranged on individual plates).

During the mid-eighteenth century the first menus appeared, and meals now progressed from savoury dishes to sweet, whereas previously the two had mingled. The French moved their evening meal from late afternoon to the more sophisticated hour of seven in the evening; they invented the domestic dining room – again; and formulated a whole new set of table manners to match (out went singing with dessert, for instance, in came all the kind of things designed to make me feel like a Beverley Hillbilly every time I eat in a posh restaurant).

The French also claim to have invented the restaurant – at least in the modern sense of the word. The first, they say, was the Grande Taverne de Londres, opened at 26 rue de Richelieu, Paris, in 1782 by Antoine Beauvilliers. That said, many cite a Monsieur Boulanger's decision in 1765 to offer boiled sheep's feet to drinkers at his inn on the rue du Louvre as the precedent. Yet others point out that there were public eating houses, or 'cookshops', in London a hundred years before that and there are places a century older still in Japan. That may be true, but the world still thinks that the French invented the restaurant – another victory for national mythology over *actualité*.

Following the Revolution, with no aristocracy left to cook for, many of the best Parisian chefs had to look elsewhere for work (the Prince of Condé's last chef, Méot, set up a restaurant on the rue de Valois, for instance), and by the turn of the nineteenth century there were over two thousand restaurants in Paris. They were in turn plagued by the first restaurant critic, Alexandre Balthazar Laurent Grimod de la Reynière, and plagiarised by the first gourmet food writer, Jean-Anthelme Brillat-Savarin.

Towering over all the chefs of his era was Antonin Carême, generally held to be the great pioneer of French cuisine, who surfed this wave of post-revolutionary, culinary democratisation to bring haute cuisine, if not to the masses, then at least to more than had ever been able to enjoy it in the past. Translations of his rationalised recipes and codified system of cooking helped spread the gospel of French cooking throughout the kitchens of the world, establishing a supremacy that would brook no rivals for over a century and a half. It was Carême who invented the concept of the four 'mother' sauces: *velouté*, made by pouring hot white stock into a light roux;

l'espagnole, a roux-thickened brown stock; *béchamel*, made by thickening milk; and egg-based emulsions, such as hollandaise – from which all other sauces of the day were derived. Among many other innovations, he also devised the formula for the bouquet garni (bay, thyme and leek) that is still taught at Le Cordon Bleu to this day.

France was slow to kick off its Industrial Revolution but when it did finally get round to building canals and railways it meant that the country's wondrous regional produce could be whisked to the *grandes tables* of Paris within hours (one might almost suspect this was the prime reason for building them). Paris was now the terminus for Europe's, if not the world's, greatest produce-supply network. 'When Paris sits down to the table,' wrote Eugene Briffault at the time, 'the entire earth stirs.' The city's chefs were now able to exploit the bounteous produce from the six hundred regions of France and their even more numerous *terroirs* – from Mediterranean to Alpine to Atlantic; freshwater and saltwater; and every type of soil imaginable, not to mention a dramatic diversity of climates. As Auguste Escoffier (from whose name I like to think is derived the verb 'to scoff') wrote, 'French soil has the privilege of producing, naturally and in abundance, the best vegetables, the best fruits, and the best wines in the world. France also possesses the finest poultry, the most tender meat, the most delicate and varied game. Its sea coast provides it with the most beautiful fish and crustaceans. Thus, it is completely natural for the French to become both gourmands and great cooks.' Whether this is true or not, the great French trick, yet again, was to convince the rest of the world that this was, indeed, the case.

Following the example of Carême, who cooked in the kitchens of George IV, Tsar Alexander in St Petersburg and at the Rothschilds' home in Paris, French chefs travelled widely across both the Channel and the Atlantic. Carême's successor in the greatest chefs stakes, Auguste Escoffier, followed later in the century, helping to invent the modern hotel with Cesar Ritz and training over two thousand chefs under his slick new 'brigade' system.

Escoffier's legacy lasted well into the middle of the twentieth century, remaining virtually unchallenged until the arrival of nouvelle cuisine. Though this was perhaps the last time that the French were to revolutionise restaurant cooking, its influence of nouvelle cuisine endures to this day in the simplified, seasonal cooking preached by virtually every contemporary chef.

The term nouvelle cuisine was first used by the *Gault et Millau* guide, but many trace its origins to the time the famous French chef, Raymond Oliver, cooked for the teams at the Tokyo Olympics in 1964. Oliver was hugely influenced by Japanese food and, on his return, urged his countrymen to simplify and lighten their cuisine. By 1973 chefs such as Paul Bocuse, Michel Guérard and Alain Chapel were preaching the Ten Commandments of Nouvelle Cuisine ('You will use fresh, high quality produce'; 'You will eliminate brown and white sauces'; You will avoid marinades' and so on). The food was lower in fat and used fewer sauces you could see what you were eating and it tasted of what it was. The increased popularity of the food processor meant the French went purée crazy for a while – and haven't really stopped. Flour was banned as a thickening agent, instead sauces were reduced to a sticky glaze; fruit appeared alongside meat on the plate; and terrines were made from vegetables instead of offal, meat and fat. Don't tell Chef Bruno, but vegetables were cooked al dente.

This was all good stuff of course but, in the early 1980s nouvelle cuisine descended into caricature with chefs becomingly obsessed with fussy plating, elaborate menu descriptions, and reducing quantities of food on the plate to absurdly small portions. As Elizabeth David wrote, 'It is not so much the cooking that is wrong . . . as a certain coldness and ungenerosity of spirit, an indifference to the customer.'

All of this served to reinforce the prevailing view of French chefs as being remote, arrogant and stingy. Things went further awry when the mania for fusion cooking – an often inspired, though occasionally ill-advised marrying of Asian ingredients and Western cuisines – gripped the rest of the western world. The French never really got to grips with fusion cooking, indeed many French chefs still believe that a token slice of mango or a sprinkling of curry powder around the edge of the plate is enough to show willing. The restaurants of New York, Sydney, San Francisco and Singapore supplanted those of the French capital as the world's prime foodie destinations, while Italian food, took over as the most popular food for busy, health-conscious folk in Western Europe and the United States. The French never really recovered. These days, the jet-setting food lover is as likely to travel to Barcelona, Osaka, London or Stockholm as they are to Paris while, in their own homes, keen cooks may well make their own pasta or slow cook tomato sauces for an eternity, but they would never think of making similarly time-consuming and tricky French food.

Following fusion, the next global food fad was molecular gastronomy which, as I write, shows little sign of abating; but, other than in the kitchens of Pierre Gagnaire, it has never really caught on in Paris either. 'The old French chefs are afraid, of course,' Hervé This, the inventor of molecular gastronomy and close friend of Gagnaire, told me when I met him at his chaotic laboratory in the Collège de France later in the year when I interviewed him for a newspaper article. 'But look at Parmentier when he tried to get the French to eat potatoes. In the end they had to put guards round the potato fields to tell the French they couldn't eat them, to convince them they were worth anything. Only then did they decide they were worth stealing!' For the same piece I interviewed Gagnaire, an elegant, leonine genius, in his equally graceful three-star dining room. Gagnaire has endured a great deal – not least bankruptcy – in pursuit of his own, uniquely adventurous cooking. I asked him why the French were so reticent to embrace molecular cuisine. He sighed heavily, 'We just don't know how to go to that next level of international cuisine. We're not the most efficient people.'

At least Gagnaire remains in business. Others have been less fortunate, not least the three-star chef Bernard Loiseau who committed suicide in 2003, his death blamed at the time on the pressures of making a top restaurant work and his terror of losing one of his three Michelin stars. Life has not been easy for the haute cuisine chef this last decade as changing tastes, rising prices, increasing costs and a growing awareness of just how much animal fat is present in classical French food has dented trade. 'Few people have time to sit down for a two-hour lunch,' François Simon, the revered and feared restaurant critic of *Le Figaro* told me. 'There are now twenty ways to each lunch in this city, from sandwiches to sushi, all of them cheaper and quicker than a classic French lunch.' The costs of employing sommeliers, a waiter for every two customers and a vast kitchen brigade, coupled with the investment in decor and cutlery, not to mention rare and expensive ingredients, means that it is virtually impossible for a three-star restaurant to survive without the chef having various publishing or TV deals, the rolling out of a concept or 'chain' (in the manner of Joël Robuchon's Atelier), or product endorsements (both Bocuse and Robuchon have a line of frozen foods, for instance). These days many of Paris' three-star restaurants rely on the patronage of Japanese, Russian or, latterly, Chinese diners, and the manpower of Korean or Japanese *stagières* (interns) prepared to work for free in their kitchens. One commentator has gone as far as to speculate that the *grande tables* of Paris will one day need to be subsidised by the government as a part of the tourist industry.

Meanwhile, the French continue to torture themselves about their supposed declining food culture. Hardly a week goes by without a newspaper poll revealing that eighty per cent of under-thirties don't know how to boil an egg, and think puff pastry grows on trees, or whatever. It is true that the French consume the most frozen food per capita of any European nation and, despite the protests of José Bové and the *anti-mondialism* bunch, it can sometimes seem as if there is a McDo on every corner but, still, Simon, Gagnaire and This remained upbeat about Paris' and France's claim to be one of the great food destinations, citing its fabulous produce, the technical

brilliance of its chefs and the deep-seated appreciation and understanding of food that still flourishes here.

'The French are terribly self-critical,' Gagnaire told me when I
asked if he really thought there was a crisis in French cooking. 'No,
no, no. It gives quite the wrong impression to the rest of the world,'
he said. 'It is never at all as bad as we say it is.' François Simon, who
has been one of the sternest critics of the food of his home city
was, surprisingly, equally positive about Paris: 'Crisis is so good for
us! It has given us a kick. Paris is always a terrific city for food,' he
said. 'We might not be so good to imagine the food of the future
but that kind of molecular "funny" food is only really interesting
once or twice a year. Tokyo or Osaka might be more modern, more
challenging, but when I eat out I want something gentle, I want love
and good food. If you know where to look in Paris you will always
find that.'

Simon reminded me about the *bistrots modernes*, the small, local
bistros run by some of the city's most innovative and exciting chefs,
which evolved in the late 1990s. Chefs like Yves Camdeborde and
François Pasteau who had worked in the kitchens of Michelin-starred
venues, left them to open their own places which, though far cheaper
and less formal, still serve exceptional, creative food. The refined,
rustic cooking of the *bistrots modernes* has had a huge influence on a
new wave of restaurants in London or even places like Heston
Blumenthal's Hind's Head pub in Bray, which tend to serve cheaper
cuts of meat and a simple but satisfying vegetable garnish. Their
food is certainly more relevant to most people's lives than the smoked
foams and flavoured gas-filled balloons of Ferran Adriá. Le Epi
Dupin, Avant Goût and Le Pré Verre are among my very favourite
places to eat in Paris: you can have three deeply satisfying, often
surprising courses there for around thirty-five euro.

Personally, when I see the week's menu – cassoulet one day,
Basque-style chicken the next – printed at the entrance to my children's school; when I wait in the mile long queue at Jöel Thibault's
stall in the Marché Avenue President Wilson to buy the kind of

vegetables Sainsbury's shoppers could only dream of; when I see the lunchtime queues outside my local *chocolatier* – where, as with many bakeries, butchers and patisseries in Paris, they sell traditional French dishes like *boeuf bourguignon* or *blanquette de veau* in takeaway form; or when I visit the herb garden in the children's amusement park, the *jardin d'acclimatisation* (can you imagine Disneyland having a herb garden?), and see children genuinely interested in seeing thyme or basil grow; when I witness all of these things and dozens more, I always feel optimistic about the future of French food.

I knew I had chosen the right city for my culinary improvement – the passion; the in-depth, inborn knowledge; the discernment; the sheer amount of time that the French allocate to the contemplation of what they put in their mouths still exceeds that of any other race on earth except, perhaps, the Japanese, by a factor of, I'd say, ten, Paris is the showcase for that glorious national obsession. But still, I do wish they would stop doing that thing with the curry powder.

Here is a recipe that combines some of my favourite things from a French market. Every time I make it, it reaffirms everything I know to be good and true about French cooking (not least because some might well claim it to be an Italian dish).

Meltingly Tender Veal Shank (*Jarret de Veau*) in a Wine Sauce

There nothing more satisfying to cook or eat than a tough piece of meat from a hard-working part of an animal – be it shoulder, shin or leg – gently braised in wine, low and slow over an afternoon. You can jazz it up or keep it simple as you like, but it is embarrassingly easy to make.

Simple version

Take a whole veal shank or shin, with the bone still in. Salt it well. Put it in a pot, glug in a bottle of white wine and cook it for three or four hours at 160°C. Remove the meat to rest, and reduce the wine to make a sauce.

Ever so slightly more complicated version (serves 6-8 depending on the size of the joint and your guests' greed)

1 veal shank

Nut or Sunflower oil

200g of dried, white haricot beans

A small handful of lardons

2 garlic cloves, sliced

2 sprigs of rosemary

A carrot

An onion

A stick of celery

1 Bouquet garni (thyme, bay leaves and parsley stalks wrapped in a green leek leaf)

Spices of your choice

Around a dozen shallots

A tin of tomatoes (optional)

Some thyme — fresh is best of course, but dried is fine

A bottle of white wine — anything drinkable will do, although I prefer to use something a bit sweet. You can always add a sugar cube if you want a sweeter sauce, or stir in a teaspoon of mustard or crème fraiche to serve

Seasoning

Butter

Another bouquet garni

The day before, put the beans in a bowl of water to soak overnight. Freeze the lardons to make them easier to stuff into the veal shank. Make fifteen or so slits all over the veal shank, and stuff them with the lardons and slivers of garlic. Stuff a couple of rosemary sprigs between the bone and the flesh and put it back in the fridge. You don't really need to trim the shank of its fat because it will turn deliciously gelatinous when you cook it and will add flavour to the sauce. If there are some particularly frightening bits you can remove them but otherwise, don't worry.

The next day, drain the beans and rinse in fresh water, then boil ferociously for ten minutes in fresh water, reduce to a simmer and add the peeled carrot and onion, celery and bouquet garni. Cook for around an hour, or until the beans are soft yet still have some bite left. Remove the vegetables and bouquet garni (bin them, they've given their all) and drain the beans.

An hour before cooking, remove the veal shank from the fridge and squeeze out all the garlic pieces – strangely satisfying that. Dry well and sprinkle with salt. Take a large metal casserole and heat it. When it is hot add some nut oil. Once that is hot, add the veal shank and brown it well on all sides. Remove the veal shank, turn down the heat and add any spices you fancy – ground coriander seeds or perhaps some nutmeg – then the white wine, bringing it to the boil and scraping any brownings from the bottom of the casserole. Reduce the wine a little to burn off the alcohol. Return the meat to the pot with the shallots, beans, tomatoes (though, personally, I'd only add tomatoes if I was using a sweet wine) and a second bouquet garni.

Place the casserole, lid on, in the oven at 160°C and cook for three to four hours, turning the shank once at the halfway mark and skimming the surface of the wine when you can be bothered.

When it is cooked, the meat should fall from the bone. Gently lift it from the wine and beans using a couple of slotted spoons. Strain the wine into another pan, place the beans, tomatoes and shallots somewhere warm and reduce the wine vigorously until it thickens and you achieve a flavour you feel proud of. Check the seasoning, grind in a little fresh pepper and, if you like (and I invariably do), swirl in a knob of chilled butter. You can add some mustard or crème fraiche at the end if you fancy it.

Serve with something green – spinach or a salad dressed with one part balsamic vinegar to six parts olive oil, salt, pepper and a soupçon of maple syrup.

If – by dint of an unforeseen Act of God which meant you had to abandon the dinner table – you have some left-over meat, it is sensational shredded and added to a thick, slow-cooked tomato sauce the next day and tossed with pasta and parmesan.

Chapter 10

Du beurre, du beurre, et encore du beurre.
Auguste Escoffier on the essence of French cuisine

As I may have hinted, some chefs can often seem a bit – how can I put this sensitively? – retarded, maybe autistic even. This is particularly evident in the way that they seek refuge from the troubling realities of the real world in obsession and repetition. Keeping the chlorophyll in green vegetables was one major fixation of our chefs, for instance. I lost count of the times we were told to heavily salt the water we used to boil broccoli or beans to 'lock in the chlorophyll' and keep them looking fresh and verdant. Woe betide any student who presented a grey, wilted *haricot vert* at the end of a practical: the chef marking the plate would hold one up like an errant worm for all to see, shaking his head sadly. To them, chlorophyll was as precious as the vegetable's flavour itself and to be so careless as to allow it to evaporate was criminally negligent. We were even shown how to extract chlorophyll (technically 'culinary chlorophyll'), from herbs by blending parsley, spinach and tarragon with a little water, straining through a cheesecloth and gently reducing the liquid over a low heat. The chlorophyll rises quickly to the surface and you can then skim it off to use as a vivid colouring for sauces or mayonnaise. It was probably the closest we would come to the scientific approach of molecular gastronomy during Basic Cuisine.

Ironically, though they were pedantic about many things, the chefs were infuriatingly vague about others – in particular oven temperatures. During each demonstration someone would invariably ask at what temperature we should cook, to which the answer would be, variously, 'Not too hot', 'Just hot enough', or 'Very hot'. Though this didn't seem terribly helpful at the time, the reasoning was sound: to get us used to the idea that it was far better to use your eyes to judge how something was cooking than to rely on an oven's, usually unreliable, thermostat (for that same reason we were told that pressure cookers were 'for housewives'). Even the school ovens could vary by as much as thirty degrees from the dial setting. 'You must build a relationship with your oven,' Chef Bruno advised. 'Always try to use the same oven in the practicals; learn its ways'.

On the other hand, there were very firm rules about presentation. You should never pour *jus* or sauce over sliced red meat, for example, the idea is that the customer should see how perfectly you have cooked it. In fact, coming up with our own approaches to plate decoration was a routine cause for displeasure among the chefs, as I discovered when I took it upon myself to arrange some anchovies on an onion tart to form an, admittedly slightly wonky, Union Jack. Chef Didier frowned when he saw it and simply removed four of them. And then there was the turning (in French *tourner*, or 'to round') of vegetables – perhaps the ultimate expression of the French chef's latent autism. Carrots, potatoes, turnips, even mushrooms – no vegetable could escape the fussy sculpting of the chefs' paring knives. Turning usually involved carving root vegetables into small rugby balls, but in the case of mushrooms required us to sculpt them in to spiral spinning tops, and it drove us students to the very cusp of insanity. It was fiddly and time-consuming and had no obvious virtues other than making the plate look like some arcane board game.

Actually, there were good reasons for turning vegetables: by making the potatoes, carrots or turnips the same shape and size you could ensure that each one achieved the same degree of *cuisson* (or 'cookedness'). Unfortunately, this usually meant discarding around seventy per cent of each vegetable. This appeared contrary to the chefs' customary dedication to eliminating waste of any kind, but they assured us that the trimmings could be used for making potato purée or, in the case of mushrooms, as an invaluable addition to a stock.

After a couple of week's worth of potato sculpting sessions, I came to look upon the turning of vegetables as the Mr Miyagi phase of our journey to becoming professional chefs (inspired by the endless 'Wipe on, wipe off' training the martial arts guru puts the *Karate Kid* through early on in the film); there were times when I drifted into a kind of meditative state when chiselling away at my potatoes: Zen and the Art of Root Vegetable Maintenance, if you like.

The turning of vegetables was one of several classical French cooking techniques we were introduced to during those first weeks that usually prompted a mass eye-roll among the students. The chefs were well aware that much of what they showed us seemed anti-quated or overly elaborate – especially to those of us schooled in the 'rip it up and stuff it in' way of doing things – but they revelled in it. 'Recipes and techniques come in and out of fashion,' Chef Bruno told us a little wistfully during a béchamel sauce demo. 'Like Sacha Distel.' They seemed to relish the historical nature of many dishes: Bruno proudly informed us that *sauté de veau Marengo* (a heavy-weight veal stew topped with a fried egg) was so named by Napoleon's chef following his victory in the battle of the same name. Thivet trumped him a few days later with a recipe for Genoan almond cake that was three hundred years old.

There was another relic from a bygone culinary era on the wall of the demonstration room: a faded publicity shot taken, I would guess, sometime in the mid-1970s, showing the late Julia Child, doyenne of American TV cooking, surrounded by racks of lamb and ornately decorated cakes. 'The most famous cook in the world presents scrumptious menus for every occasion!' read the caption. As great as Child was, even back in the early 1970s she was hardly what you'd call cutting edge (nor was she 'world famous', at least not unless we are using the 'World Famous in America' criteria they also use for the baseball 'World Series'). Meanwhile, on the stair-case, next to photos of Dustin Hoffman taken during his two visits to the school, hung framed, early-twentieth-century newspaper reports about Le Cordon Bleu and the menu from the coronation dinner of Queen Elizabeth II, catered by the school and featuring Coronation Chicken, devised specially by its chefs.

Of course, the school's traditional approach was the whole point. We were here to learn the classic techniques of French cookery, not how to make parmesan ice cream, or a hundred ways with gelatine. At Basic Cuisine level at least, this meant plenty of simply roasted or fried meats, fish in buttery sauces, bisques, parfaits and gratins.

In accordance with Auguste Escoffier's advice, our chefs employed vast quantities of butter in their recipes, which distressed the Americans especially. 'I can smell the butter already,' Veronica, an economist at the World Bank in Washington, whispered to me at the start of one demonstration of *poularde pochée sauce supreme, riz au gras* during week four (she was right, the chef must have used at least two packets for that one). And if it wasn't butter, cream would be the artery-lagging ingredient of the day. Meanwhile, it took little more than some dripping blood from a steak or a whole, naked chicken to draw further gasps of horror from the Japanese women in the class.

Then there were the alarming quantities of salt, which the chefs would toss liberally into dishes, sometimes fistfuls at a time, or so it seemed. I tried to imitate their saline abandon when we were deep frying battered sole goujons and ended up with something that tasted like dehydrated anchovy. I could never get seasoning right. Judging how much salt to add to a dish presented the greatest single challenge of Basic Cuisine, and its greatest source of frustration.

While the use of pepper rarely raised any issues unless catastrophically misjudged, salt was dastardly difficult. It doesn't help that one man's palate – or an entire nation's for that matter – is invariably different from the next's. As time went on, we got to know which chefs smoked and which did not, the smokers tending to prefer saltier food, but it was hard to argue with the chefs, smokers or not, when they pointed out that I had added too much salt too early when reducing a stock or a sauce which meant that as the liquid content concentrated, so too did the salt; or too late in another dish, which meant that it didn't have time to dissolve properly and left that harsh, just-salted flavour. And did you know that lemon juice intensifies the salt in a dish? Me neither. The Asian students, more used to using soy sauce as a seasoning, found salt an even trickier substance to work with. I'd been using it all my adult life: what was my excuse?

The chefs used more salt than a home cook, of that there was no doubt, but the key was that they knew better *when* to use it – adding a little at the start, for instance, then more later on during cooking, but rarely any at the end unless absolutely necessary or to deliberately add bite to a dish, in which case they would use coarse sea salt. For example, a simple side dish that we were taught which works really well with fish was braised fennel – simply *julienne* of fennel bulb, cook in a pan over a very low heat with a couple of tablespoons of water and, of course, a good dose of butter. The success of the dish depended on three things: the precision and regularity of your *juliennes*; cooking the fennel without browning it (the chef showed us how to fold and cut a circle of parchment paper to cover the pan and keep the fennel moist); and the seasoning. The key to the latter, as with all braised vegetables, was to add the salt only halfway through cooking, and then to err on the side of caution. That way the vegetables will have had time to soften and reduce in quantity. Instead of having a mountain of fennel to salt, you are left with half a pan and you can judge more easily how much is needed.

In week five, early in October, we made *filets de barbue Dugléré* (brill fillets in a white wine sauce). All was going well during the practical for perhaps the first time since I had started at the school. I wasn't looking out of the corner of my eye at the others; I was referring less and less to my notes; and starting almost to feel confident. By the end, my fish was perfectly cooked; I had made a decent fist of shaping my potatoes into little rugby balls; and the consistency of my sauce was perfect – like cold olive oil, just as the chef had shown us. Chef Patrick Terrien, head of Intermediate Cuisine but supervising us that day, inspected my final plate with his usual diligence. Some of the older chefs often gave our plates little more than a quick once-over, tasting the main feature and then just breaking into the potatoes to check they were cooked well enough, but Terrien tasted everything. He tried my fish: *parfait*. He admired my potatoes: *trés bon*. My tomatoes were diced with a regimental precision: *impeccable*. Then he tasted the sauce. I could see the disappointment register. There was too much salt. Not so much to render it inedible, just more than was comfortable. Eat the whole dish and, half an hour down the line, you would be parched. The reason? I had added salt to the sauce *before* reducing. The chef congratulated me on the rest of my work, but I could see he'd marked me down as an also-ran, someone who didn't quite make the grade, who couldn't quite hold all the elements of a plate together.

He would have had more evidence of this the next day when it was Chef Bruno who picked up my mistake. We had been cooking *côtes de veau grand-mère* (gigantic, Jurassic-sized veal chops, 'like Grandma used to make them'), with a garnish of glazed pearl onions, mushrooms and lardons. It's not an especially complex dish to prepare; you simply fry and baste the chop for twenty minutes or so, although this does require some vigilance to avoid burning. The tricky thing, as ever, is to judge when the meat is cooked to perfection, which in this case meant nicely caramelised on the outside but pink and juicy within. Often though, having too much time in the kitchen can be just as problematic as being rushed off your feet and, consequently, my onions turned to marmalade, my mushrooms were turned half to death and I had a brain fade about how to chop the bacon into lardons. While the meat was resting, I had time to over-reduce my *jus*, ending up with a couple of teaspoons. Plating this into something remotely presentable was going to be quite a challenge.

I picked the three onions that had somehow managed to hold themselves together, browned them a little and hoped the chef had had enough onions that day and wouldn't taste them. I then mustered all my *jus* and selected my two best mushrooms. I let out a little whistle of satisfaction when I came to slice the veal chop and it was perfectly pink inside. I made a special effort to have a clean, hot plate, chopped some parsley to scatter over for a bit of distracting colour and presented it to the chef. '*Parfait jus!*' he exclaimed. '*Parfait cuisson!*' The meat, he agreed, was good too. '*Superbe!*' He even ignored my onions, but then, just as I was about to pick the plate up and float away on a cloud of elation, he did a double take. He had noticed my overly large lardons. His face dropped. 'Not so big next time, you don't want the customer to have to . . .' He mimed someone chewing an old boot.

I was pleased that most of the components of the dish were as they should have been (although, admittedly, if the chef had taken a look in my pans they would have told another story). It was the first plate I had presented that might realistically have been good enough to be given to a customer in, say, a second-rate bistro on a quiet Monday night. But I was disappointed to have been so close to perfection only to be let down by a bit of bacon. I mulled over my error for several hours after the session, returning to the subject like a tongue toying with a sore tooth late into the night, until Lissen pointedly walked over to the stereo and turned the volume up.

Chapter 11

Animals feed themselves, people eat, intelligent people alone know how to eat.

Brillat-Savarin

Never eat more than you can lift.

Miss Piggy

Having lived in Paris for a couple of months I felt it was about time we dined out somewhere that didn't have vinyl banquettes and a row of builders' bums gazing at us from the bar. One evening, having bound and gagged the children and locked them in a cupboard (I'm joking, that was the babysitter's job), Lissen and I headed out. Our destination was L'Atelier Joël Robuchon, beside the Hotel Pont Royal in St Germain.

Joël Robuchon is a legend. In 1990 the Gault Millau guide crowned him 'the greatest chef of the twentieth century' and, though there are a few who might quibble with this (not least Alain Ducasse and his henchmen), it is not without substance. Back in the 1990s Robuchon ran two restaurants, each with three Michelin stars – at the time an unprecedented achievement. Long before Ducasse began his rampant empire building, Robuchon was advocating the highest-quality ingredients prepared with simplicity and clarity – with vegetables cooked al dente, sauces thickened without cream or roux and innovative plating. A generation of chefs, Gordon Ramsay among them, were tutored the Robuchon way. It was by all accounts a tough education with Robuchon, who had studied at a seminary to become a priest until the age of fifteen, and was remorselessly demanding of his chefs (Ramsay tells a story of being deafened for a week when a disgruntled Robuchon threw a langoustine at his ear, for instance). Yet, in 1996, at the age of fifty-one, Joël Robuchon quit the restaurant world. Though hardly a Garbo-style disappearance – he continued to present a popular cooking show on French TV – gourmands and gourmets the world over were bereft. His return to the professional kitchen a few years ago was the culinary equivalent of a Sinatra comeback. But he didn't just come back singing 'My Way' again in a slightly less plausible wig, his was the full Madonna-esque reinvention. Robuchon had clearly had his fill of the *Guide Michelin*, with its arcane service criteria and obsession with fancy toilet facilities. His new *atelier* concept would be the antidote to stuffy, starred dining. Influenced by his time working as a consultant in Japan, Robuchon wanted to try something different, something less formal, on his return to Paris; thus there is no reservation policy at L'Atelier, even celebrities must queue; and once in, diners sit on high stools ranged around a bar that encloses an open plan kitchen.

The French press were initially sceptical: Parisians might queue for the first few weeks, they said, but once the weather changed there was no way they were going to wait in line in their best frocks for a one-hundred-euro dinner. But wait they did, and come they did, not just from Paris or France, but from around the world. And they haven't stopped coming, which is why, if you want to be sure of a table, you must be there for the first sitting at six thirty, as we were.

Spotlit olive trees flank L'Atelier's front entrance beyond them a wall is taken up by a glass display case filled with spices and nuts from North Africa. Inside, just to confuse us further, the decor is Japanese-ish, with a red and black lacquered wood counter and staff dress in pseudo-oriental, black Mao jackets. Meanwhile, Spanish hams and sausages hang from the ceiling. It oozes class, of course, but there are no linen tablecloths and no penguin maître d'. Instead, we were shown to our perches, beside an obviously wealthy, late middle-aged American couple, by a slinky young waitress, dressed as if for the office, and offered menus.

One interesting effect of the piano-bar-style layout is that it directs your focus to the food, rather than your companion. It must make dining as a threesome or more tricky but you can imagine how this might appeal to a megalomaniac chef. A reviewer once described it as being 'like receiving a highly advanced private medical treatment' with the waiter as consultant, but it reminded me more of receiving Holy Communion. We still managed to get talking to our neighbours. 'This is my fifteenth time at a Robuchon restaurant!' Ken, a Californian in his early sixties, told me proudly. 'Our sixth time here!' piped up his wife, Joanne-Jo. In keeping with the restaurant's informal atmosphere, both were dressed in upscale, highly flammable nylon leisure suits. They spoke of Robuchon's lightness of touch and his 'crazy genius'. 'You gotta try the mash!' said Ken, referring to Robuchon's legendary potato purée which, far from being 'light', is a potted coronary made from one part butter to one part potato ('just plain silly', the *New York Times* called it). I did and it was silken, creamy and delicious – but it didn't really fit with the rest of the *atelier*'s ethos, and I got the feeling it was on the menu because people expected it, like Sinatra singing 'My Way'.

As for the rest of the ten-course tasting menu, with its signature avocado and almond *coulis*; a sweet, pink lamb cutlet accompanied by a rustic brush of thyme; and the fittingly named 'Chocolate Sensation' dessert, it made of me a devotee within a few mouthfuls. The Sensation wasn't the only dessert, nor the highlight of the evening, come to that; that accolade went to a small quenelle of lime and basil sorbet with strawberries, pineapple and melon lapped by a palate-busting basil infusion. Or was the creamy chestnut soup with chunks of foie gras and a fresh, background hint of celery the best thing? What about that fat, glistening scallop with browned truffle butter? Then there were the *amuse bouche*, which included gazpacho and a single crevette tempura paired, like a question mark, with a vivacious blob of basil dressing. Little flavour bombs each. The presentation was studied yet casual: some dishes were served on lava from a Japanese volcano, others on simple wooden boards, or porcelain. Ten courses might sound like a gargantuan blow-out, but the vitality of the ingredients and the deftness with which they were used meant that, as we left at the end of an evening of sensual ecstasy, we didn't feel bloated at all. I waddled only slightly.

These days you can't move for posh, Modern European tapas joints in London (where the latest branch of L'Atelier opened in 2006 to excited reviews), Paris and New York but Robuchon was among the first to experiment with smaller-sized dishes that still had the complexity and quality of haute cuisine, and I can't imagine it being done any better than this. Indeed, despite setting out as an almost anti-Michelin statement, L'Atelier has even won a star – it is as if Robuchon can not help gathering the things.

For me, though, the most fascinating aspect of the atelier was watching the kitchen brigade at work, silently, studiously and without hesitation. They moved with an economy of motion and fluidity clearly honed over the years, and worked with the concentration of air-traffic controllers. I could no more imagine myself joining them than I could imagine directing the traffic around the Arc de Triomphe.

One of the perks of attending Le Cordon Bleu was that we got to take any food we made home with us. With our budget diminishing at an alarming rate, this was a boon and I would eagerly vacuum up any leftovers from the other students, stuffing them into my giant Tupperware tub to carry home in my string bag for dinner that night.

The reaction at home was, however, mixed, Lissen appreciated the food and hates cooking herself (except for baking, which she excels at – which is fortunate as yeast makes me panic), but there was an undeniable tension between how much she enjoyed eating the food I brought home, and the impact the large quantities of butter and cream used in its preparation were having on her ability to fit into her jeans.

Asger and Emil were less appreciative. Asger, his mind clearly influenced by some new playground revolutionary, had become aware that he had a choice over what he ate and was refusing anything that wasn't frankfurters. Each evening I would place a token vegetable on his plate in the vain hope that – perhaps distracted by one of Emil's water-throwing fits – he would eat it absentmindedly. But upon entering the kitchen, he would instantly see that his plate had been violated by a small broccoli floret or a pea. He would scream, he would cry, he would stamp his feet and roll around on the floor, and end up eating only the starch and animal bits. It was, I realised, divine retribution for all I had put my parents through as a child. As for Emil, being of an age at which he wolfed down anything placed before him, he seemed to appreciate my cooking most of all. Then again, bearing in mind that we would often catch him eating soil, this was no ringing endorsement.

Another of the perks of the school was sampling the cooking of other students, especially the patisserie students. After a couple of weeks they had had their fill of the cakes, biscuits, desserts and gateaux they were making and, instead of taking them home, they would leave them on a round table in the corner of the Winter Garden for the rest of us to devour. Naturally this table became a rallying point for especially gluttonous students or those, like me, with a high-minded, research-based interest in the techniques of patisserie.

It was while shovelling fistfuls of chocolate gateau into my mouth that I got chatting to Dingbang, another member of my practical group, Basic Cuisine E. Dingbang was a twenty-one-year-old Thai, though he looked even younger with his bum-fluff moustache and a fixed grin. Back home he had cultivated what presumably passed for a 'bad boy' image, smoking red Marlboros and wearing wrap-around glasses and a leather jacket. Dingbang had been a bit of a tearaway at school, he confessed with a hint of pride, growing his hair long, listening to pop music and getting up to mischief. He had friends, he said looking round to check no one was listening, who were in the Mafia. I asked him how and why he came to be at the school and he explained.

101

One day, he said, a teacher had been picking on him, before finally pulling him out of his chair by his collar for something he hadn't done. Dingbang had exploded and hit the teacher, who unfortunately turned out to be a friend of his father's – a commander in the Thai air force. By the time he arrived home that evening, Dingbang's father was already waiting: 'He look like this,' said Dingbang, making a constipated face. He told Dingbang he would be removed from school and offered him a hat in which he had placed two pieces of paper. 'Pick one,' said the father, 'This is what you are going to do.' Dingbang unfolded the paper and read what was written there: 'Cook'. 'What was on the other paper?' I asked him. 'Diver,' shrugged Dingbang, clearly still kicking himself. Dingbang would be sent to live with his aunt in Paris where he would learn to be a chef. If he failed he would have to repay his father ten times the amount the course had cost. So here he was, a world away from home, learning how to make *pintadeau pôelé vallée d'Auge* and *blanquette de veau*, without having the slightest interest in food. To compound the indignity, at the weekends his aunt made him work on her roast-chicken stand in the local market to pay his rent. 'She very strict, many rules,' he said. His only real escape was playing arcade games. Would I like to come with him to Les Halles to play? I hadn't had an invitation to play after school for about twenty years, so agreed immediately.

'Welcome to hell!' grinned Dingbang as our Metro train pulled into the station beneath Les Halles, a soulless underground shopping centre, built on the site of the city's central food market. This was Emil Zola's 'belly of Paris', which, overrun with rats and garbage and struggling to feed the growing city, was finally moved outside of Paris to Rungis in 1969. The modern-day shopping centre that replaced it is indeed my idea of hell – how many hair accessory shops do people need? – but Dingbang's arcade of choice was in the even less salubrious rue St Denis, a strip-joint and sex-shop street close to the Centre Pompidou.

We entered the arcade and I followed Dingbang upstairs where a group of black French teenagers was standing intently in front of their machines vicariously beating the stuffing out of each other via on-screen warriors. Dingbang fell into a virtual bout with one of the boys – the best player, as it turned out – winning a round or two before being having his entrails splattered over the Hong Kong skyline in the final. He stepped back to allow another to take his place at the podium. I asked Dingbang what his opponent's name was and what he did. 'I don't know, we don't talk, just play,' he replied. Though I was surprised at how little computer games had changed since I last played them as a teenager, my reactions, it seemed, had dimmed. After repeatedly being beaten senseless – as a two-headed ogre, a small girl with pigtails, and a mouse-dog-type thing – I suggested we go elsewhere.

Dingbang took me to a nearby café where the clientele were staring intently at the table tops, playing a board game with black and white counters. 'Chinese chess!' Dingbang told me, 'Want to play?' I fared little better at this, becoming counter blind after a few minutes, but it gave Dingbang a chance to offload his heart's burden. We talked about women. Did he have a girlfriend? Never, but, it turned out, he had a crush on Michelle, the pretty, bespectacled receptionist at school. 'She beautiful,' he beamed. So why don't he ask her out? He turned down the corners of his mouth in mock fear, 'Nooo, never.' 'Is it because of your dad?' I asked. 'He sounds really strict.' 'Yes he is,' Dingbang agreed. 'But I still love him. If you don't love parents, who do you love?'

Dingbang had not been faring too well at the school, which was hardly surprising given his complete lack of experience in a kitchen and his ambivalence about the entire project. Chef Didier Chantefort, who usually taught at Superior level, had been supervising us the day before and had laughingly called Dingbang's *duck à l'orange* sauce '*sheet* water' and tossed the plate back at him across the worktop. 'This is a sauce,' he had said pointing at my plate. 'But this, this is *sheet* water.' At the time I was elated that a chef had held up something I'd made as an example to another student, but looking back I did feel sorry for Dingbang.

Then again, with him around, at least I might be spared the indignity of coming last in the end-of-term exams.

Chapter 12

Mustard's no good without roast beef.

Chico Marx

Autumn came to Paris overnight. Until that moment it had been an Indian summer like none I have ever experienced. This had confused the Parisians greatly. You would see them sweating under heavy woollen coats and the ubiquitous stripy scarves which, logic told them, they normally wore at this time of year although, in fact, it was virtually beach weather. Up until the first week in November the air had remained warm and cosseting with that faintly sour summer Paris smell, but suddenly one Wednesday night, the leaves gave up their chlorophyll, and fell from the plane trees that lined avenue Marceau, leaving fuzzy golf balls in their place. The sun dissolved behind white clouds, its rheumy light bathing the masonry and sky with a more sombre palette.

Things were getting more serious at school too. At the end of November the students of Basic Cuisine would face a written and practical exam, but before that we had the mid-term party to look forward to. As the result of various conspiring misfortunes the former would turn out to be one of the most traumatic episodes of my adult life, while the latter would provide one of its more embarrassing experiences. And I had yet to pan-fry my hand.

This notably humiliating incident occurred towards the end of what had, up until that point, been a successful attempt to roast a side of beef and make a *jus* – a sauce made of the brownings from the meat, dissolved in water – to accompany it. We had first seared the beef in a *sautoise*, a high-sided, stainless steel frying pan with

105

stainless steel handle. Searing was important in order to create the flavoursome crust around the meat, leaving those precious brown bits at the bottom of the pan which would give the accompanying *jus* much of its flavour. This crust was a result of the *Maillard* effect, a kind of caramelisation involving a reaction between amino acids and sugars, named, after Louis-Camille Maillard (1878–1936), the chemist who discovered it.

As Basic Cuisine progressed I had come to realise that caramelisation – a *true* caramelisation occurs only with sugar, but it's as good a word as any to use here – creates one of the most important flavour elements in French cooking. The crusty residue that it leaves in the bottom of the pan is a vital ingredient in its own right. Usually this is referred to in cookbooks as a kind of by-product of frying meat, but it is far more than that and should in fact be your number one priority if you want to make a sauce. Whether you are cooking meat or vegetables, or even fish or fruit, the complex savoury-sweetness that comes from applying a high heat to raw ingredients in an oiled pan, or in an oven, is as precious a flavour as truffles, saffron stems or foie gras – and it's free.

I don't think anyone clings any more to the old notion that searing meat seals in its juices, except perhaps for my mother who still doesn't really believe me when I try to explain the truth. It does no such thing, but the browning of the exterior of meat is crucial to give it its complex flavour and, time and again, the chefs would stress both the need to brown meat and its vegetable garnish and – equally important – to recuperate the brownings that formed on the bottom of the pan.

It works like this. Let the meat come up to room temperature for at least half an hour before cooking so that you stand a fighting chance of cooking the interior without overcooking the exterior (the American food writer Harold McGee goes as far as to advocate letting the meat sit, well wrapped in clingfilm, in warm water for an hour. It is equally essential that the meat is as dry as possible (a thorough dab with kitchen paper ought to do it), otherwise it will boil and toughen and you won't get the flavoursome brown crust. Now, heat the pan until the air above it starts to shimmer, then add some peanut oil and a knob of butter. Start frying the meat – in this instance we were, as I said, cooking beef – over this high heat (the oil is supposed to prevent the butter from burning, but this isn't always the case so be vigilant). Brown the meat on all sides, trying cover as much of bottom of the pan with crusty brownings as possible. *Don't* stir fry if you are cooking small pieces of meat, because the brownings won't settle and stick; use tongs to turn the pieces individually. Remove the meat from the pan and, if it is a joint of some sort, place it in a clean pan in the oven to roast or braise – depending on the dish you are making.

Meanwhile, chop any bones that might have come with the meat (if the joint is off the bone, ask your butcher for some extra), and add them to the frying pan along with any non-fatty meat trimmings left over from preparing the joint. Fry all of this for ten minutes or so to build up that brown crust on the bottom of the pan even further, then add a *mirepoix* – the finely chopped vegetable garnish, usually a blend of chopped celery, shallot, onion, garlic and carrot.

If you are aiming for a richer sauce rather than a simple, pure *jus*, a teaspoon of tomato paste might be called for at this point. Fry the bones, *mirepoix* and tomato paste for a few more minutes until the base of the pan is totally covered by a thin crust of brownings (I am actually beginning to salivate as I write this) then tip it all out into a fine sieve, or *chinois,* to drain the oil. If the pan still glistens with oil, dab it out ever so gently, so as not to remove the crust, with some kitchen towel (imagine you are cleaning a priceless Old Master painting), and return the bones to the pan. All the time you must remain vigilant to ensure your brownings don't turn to burnings. If you see any blackening at all, remove the pan from the heat at once and try to scrape any black bits from the pan. It is a thin line between sweet, meaty caramelisation and bitter burnt bits, but once you have burnt bits in your pan there is little you can do to rectify the situation. The bitter burnt flavour will linger in any sauce that you try to make from what remains in the pan and, at school, we could be certain that the chefs' fine-tuned palates would spot it at the end-of-session tasting.

You should now be left with perhaps the ultimate prize in French cooking: a pan covered in a rich, brown crust, bursting with meaty flavours just waiting to bring taste and colour to your sauce. For this reason, I urge you to throw out your Teflon-coated, or any kind of non-stick pans, *immediately*.

The Space Programme, from which Teflon is famously a by product, didn't just waste zillions of dollars allowing Buzz Aldrin to practise his golf swing. It set back flavour and the advance of global cuisine by a generation. Teflon is the enemy of flavour because it renders caramelisation and the Maillard effect virtually impossible to achieve. In other words, YOU DON'T WANT NON-STICK; YOU WANT STICK!

If you take away nothing more from this book than this, my work here will be done. (And if any kitchenware companies would like me to endorse a range of non-*non*-stick pans, they should feel free to get in touch.)

Next comes the alchemy: deglazing – introducing a liquid to the roasting pan – which helps to recuperate that tasty brown crust and, depending on the liquid, can often add a flavour note itself. For a *jus*, which is the purest of sauces – the *über* sauce in fact – containing the very essence of the meat you are cooking with, you would normally deglaze with just a tumblerful or so of water, which adds no flavour but allows the brownings to lift and dissolve (give them a helping hand with a scraper, you don't want to waste any) and, with a little boiling and reducing, draws more flavour from the *mirepoix* and bones. But deglaze with alcohol – wine, port, Madeira, or spirits like Calvados or cognac – and not only does the room fill with the most heavenly aroma, but it will also add a new note to the resulting sauce.

This you create by first evaporating the alcohol entirely (this is crucial, otherwise there's a risk of a sharp background alcohol flavour). I often deglaze first with a splash of cognac or brandy, reduce it until it is a mere sticky residue, then add a glass of white wine and reduce that by a half or more. Then add water or the relevant stock (chicken if you have used chopped chicken carcass, veal or beef if you're roasting veal or beef, and so on), or most likely both stock and water, and reduce gently for half an hour. If you are cooking veal or beef but don't have any stock, you could just add three or four sliced shin bones to the pan at the browning stage instead – the bones will caramelise, and the water will recuperated those brownings, and the marrow will melt and create a lovely rich, glossy sauce.

You should also throw in a couple of bay leaves at this point (though quite what they bring to the party has always been a mystery to me – I think they are one of those ingredients noted more if absent), some thyme (dried is fine), and, if you have any, some parsley stalks, one of those precious ingredients French chefs will rifle rubbish bins to scavenge.

Whatever kind of sauce you are making you must then strain it one more time, discarding the garnish and bones which will have rendered all their flavour. Reduce it yet more still, gently skimming the surface for any impurities, and you can serve it as it is. You may have just a few spoonfuls left in the pan, but it will be so intensely flavoured that you'll need just a trickle on each plate – the French rarely drench their plates in great jugfuls of gravy like northern Europeans. Alternatively, add cream, butter or a thickener to turn it into one of literally dozens of different types of French sauce. The thickener might simply be a corn starch, arrowroot or potato starch mixed to a paste with water then whisked well into the hot sauce, or an equal parts butter and flour mixture. Used cold, this is called a *beurre manière*, but for the full-on, classical French sauce experience, you will need a roux, in which you melt some butter, then mix in an equal quantity of flour. Depending on how dark a sauce you are aiming for, cook the roux for three minutes or so – for a light, 'white' sauce – or longer until the flour turns a rich brown. Let the roux cool before pouring over the sauce because a hot roux and a hot liquid will repel each other like the same poles of a magnet, and they won't mix successfully – one needs to be cold, the other hot, it doesn't matter which is which. If you are pulling out all the stops on the way to the cardiac centre, you can even *monté au beurre* at the very end, by adding some butter cubes – chilled are best – taking care to incorporate them into the sauce by gently moving the pan around on the hob in a circular motion as if panning for gold, rather than stirring or whisking. For some complex molecular reason whisking doesn't work as well, but 'panning' keeps the sauce looking more glossy.

I usually do without the flour and cream unless I want to impress elderly relatives, but always make sure the sauce is well-skimmed. And, of course, you should check the seasoning carefully at the end – and don't be afraid to add a tiny pinch of sugar if you think it will help.

Meanwhile, your meat will have finished cooking. Remove it from the oven and leave it to rest on a pastry rack for half its cooking time (a practice which rendered the Patisserie students incandescent with rage when they came to use the racks and found them encrusted with fossilised meat remnants), in a warm place (that shelf over the oven again), loosely covered with baking paper. Don't wrap the meat tightly in foil, as some advise, or it will continue to cook. If there are any more brownings in the pan you cooked the meat in, recuperate them with a little water and add it to your sauce.

And that's it. It sounds complicated, and it is, but essentially there are three stages to a basic but magnificent sauce: create the brown crust with meat, bones and *mirepoix*; degrease, deglaze and reduce; then strain and finish with butter, cream or a thickener, and season. To simplify the process further, you could brown the meat, remove it from the pan, then add the bones and *mirepoix* and fry them a bit more, put the meat on top of it all and stick the whole pan in the oven. Then, when the meat is cooked, removed it from the pan, tip the bones and *mirepoix* into a sieve, and degrease, and deglaze the pan and continue from there.

The day I fried my hand I had removed my beef from a 220°C oven, carefully wrapped a dry tea towel around the handle (Do you think I'm stupid?) and placed it on a hot hob. Distracted for a second by some potatoes that were boiling too fast, I looked back to see that my roast was in danger of ending up like something you might find floating in the Ganges, and went to remove the pan from the heat. Unfortunately, by then I had tucked my tea towel back into my apron. I now had a burning hot pan-handle sticking out just begging to be grasped. And grasp it I did, with my left hand.

For a split second there was no pain; as with the knife cut on day one, there was even time between the burn occurring and the news travelling to my brain to wonder if damage had been averted. But then the pain began, literally searing through my hand. I dropped the *sautoise* back on the hob. My palm contracted like a steak in a hot pan and, as I stretched my fingers out, I could feel the burnt sinew pulling them back. 'Did you forget that was hot?' asked Paul, helpfully.

Chef Bruno was again quick and sympathetic, ushering me to the sink where I stood as he held my hand under cold, running water for a while before walking me downstairs where one of the receptionists helped me apply some cream and a plastic glove. This, along with a magic potion Lissen concocted that night (from lavender water), helped avoid any serious blistering the next day.

More happily, my beef turned out perfectly: crusty and caramelised on the outside, moist and pink on the inside (much like my hand). Crucially, during the kerfuffle it had had plenty of time to rest. Before I started at Le Cordon Bleu I had a vague idea that you should let meat stand for a few minutes after it comes out of the oven, but none of the TV cookery books I'd read had properly explained why. The molecular gastronomist Hervé This – whom the Cordon Bleu chefs, in a rare concession to modern scientific knowledge, would occasionally cite as the final authority on such matters – shed light on why we do this in his fascinating book, *Molecular Gastronomy – Exploring the Science of Flavour*. He says that when you leave meat to rest its fibres relax and allow the juices to flow from the centre back out to the edges of the meat which will have dried out during cooking, making it more moist and tender. He goes as far as to advocate that chefs use a syringe to re-inject any juices that have been lost during cooking back into the centre of the meat. More useful is the knowledge that, due to thermal inertia, meat will continue to cook after it comes out of the oven, particularly towards the centre, which is why you should remove meat before it is quite as cooked as you require

'Resting meat is not optional,' Chalopin had told us. 'It is a mandatory part of cooking meat. The resting time for any meat should be a half of its cooking time; and with large pieces of fish you should rest them for as long as you have cooked them. Turn fish halfway through to keep the juices inside. Rest chickens breast-side down.' As usual, he was right; resting meat – on an upturned plate so that the air can circulate to keep the temperature even throughout – made as much a difference to its flavour and texture as decanting does to red wine. You should try and keep it warm, of course, by placing it on the open door of the oven, perhaps, or on a shelf above the hob, but if it does go cold, resist the temptation to reheat meat as it will toughen. Tepid, tender meat, is always preferable to uptight, hot meat and, besides, the sauce will warm it on the plate.

From hostile first impressions I was beginning to, if not like, then at least understand Chalopin. He was bad cop to Bruno's good cop: the enforcer of Cordon Bleu. His rimless glasses gave him the appearance of an angry mole and his meticulous precision bordered on the pathological but his wisdom was without doubt. He insisted we weigh water rather than use a measuring jug, for instance, and advised us to use only one hand when working with dough, to keep the other clean – both of which are sound pieces of advice. 'In a kitchen it is just as important to use your ears as your taste and smell,' he told

us. 'If you are reducing wine, it won't make any noise until it is
almost gone. If it starts sizzling, move quickly. You will learn to
listen to your pans, they can tell you a lot about how your food is
cooking. A good chef has his ears open all the time. And a good
chef never trusts anyone – he makes sure a fish has been de-scaled
properly; he smells the blender to check the last person has cleaned
it properly; he always checks whether a stock has been salted before
he reduces it.

'It has come to my attention that we had a few bad burns yesterday,'
he continued. My face flushed gammon pink and there was some
sniggering from behind me. 'If you have a hot pan-handle, sprinkle
it with flour so that everyone can see it, okay?' He then launched
into an impression of the students he had observed – like Soon Yuk
– who shook their pans around when frying. 'Do you feel like a
grand chef when you do like this? Don't! It cools the meat.'

At the start of his next demonstration – *artichauts poivrade à la
Grecque aux legumes printaniers* – Chalopin had launched into a scathing
attack on those who had ignored the advice of the past six weeks.
Why weren't we placing layers of damp kitchen roll under our chopping boards, as we had been shown? he demanded. 'Do you think
we tell you this to make work for the people who make the paper?
No!' Why were we leaving our knives lined up on the chopping
boards like Japanese chefs when we were using them, he said, instead
of placing them on a tray, out of the way on the shelf above our
hobs? 'Do you all like looking at your knives? You are too messy,
when I go to your practicals it looks like a bordello!' he added, tossing
screwed-up paper and potato peelings across his work surface by
way of imitation. 'Get organised! You have paid a scandalous amount
of money to be here so why don't you want to learn properly?'

A week earlier, some of the female students had found Veronica,
a petite economist from Washington, in tears in the changing room
following a Chalopin rant. She spoke excellent French but he had
delivered the ultimate insult by raging at her in his bad English for
not placing kitchen roll under her chopping board.

Despite his protestations that he wasn't a 'kitchen ayatollah', one could easily imagine Chalopin issuing *fatwas* to students who committed such errors. He could make even the most harmless advice sound like an admonishment: 'Melting butter makes no noise! If you can hear it, it's cooking!' Another thing that stoked his fire was chatty cooks, he hated to enter a kitchen and hear voices chatting above the sizzling of pans. 'Chefs don't talk when they're cooking,' he would shout above the noise. Again, he was right. You could never argue with the man's experience and, if you did, he could freeze you in an instant with his withering, purse-lipped stare.

Fortunately, I think Chef Chalopin appreciated that I was at least trying my best in the kitchen and I was even beginning to detect the faintest traces of a sense of humour behind the fierceness. The first inkling – unless you count the Englishmen's brains diagram, which I don't – of this came when he explained the dietary factors that killed the French, region by region: 'In Normandy, it's the butter or they die of diabetes from all the sugar,' he said. 'In the Auvergne it's the charcuterie that kills them; in the Basque country it's goose fat; in Provence it's the driving, their diet is very healthy.'

Though our kitchen back at home was reasonably well-equipped there was one piece of equipment which those first weeks at school had taught me was invaluable: the *chinois*, or Chinese hat sieve. Finer than a flour sieve, and conical in shape, the *chinois* is essential for straining stocks, soups and sauces; degreasing fried food; and basting roasting meats without covering them with bits of garnish. I had to have one and, on the advice of the chefs, learned that the best place in Paris to buy a *chinois* – or any other piece of kitchen equipment, for that matter – is E. Dehillerin.

Founded in 1820, Dehillerin is close to Les Halles in the second arrondissement. It is the kind of shop Harry Potter would go to if he were a chef – a maze of dark, narrow corridors filled with every conceivable piece of culinary equipment, from stockpots big enough to boil a whole cow, to those curious razors waiters use to scrape the crumbs from tablecloths between courses. Visit more than a couple of times and the staff greet you by name. On my first visit I was welcomed by a member of staff as I entered the store.

'Can I help you?' he asked.

'Yes, I am looking for a *chinois*,' I replied.

'Yes sir, I will go and find one of my relatives.'

This was clearly a well-rehearsed joke. The man was Chinese and *chinois* also translates as Chinese or Chinaman. After finding me a *chinois* he helped me choose a roasting tray, kindly responding when I winced at the price of a thick aluminium tray by taking me to the cheaper stainless steel ones.

Dehillerin is on the edge of one of the best food shopping districts in Paris, centred on rue Montergeuil. Together with the infamous sex street, rue St Denis, and the restaurant Le Pied de Cochon, it is one of the last traces of the old Les Halles produce market which stood here from the reign of Phillipe August in the twelfth century until its demolition in the late 1960s. As I said, the produce market moved out to a purpose-built site in Rungis, near Orly airport, in the early 1970s, and was redeveloped as the miserable underground shopping centre, loathed by all but the junkies and alcoholics who linger there. But around Montergeuil is a compelling array of gourmet grocers selling the best foie gras, truffles and charcuterie in Paris; as well as rival equipment stores like Mora and Bovida; fishmongers; butchers; cheese shops; and greengrocers. My favourite food shop in all of Paris, G. Detou on rue Tiquetonne, is close by as well. This tiny, old-fashioned place is packed with wholesale bags of professional cooking ingredients like *couverture* chocolate pastilles, powdered stocks, nuts, ground almonds and, perhaps my favourite secret ingredient, pistachio paste – a dense, intense, oily paste made from ground pistachios and almonds and used in cake-making and desserts. I use it mixed – you have to leave it to soften at room temperature for some time beforehand – with whipped cream and mascarpone as a filling for shortbread biscuits (mix in some shredded basil too if you like) or to flavour the milk and sugar infusion for a crème anglais which makes a great sauce for chocolate desserts or, when frozen, turns into the most wonderful pistachio ice cream. Foodie visitors to our house would invariably leave with a sample wrapped in a small freezer bag and sealed with rubber bands, like cocaine ready to be swallowed by a drug mule.

I would often come to this part of Paris alone to indulge in a morning or afternoon of gourmet 'window licking'. This wasn't just because Asger and Emil's tolerance for food shopping was low but more that Paris, as we soon found out, is one of the least child-friendly cities in Europe. The city zoo has seen better centuries; triumphal arches outnumber play parks; and I can only assume the Metro was designed by some child-hating bachelor, or at least someone who never had to conquer a flight of stairs carrying a baby buggy, its cargo and a rucksack and hauling a truculent four year old behind him. The city's few parks may be immaculately tended, but are only really meant for looking at. Each has the same brand of meagre climbing frames and no swings – far too dangerous. Their lawns are usually cordoned off and, quite possibly, booby-trapped to protect the grass, while a list of rules longer than the Magna Carta is posted by each gate. The notion of a lawn only meant for looking at was a difficult one for Asger and, particularly, Emil to grasp. He would stare intently at me as I explained that he was not allowed to walk on the grass, that the grass would die if he set foot on it, and then the park guard would get cross. He would nod at me indicating that he understood perfectly, but the moment I had finished would turn and sprint off across the lawn as fast as his chubby legs would carry him.

This would invoke the wrath of the park guards whose job it is to emerge from their little windowed kiosks at frequent intervals to berate small children. Our local one – Claude – would, over the course of just a few weeks, accost us for, variously, playing with the wrong kind of football (plastic, but not soft enough, apparently); walking on the grass, of course; and using the climbing frame when it had a very slight dusting of snow, which was particularly tricky to explain to children who had spent most of their lives in Scandinavia and were, at the time, clad in all-weather, one-piece body suits that would have served them well for an Arctic expedition.

Luckily, an alternative attraction had taken Asger's and Emil's fancy. In fact, they were besotted. From the first moment they set eyes on them, they were hooked like a Glasgow tenement dosser to his crack pipe. These were the toy sailing boats which, when the wind is gusting, you can rent at the central fountain of the Jardin des Tuilleries in front of the Louvre. Like all the best playthings, these tatty old wooden boats were a simple idea with a cunning twist: for two euro you got to choose a boat but – and this, I believe, was the key to their vice-like grip on the imaginations of all the under-eights who saw them – you were also given a stick to steer it with. The stick was the thing. In fact, I suspect Asger and Emil could quite happily have done without the boat altogether and just spent an hour running around the fountain waving them like crazed Herbert von Karajans. I would often have to remind them that they had boats to look after but they would be too busy poking the haunches of distressed poodles or sword fighting startled Parisian children to care.

Chapter 13

A hangover is the wrath of grapes.

Anon

After the tension of the first two months at Le Cordon Bleu – which had prompted the appearance of a curious stress rash on my arm that looked exactly like a map of Tunisia – I had at last begun to find my feet. I was fretting just as much about everything, but it seemed the fretting was starting to have results rather than just annoying everyone around me.

The credit for this goes entirely to the chefs. Even with the most mundane procedures, things I had done literally hundreds of times before, they had tips and explanations that shed new light. Take boiling potatoes. The chief satisfactions of one's daily life are, I believe, made up of inconsequential challenges – brushing your teeth before the shower warms up; grabbing the ticket at the entrance to the car park without stopping the car; or cramming all the chocolates into your mouth in one go before the kids enter the room. One of mine has always been to see if I can peel the potatoes before the water boils. Though this obviously adds an edge of suspense to a mundane chore, it turns out it is quite the wrong thing to do. You should always bring potatoes to the boil in the water from cold, never add them to water that's already boiling, because it gives the interior of the spuds a chance to cook before their exterior is overcooked. Neither should you add salt until you have a rolling boil, otherwise the potatoes form a tough outer skin.

It was Chef Bruno, the avuncular head of Basic Cuisine, who explained all this. Bruno was a model of precision and clarity. (The

119

only time I saw him remotely ruffled was when he put coffee extract instead of vanilla extract in a chantilly: he flushed a bright pink.) A kindly man, Bruno was one of the only chefs who really tried to learn the students' names. One of his favourite students was Sarah, a forty-something American whom I came to know well. Few of the students made any great impact on the chefs; you could hardly blame them as the student body at Le Cordon Bleu was in constant flux with students arriving for short intensive courses, as well as the full-timers like me. But Sarah stood out. A former fashion stylist for Condé Nast in New York, she lived in the Marais with her two teenage sons, and loved entertaining at home. This elegant, slim redhead spoke fluent French, which endeared her to all the chefs; they flocked around her during practicals, to gossip and flirt and, as the only students in our practical class to have children – and children with dual nationality at that – she and I also became friends. Along with the resident nut allergic, Samantha, I was one of only two English students at the school at the time and was grateful that, via Sarah, I was welcomed into the American fold, befriending many of the other Americans students, like Christine, the food-obsessed Chinese American from San Francisco. Hayden, the Boston blue blood; the boundlessly enthusiastic Tessa; and Danielle, the daughter of a Miami real estate trader.

I got to know Christine and Hayden better during an unexpectedly debauched wine trip to the Loire. Each term the Cordon Bleu Wine Group takes a field trip to vineyards outside of Paris, inviting along any Cuisine or Patisserie students who feel like joining them. Personally, I rarely touch alcohol, except with food and after food, and sometimes a little before food – in the pub, for instance, or at parties, or sitting slumped in front of the snooker, – but Lissen is interested in wine and so we met up outside the school with a coachload of fellow, let's call them *bon viveurs*, at eight o'clock one Saturday morning.

Our destination was the northern part of the Loire, specifically the hilltop village of Sancerre, and the Pouilly sur Loire vineyard of the fourteenth-century Château Tracy, owned by the Assay family. We arrived at our first vineyard mid-morning. By eleven o'clock we were tipsy, by lunchtime we were sloshed and even a hefty portion of chicken in Sancerre sauce did little to allay our slide into wanton drunkenness. This was all the more shameful as we were shown around the chateau by the suave Count Henri D'Assay himself and our trip was being led by Jean-Michel Deluc, the president of the Association of Paris Sommeliers. I like to think that Lissen and I managed to maintain a sober façade – although that's unlikely – but there were plenty of others far worse for wear than us: Fabia and Henrique, the golden couple of Basic Cuisine, for instance.

She was the spitting image of Colombian pop star Shakira, blonde, shapely and, I suspect, rather high-maintenance; he was a young, Brazilian George Clooney, tall, dark and dashing. They had hooked up a couple of weeks earlier but unfortunately, on the coach home the cumulative affect of tasting about twenty wines without spitting took its toll on their relationship as they and the rest of the South Americans gathered for an impromptu party – replete with ciga-rettes, more booze and a raucous singalong – at the back of the bus. At a toilet stop outside Paris Jean-Michel took Henrique aside to see if he could calm things down. Henrique took his new authority very seriously and instructed Fabia to pipe down rather too firmly for her liking (she was a few years older than he). She promptly dumped him and he spent the rest of the journey sobbing quietly – I tried not to but couldn't help overhearing – to Tessa on his mobile phone. We arrived back in Paris late, all of us rather tired and emotional. About all I can remember about the actual wines that is worth passing on is that red Sancerres give you truly harrowing hangovers.

Chatting with Hayden – who, when the movie of his life is made, will be played by Matt Damon – during lunch I learned that he was taking a break after completing his economics degree at Yale, before heading for MIT with a view to becoming a hedge-fund manager/Master of the Universe. His parents were paying for his

Parisian sojourn on the understanding that he promised to return to his studies. 'But I quite like the idea of doing private catering in people's homes, you know, dinner parties and things,' he told me. Hayden's nickname at college had been the Punisher, which I took as a direct challenge to my own talent for excruciating wordplay: 'There's not *mushroom* in here,' I said proudly and – you understand – entirely off the cuff one morning, as we chopped mushrooms during a practical in a particularly crowded kitchen. I put my knife down, stepped back and opened my palms upwards in the universal symbol of victory. Seemingly without having to think, Hayden shot back a withering, 'Oh. I see. A pun. What? You think you're the *champignon* then do you?' I was crushed. Quietly, I returned to my chopping.

Christine, meanwhile, was a born foodie, her fascination having been passed on from her Baptist minister father. 'When I was a kid we ate out every night,' she told us. 'We would be taken out in our pyjamas to Asian restaurants in the Bay Area. For us that was perfectly normal, we didn't realise anything was strange about eating out every night.' From that she had developed an insatiable fascination with food which, she hoped, would parlay into a career as a food stylist or in a teaching capacity after her stint at Le Cordon Bleu.

A local market trip followed soon after the wine trip. Chef Boucheret, our guide, was in an unusually jolly mood that crisp, blue-skied November morning as we set out for the market on Boulevard Raspail. On Sundays this market is famous for being all-organic, when it attracts the *Bobo* (*bourgeois bohème*) crowd, dressed in pseudo English casual wear with carefully colour co-ordinated kids (the week before Brad Pitt and Angelina Jolie had been spotted there). During the week the market sells the standard, non-organic range of fruits, vegetables, charcuteries, cheeses and meats which the chef talked us through, inviting us to pick out some things for a 'picnic' back at the school. 'Look out for the old ladies with their shopping trolleys,' he warned as we entered the market. 'They can be deadly.'

Shopping trolleys, which in the UK remain the sole preserve of elderly ladies in knitted hats, are a must in Paris and you see people of all demographics – middle-aged men in suits, trendy teenagers and, of course, old ladies – lugging them around markets and shops. I resisted for a few weeks but after heaving bulging rucksacks and carrier bags that scythed through my palms like a cheese wire, and even experimenting with a suitcase on wheels on one supermarket trip, I finally gave in and bought a psychedelic flowery number, which I now trail behind me, entirely at ease with my sexuality, on my twice-weekly market trips.

Chef Boucheret showed us how to tell a good stall from a bad, drawing our attention to the limp leaves on a head of celery on one and how they had disguised the age of their cauliflower by removing its greenery. Another stall had arranged its produce in a specific order, with over-ripe melons and deliciously fragrant, curious-looking flat, white peaches (which I had never encountered before coming to Paris but became my favourite fruit) on one side, and fresh grapes and autumnal wild mushrooms on the other. It was, the chef pointed out, arranged in seasonal order, with the end of season produce on one side and the new stuff on the other. At that moment I was being vigorously pummelled from behind by an elderly woman pushing a tartan trolley as if it were a battering ram and my back-side was a castle drawbridge. I took her prompt and moved on with the group, sampling my first ever fresh prune – delicious but over-poweringly starchy – as I went. The chef stopped a little further on to talk about some of the cheeses. Yeng Chan, from Taiwan, and Dingbang were wrinkling their noses in disgust. 'I no like,' said Yeng Chan. 'Never eat!' Dingbang felt the same, but for different reasons: he told me that his dad had tricked him into eating some cheese by telling him to close his eyes and offering it as a special type of mango. Dingbang had thrown up. For my contribution to our picnic I chose, from the charcuterie stall, some *boudin noir*, blood sausage, which I had been eyeing up at my local market but hadn't quite had the nerve to buy. 'It is great served with thinly sliced apple on buttered Poilâne bread, then toasted,' the chef explained.

By happy coincidence the Poilâne bakery was our next stop, on nearby rue du Cherche-Midi in St Germain. The bakery – probably the most famous in France, if not the world – was founded in the 1930s by Pierre Poilâne. It passed to his son, Lionel, and then, following Lionel's death in a helicopter crash in 2002, to his daughter Apollonia – who was just nineteen at the time. Poilâne is now an international brand with a branch in London and daily exports as far as New York. Every morning a chauffeur – driven limousine arrives here to take loaves to Charles de Gaulle airport to be flown to an oil sheikh in the Emirates; Robert de Niro is a regular at the New York branch; and Frank Sinatra used to insist on eating only Poilâne bread wherever he was on tour in the world. Back in the 1970s Salvador Dali commissioned his bedroom furniture to be made from Poilâne bread, sending in return the message: 'Surrealism is not yet dead!'

These days six thousand Poilâne loaves are manufactured every day at a factory outside of Paris in Bièvres to be sold in supermarkets throughout France. But the rue du Cherche-Midi branch is the original, and its distinctive round loaves, marked with a rococo 'P', are still baked in its subterranean wood-burning oven. We were shown down some narrow marble steps into a room with a low, blackened ceiling, where a man in white shorts and T-shirt was busy pulling steaming hot loaves from a small door in an oven using a gigantic wooden paddle. Every surface you touched left an imprint of flour dust and, as I was dressed mostly in black, I left looking like a pantomime cow.

The baker explained that the famous pain Poilâne is made from thirty per cent spelt flour and seventy per cent stoneground wheat flour, and seasoned with Guérande salt from the marshes of Brittany. It is a sourdough bread which means that, instead of adding yeast to the dough, the chef keeps a 'header' from the previous dough to start the fermentation of the next batch. This results in a sharper, slightly acidic taste (although the French prefer their sourdough less sour than Americans) and lovely stretchy fibres. Back at the school we gobbled chewy slices of the bread with hare pâté, weepy cheeses and my sugary, pungent, herby black sausage, all washed down with a flowery rosé. All that was missing was a nice piece of chocolate.

Chapter 14

Parisians are a surly, fretful, envious people in a perpetual state of dissatisfaction.

Stendhal

The most eagerly anticipated event for food lovers in Paris in late autumn is the Salon du Chocolat. Held over seven days in the cavernous exhibition halls at the Porte de Versailles, the Salon is the world's largest gathering of chocolate makers. There is plenty of other choco-late-related action too, including a fashion show with dresses made from chocolate and a Miss Cacao pageant. The brochure also promised a 'Choco-Dance Space' featuring chocolate-themed dancing, and a chocolate beauty parlour offering cocoa therapy with beauty products you could eat after you had used them, should you feel so inclined. More importantly, I had also heard there were endless free samples, and had considerably reduced my intake of chocolate during the preceding days to sharpen my appetite. Lissen and I arrived as the doors were opening on the first day. The smell was heavenly, the air thick with rich, wafting chocolate aromas, and I am proud to say that I don't believe I passed up one free sample in the entire exhibition.

I soon discovered that the trick to hustling for freebies was to approach each stall, express an almost concerned level of interest in their products, peer at one type of chocolate in particular while furrowing my brow, and ask for a catalogue. It worked every time. I must have eaten a kilo of free chocolate in under an hour. I tried smoked chocolates; geranium-flavoured chocolates; chocolates laced with herbs like thyme and rosemary; chilli chocolate; and hemp chocolates, which were surprisingly tasty. There were chocolate wines

– not wines to go with chocolate, you understand, but wines that tasted of chocolate – onion and chocolate *confit* served with foie gras (surprisingly edible), and a fascinating educational exhibition on the history of chocolate, or at least that's what Lissen said.

At one stall I overcame initial reservations to taste some chocolates filled with cheese. Though this sounds like something that ought only to come to pass following a traffic accident between two delivery trucks, these small, square *ganaches* made by the magisterial Parisian *chocolatier,* Jean-Paul Hévin, were intriguing. It took some courage to try the Roquefort-filled one, but the staff at the Hévin stall assured me that chocolate and cheese have an unusually compatible molecular structure. They complement each other very well, blue cheeses especially. Hévin uses four different cheeses, none of them mild: Epoisses, with a little cumin; a goat cheese with hazelnut; Pont l'Evêque with a touch of thyme; and Roquefort with walnut; all of them intended to be served with dessert wine.

I wasn't so taken by one of the other free samples I came across at a stall tucked away in a far corner of the hall. By the time I reached the stall, run by a woman with, essentially, the same physique as a snowman, dressed in a gigantic floral print dress, I was in automatic scrounge mode. As I had done at countless stalls before, I reached for the plate as it was offered, instinctively taking the largest morsel. I tasted the chocolate coating first. That was good; probably Valrhona like most of the rest of the chocolate I had tried. But then, once the chocolate flavour had cleared from my palate, another, less familiar, and less welcome, taste began to emerge: fish. 'It's seaweed!' the woman told me cheerily, as my frown began to deepen. 'From Wales!' 'Oh, seaweed, how *interesting!*' I replied, desperately wondering how I could avoid swallowing. 'There are many different types,' she continued, offering me another silver tray. I had walked into a Monty Python sketch. What could I do? I was like an oil tanker attempting an emergency stop; my chocolate-eating momentum was irreversible. Having been the recipient of more free chocolate than a gatecrasher at the Weight Watchers Easter party, I had forgotten how to politely decline.

I took another. The woman looked on eagerly. A crowd of interested – and then, one by one as they read the ingredients blurb on the wall behind the stall, faintly appalled – onlookers gathered. I had no choice but to feign interest and take another morsel. And swallow both.

We left soon after, heavy with cocoa fats, sugar and cream and feeling not a little nauseous. Outside the exhibition hall the pavement was coated with chocolate debris. I caught a glimpse of my face in a car's wing mirror – my mouth was smeared with chocolate sauce, my clothes dusted with cocoa powder. I looked like Augustus Gloop, but my fascination with chocolate had been fuelled as never before. I wanted to know more about how to work with chocolate at home and began to look into doing a chocolate course during the pre-Christmas break from Le Cordon Bleu.

Chocolate Risotto

This recipe is based on one by Anna Notari of the Atelier des Chefs cooking school but I add parmesan shavings because their umami savouriness works well with a dark, bitter chocolate, as does the chilli (Notari uses cumin). Served in small scoops, it makes an interesting starter, perhaps before a light fish dish.

Ingredients – (Serves 6 as a starter)

1 onion

Olive oil

500g risotto rice

20cl white wine

1.5l of hot vegetable stock

7.5cl single cream

20g cocoa powder

Half a dried chilli

80g butter

Salt

Parmesan

Finely chop and then sweat the onion in olive oil for five minutes. Add the rice and turn up the heat. Cook the rice for a minute or so until it starts to crack. Pour in the white wine and reduce completely. Begin to add your hot stock a ladle at a time, waiting until each ladle has been absorbed by the rice seasoning gently as you go. Meanwhile, boil the cream and add the cocoa powder and the dried chilli, finely ground.

When the rice is cooked – soft but crunchy – add the chocolate cream and cook for a further two minutes. Remove from the heat, add the butter and mix. Serve topped with some parmesan shavings and a lightly dressed salad.

Though my cooking had begun to improve at school – I had now almost entirely stopped flambéing, chopping and roasting parts of my anatomy – my food was invariably let down by my lack of presentational skills. Time after time I would bung my lovingly crafted food onto a plate with little thought for how it looked, and rush it under the chef's nose for evaluation while other, more measured students would spend a few moments thinking how best to present something, carefully selecting some chervil for decoration (the sole purpose of chervil, as far as I can make out), or using a ring mould to form a neat circle on the plate, for instance. I usually forgot to wipe down the rim of my plate too, so that greasy fingerprints would catch the light making it look more like a crime scene than dinner. Because I rarely took the trouble to warm my plate, my sauces would congeal in the breeze. This would all have to be taken in hand before the Basic Cuisine exam which was looming at the end of November. Presentation, Chef Bruno had warned us, was a key factor in achieving a good mark.

A long weekend in Provence would give me the time to revise the ten recipes from which the two exam dishes would be taken (half the class would do one recipe, half the other). Some friends, who live in Provence, had told me that a wonderful gourmet market, *Les Journées Gourmands*, was going to be held in Vaison la Romaine that weekend.

Like everyone else on the planet, I have fallen for Provence – the landscape, the light, the food, the wine, the pace of life. The English are especially guilty of romanticising what is – away from the oligarchs and dancing girls of the Côte d'Azur – quite a harsh and impover-ished part of France but, frankly, I bought into the hopelessly idealised fantasy long ago and refuse to relinquish it. To me every gnarled peasant is a truffle snuffler; every farmer an organic friend of the earth; every workman a loveable alcoholic; and every braying middle-class Englishman I overhear at the Tuesday market in Vaison, is an annoying reminder that I too am a middle-class Englishman living out a hopeless fantasy.

Vaison is known chiefly for its Roman ruins and its picturesque Old Town up on a rocky hilltop above the modern town, crowned by a castle ruin. But the surrounding region boasts impressive produce including goat's cheeses, apricots, cherries, walnuts and almonds, olives and truffles, as well as some big-hitting wines – often as good as Châteauneuf du Pape but far cheaper – made in and around the local villages of Séguret, Gigondas, Vacqueyras and Beaumes de Venise. *Les Journées Gourmandes* attracts over twenty thousand visitors who come to celebrate this thriving food culture every autumn in a giant tent in the town's main car park. As we arrived at lunchtime on the Saturday we were handed a free wine glass for tasting. Inside a jazz band played beneath palm trees; children scurried excitedly as their parents, dressed in blazers and best frocks, tucked into plates loaded with roast lamb and *aligot* (a dauntingly heavy, chewy, potato mash from Aubrac made with Cantal cheese and garlic and so elastic it can stretch up to ten feet). Others were enjoying truffle omelettes and oysters by the dozen. There were stalls selling hams, sausages, wine, chocolate, nougat from nearby Montelimar, marzipan fruits, pâtés, olives and patisserie.

Olives and olive oil were a recurring theme – there were even olive-oil chocolates, which were smooth and pleasantly tart. Other oddities included a beer brewed in nearby Nyons; bison sausages and an ostrich pâté, both of which I enjoyed enough to go back for thirds. Despite the quantities of wine being guzzled there was no drunkenness or unseemly grasping for free samples, other than by me. There was not a hint of foodie pretension either, and I couldn't help wonder how an event like this would pan out in my home town, assuming the frenzy of excitement concerning the opening of the drive-thru McDonald's in 1983 has at last subsided.

The most visited stall in the hall was the soup stall, where you could taste the finalists for the *Festival des Soupes*, an annual competition open to residents of the surrounding villages. My soup-making usually ends up the same way as my attempts at painting: I start with a clear idea of what I want to create; give up halfway through, turn abstract and throw in everything I can find from the larder and fridge, and end up with an indefinite reddish-mud coloured slurry, so I was curious to see what the locals had created. There were some exotic blends on offer – lemon grass was particularly popular – but the competition had been won in the end by a shy eleven-year-old girl called Camille, from the Old Town. Eschewing fancy ingredients and complex techniques, Camille had cooked up a simple courgette and olive oil soup with the clear, invigorating taste of fresh picked courgettes and grassy, peppery virgin olive oil. But the excitement didn't end there. Talking to one of the ladies running the stall, I learned that the next day, the final day of the festival, they would be making *soupe de favoulles*, a speciality from Marseille made with small, live green crabs. This I had to try.

I returned alone at opening time the next day only to find the place closed. The clocks had gone back and no one had told me. I returned an hour later and made straight for the soup stand. I did my crab mime for the *Grande Louchiere* (the Grand

132

Ladle – head of the soup competition), but she shook her head. I was too early. Come again around three, she said. I did, but the story was the same. The anticipation was by now unbearable. This soup had become the most important thing in my life and nothing was going to get in my way. I returned as instructed later that evening fearful that I might have missed my chance and driving like a local, to be directed to the rear of the stall to a Wizard of Oz-style curtained-off room where, in a cupboard-sized cubicle, several jolly, round ladies were busy massacring small, green crabs.

The resulting soup tasted fabulous – sweetly crabby but light and aromatic – but I was rather put off by the fact that they had left the bashed up crabs in the mix. It was like eating the packaging along with the soup.

With due respect to the soup ladies of Vaison, I prefer this recipe. It is quite a trauma throwing the live crabs into the hot oil, but you become inured to it after the first few occasions (and it is probably more traumatic for the crabs).

Free-Form Crab Bisque

This is my free-form, highly adaptable, improvised bisque recipe. So freeform is it, in fact, that it needn't even be crab bisque. You can use the heads and shells of prawns or lobster, whole, live crayfish or even live shrimp. Actually, I would go as far as to say that, if you cook lobsters and *don't* use the shells to make this soup, you ought never to be allowed near a crustacean again. If you are using just shells and are feeling particularly conscientious you can roast them for ten minutes or so in a high oven before you start, which will intensify their sweet, shellfishy flavour. I have left the quantities up to your judgement – it depends so much on how many crabs you have, or how flavourful you sense that the shells are going to be.

Ingredients

500g-1kg of either small, live crabs or crustacean bits (you'll need a greater weight if you are using shells rather than live crabs)

Olive oil

A *mirepoix* of around one-fifth of the quantity of the shells, made up of chopped celery, onion, carrot, leek and garlic

Cognac

White wine or vermouth

Tomato paste, or perhaps an anchovy fillet or two

Paprika

A dessertspoon of flour

1.5l of fish stock (or you can just use water if you have no stock, but a fish stock cube is probably better than water)

Cream

Dry sherry

Bouquet garni (thyme, parsley stalks and a couple of bay leaves wrapped in a leek leaf)

Croutons – small cubes of stale bread, pan fried in clarified butter. To clarify butter, place a pack in a pan and heat gently. Skim the impurities that rise to the surface when it melts. The clear, golden liquid that's left is clarified butter – with much of its water and non-fatty substances evaporated away, the fattiest butter of all in other words – which can be heated to a higher temperature than normal butter without burning

Soak the crabs in cold water, then rinse well. Heat a pan, add the oil and, I'm afraid, yes, you throw the crabs in alive, stirring as they cook – sing loudly to yourself, or go to your happy place. They will change colour to a nice deep pink. While still in the pan bash them up with one end of a rolling pin wrapped well in clingfilm (if you are using pre-roasted shells, you need only fry them briefly before the bashing commences). Cook for a few minutes then remove from the pan, taking care to save any juices.

Add the *mirepoix* – all except the garlic which cooks quicker – to the pan and sweat gently until softened; don't be afraid of a little browning here. Add the garlic and cook for around a minute more. Put the crabs and their juices back in the pan. Heat around 50ml of cognac in a separate pan (alcohol catches light more readily when warm) and pour it over the crab and *mirepoix* and stick a lit match as far in as you dare. Let it flambé for a few seconds then, if it doesn't go out of its own accord, put a lid on the pan to extinguish the blaze. If it still doesn't go out, evacuate the building and call your insurance broker.

Add about a glass of white wine and reduce almost completely (if you hear it start to sizzle, the wine has gone completely and you must move quickly to prevent burning). You could add some peeled, de-seeded, chopped tomatoes here if you want, or just squirt in a bit of tomato paste, and let it cook for a minute or so to soften the acidity, stirring well. Or, if you sense your shells might be a little anaemic, you could even mix in a finely chopped anchovy fillet. Add as much paprika as you fancy now (how much you use depends on the type of paprika – sweet or spicy – and your own predilections). If you want a thick soup you can sprinkle over a dessertspoon of flour and mix well into the crab and vegetables at this point.

Now add the stock or water to cover the contents of the pan well, but not excessively. You don't want to drown that sweet, fishy crab flavour. Add a bouquet garni. Let it bubble gently for about half an hour (if you get waylaid and it runs to forty-five minutes, it doesn't really matter – but any longer and things will get a bit sludgy). Blitz the whole shebang in the food processor. Add a little cream, mix, then strain well.

If you have belatedly decided that you *do* want a thicker soup after all, mix some cornflour with a little water in a cup, then whisk it into the soup and heat for a minute or two, then strain again. Some people like to add a bit of the slurry back into the soup, but I don't (perhaps if they called it something other than 'slurry', I don't know). To serve, you could add a drop of sherry, a quenelle of crème fraiche sprinkled with chopped chives and/or some of the crab/prawn/lobster/crayfish meat. The truly anally retentive might like to place five small croutons on the surface of the soup, one in the centre and the other four equidistant from it and each other.

Talking of crabs, here's a teaser: You've accidentally bought a large, whole, live one, foaming at the mouth in that disconcerting way they have. But how should you keep it until you are ready to cook it? Tessa did just this on her way to school one day and there was a good deal of debate in the Winter Garden as to how she should keep it alive through the day before she could take it home and cook it.

'You can't put it in the fridge,' said Stephan, 'It'll go into a coma.'

'No, put it in a bucket of water,' said Hayden

'No, no, no. Ordinary water'll kill it,' I said, with no authority at all. 'What you need is some salt water, to make it feel at home.'

'But how will I know how much salt to put in?' wailed Tessa. 'Too much and it'll overdose. Can't I just keep it wrapped in this bag?' She held up her plastic shopping bag with the crab, already motion-less, within.

'Perhaps it's dead already,' I said, 'He's not had a terribly good day so far. But if you wrap him too tightly he'll suffocate.'

'Does it really matter, he's going to die soon anyway,' said Paul. 'What do you care *how* he dies?'

'Well, I don't want him to suffer,' said Tessa. 'I'm going to ask a chef.'

Tessa disappeared down into the basement prep kitchen, returning a few minutes later looking much more reassured. 'Chef says you just cover it with a damp tea towel and leave in the salad crisper in the fridge. They're like crocodiles – if you cover their eyes they calm down completely.'

I returned from Provence re-energised. In truth I didn't need a break in paradise to find energy for Le Cordon Bleu. Even on the most miserable winter's day, even if I was slowed by flu or a night of wet beds and tantrums (you'd have thought by my age . . .), I would set off for the Metro early in the morning humming with excitement. On the train I would look up from reading the forth-coming day's recipes, gaze out of the window into the apartments on the Boulevard de Grenelle and imagine how we were going to make them, perhaps nibbling ruminatively on a *flan nature*.

The Paris Metro is a paragon of a modern transport network; the frequency of its trains, which often seem to arrive as I step on the platform, is *Truman Show*-esque. The line I took, the Sixth, crosses the Seine just across from the Eiffel Tower, launching its trains exhil-aratingly across the river from their subterranean tunnel at the same height as the third-floor windows of the neighbouring apartments. It feels like being shot from a cannon and the view is unparalleled: on the left is the Eiffel Tower – always so much *browner* than I expect – and, further north, the Sacré Coeur; to the right is the curve of the river as it turns south, and the slender Isle des Cygnes – a minia-ture Statue of Liberty standing facing towards New York, an incon-gruous sight at its far tip. It has to be one of the world's most thrilling public transport experiences, like the Star Ferry across Hong Kong harbour, the west-coast train line in Scotland, or walking briskly along the bouncy Dunlop rubber travelators at Heathrow Airport. I would fall in love with the city anew every time I took it.

The strength of my feelings for Paris and, even more unexpect-edly, its residents had quite taken me by surprise since we had moved there three months earlier. Parisians have, I think, an undeserved reputation for being difficult, arrogant and hostile – not helped by Stendhal's withering verdict. But in fact I had found them to be a well-mannered, civilised bunch. Parisians never eat or drink while walking, nor do they wear trainers to restaurants and, having lived with the Viking hordes in Denmark for five years, I appreciated the apologies Parisians were ever-ready to offer when they so much as entered your personal space. Come the springtime, Parisians have sex out of their windows; plus the shopkeepers expect you to say '*Bonjour*' when you enter their shop and '*Au revoir*' when you leave, which is fine by me. They are mostly tolerant of foreigners' poor behaviour too.

For instance, around this period I accidentally set fire to my napkin while dining in a restaurant in St Germain. Blocked in by other diners and perhaps slightly 'light-headed' after a small glass of wine, all I could do was stand up and wave the flaming napkin like some kind of distress signal. My friends though alarmed, didn't feel obliged to come to my aid (one said later that he was keen to see what I did next), but the waiter silently, calmly took it from me, stamped it out on the floor and brought me another.

Sure, once Parisians get behind the wheel of a car or are required to queue for longer than twenty seconds they regress to homicidal apes, but who doesn't? The fact that the pavements of the city are awash with dog poo – ten tons a day, apparently, visualise that if you will – is perhaps more a matter for concern. Empirical research tells me that the worst arrondissements are the Third and the Sixteenth, a state of affairs I think must have something to do with the high proportion of gay men in the former and posh, elderly ladies in the latter: both demographics sharing a penchant for Tricky-Woo-style dogs, and perhaps a squeamishness about scooping. But I have a solution. The mayor should employ a special task force whose job it is to roam the city looking out for dogs in mid-motion. They would then arrest the owner and force them to conduct *their* next bowel movement in the exact same location as their dog. Things will get rather messy for a week or so, but I suspect the learning curve would be steep thereafter.

Anyway, my train would fly across the river and then dive back underground to Pasteur, where I would change for Vaugirard, the closest station to school. By the time I reached Le Cordon Bleu, I would be as psyched up as a prize fighter entering the ring. Often I would begin undoing my shirt as I walked into the men's changing room in the manner of Superman approaching a phone box. I couldn't wait to get cooking; I was even looking forward to the exam.

('Sex out of the windows?' you ask. It's true: one memorable morning – the first day of spring, in fact – I spotted our neighbours across the street doing precisely this. I was on the phone to my sister at the time and, initially I couldn't quite believe what I was seeing as the gentleman stood behind his lady friend as she leaned out of their rooftop window and proceeded to mate. At one point during my commentary to my sister I realised we were dangerously close to having phone sex, so hung up and ran to find some binoculars. Tragically, by the time I had located them, the couple had retreated behind their net curtains. They never did put in a repeat performance.)

Chapter 15

A milkmaid, pure and playful.

> French food writer Raymond Solokov,
>
> on *blanquette de veau*

The exam took place on the last day of Basic Cuisine. Preoccupied with crabs in Provence, I had revised just two of the ten dishes that we might be asked to prepare, which meant there were eight recipes I didn't know, including a few that I could barely remember having made. This may seem irresponsible given that an exam failure would mean I would probably have to repeat Basic, and we certainly didn't have the money for that. So how come I walked to school in such a buoyant mood on the day of the exam? I had inside information.

Pre-exam rumours were rife at Le Cordon Bleu. 'It's definitely going to be the *filet de barbue Dugléré avec pommes anglaise* [brill in a white wine sauce] and the *canette rôtie aux navets* [roast duck with turnips]', Maria, a Spanish student, had told me a few days earlier, 'One of the *plongeurs* said.'

'No, it's the chicken and the lamb,' interrupted Sarah, 'I asked one of the chefs and, though he didn't say yes or no, he kind of pulled a face when I mentioned them.'

I, however, had a surefire tip from a real insider: Alicia, an Intermediate student who had been working in the basement prep kitchen, had seen the ingredients arrive the day before. She told me with some certainty that it would be the *tronçons de colin pochés* (a simple poached hake) with a hollandaise sauce, or the *filet de daurade poêlés au fenouil* (sea bream with braised fennel). She'd heard the chefs talking about it, she said. So, I had learned these two recipes, and only these two, by heart. I was relaxed about the whole thing; in fact I'd go as far as to say I was actively looking forward to the exam.

Imagine then, if you will, the look on my face – a blend of 'sudden cramp spasm' and 'just remembered you've left the iron on' – when, having arrived at school, changed and walked upstairs to the exam kitchen carrying my knife kit, I chose from a bowl of red and blue plastic discs held by Chef Didier Chantefort at the door, and took my place before a bowl of iced water with a large lump of grey meat floating in it. Not fish; meat. Not hake or sea bream; meat. Hurriedly piecing together the evidence from the other ingredients on the worktop in front of me – cream, pearl onions, bacon – it was clear what was expected here was the creation not of a light, simple seafood dish, but a hulking great *blanquette de veau*. If you recall that scene in *Jaws* when Roy Scheider spies a shark from the beach and his surroundings crash-zoom into focus, this is what happened to the kitchen for me at that moment. It was my very own Great White.

Blanquette de veau was my least favourite dish of all those we had made in Basic Cuisine. It is, essentially, boiled veal cubes with a gloopy white sauce thickened with egg yolks and cream (the 'blanket' of the title), garnished with pearl onions and button mushrooms, although of course the French dress it up as something far grander, elevating what is really a home cook's staple into haute cuisine. Sokolov, described it rather poetically as 'a milkmaid, pure and playful'. To me it is about as playful as wallpaper paste. I stood, frozen in the kitchen yet again, not really sure what to do next. Did I fry the meat and then boil it? Or boil the meat together with the vegetable garnish? I started to sweat. I swayed slightly. Thank the lord for Hermann the Austrian, who was working beside me and had also selected the veal.

Together we slowly plotted a course through our piles of ingredients – celery, mushrooms, onions, carrots, rice. In the end, though I now know that I took a slightly unconventional path to the completion of my dish (I must be the only person ever to brown the meat in a *blanquette de veau* – a dish in which the meat must remain pale – after leaving the pan with the decanted meat in it on a hot plate by mistake), I ended up with something that tasted and looked pretty good.

Having lavished pedantic attention over its presentation, I stood back from my plate with a deep exhalation of relief and began tidying up. As I was washing my knives at the sink Chef Chantefort came storming through the kitchen checking up on our progress. He stopped halfway and took down a pan from a shelf above someone's oven. 'Whose is this?' He shouted. I looked up. Ha! Some dufus had forgotten to add their mushrooms and onions to the sauce. They were certain to fail and would have to re-do Basic Cuisine. A fraction of a second later I realised I was that dufus. I rushed to grab the pan. I could virtually hear the footsteps of the judging chef – Chef Bruno – climbing the stairs to the second floor as I laboriously placed each piece of garnish around the meat, and artfully spooned sauce over each to disguise its late arrival.

Chantefort witnessed all this but kindly waved his hands as if to say, 'Don't worry, I didn't see anything.' Just as I was placing the last mushroom delicately on the plate and spooning over the sauce, Chef Bruno arrived. We were ordered to back away from the plates and leave the kitchen in order for him to pass his judgement. But my nightmare wasn't over yet. As I left the kitchen, glancing over my shoulder in relief at my plate, I had just enough time to notice the carefully measured fifty millilitre cup of cream at my work station, cream that should have been in my sauce; it was like assembling an IKEA wardrobe and finding a bag of screws in the bottom of the box.

Duvet de Veau

It was several weeks before I could so much as look at a piece of veal again but, with our fates now inextricably entwined, and the trauma of the exam fading, I thought I would attempt to revisit *blanquette de veau*. I know of several people – mostly middle-aged French men, admittedly – for whom this is their absolute favourite dish, so there must be something to it. I decided to attempt to lighten and modernise it a little, and this is the result.

Ingredients (Serves 4-5)

Around a kilo or so of veal shoulder – feel free to add more, but this is really the minimum

A couple of carrots, peeled

1 large or 2 small onions, peeled

A leek, including the green bits

2 celery stalks

2 bay leaves

A few sprigs of thyme

10 peppercorns

2 cloves

A thumb of fresh ginger, peeled and sliced lengthways

1 or 2 lemon grass stems, split lengthways

A litre of veal stock (optional)

Salt

For the *duvet*

A dessertspoon of flour

A dessertspoon of butter

A dessertspoon of crème fraiche

For the garnish

Pearl onions

Butter

Salt, pepper

Shitake mushrooms

Lemon juice

A pinch of sugar

Nut or sunflower oil

First off, don't be daunted by the list of ingredients. Essentially all you do is gently boil it all, take some of the liquid you've boiled the ingredients in, reduce it, add it to a flour and butter mix and plop in a bit of crème fraiche.

Cut the veal into large cubes around the size of a golf ball (if golf balls were cubes), then blanch the cubes. You don't have to do this but it will save you a good deal of skimming later on. Put it in a casserole dish, cover with cold water, bring to the boil, take it off the heat, skim the scum that comes to the surface so that you don't re-contaminate the veal when you remove it from the water. Rinse the casserole, add the meat back in along with all the other ingredients. A little under half the liquid should be veal stock, the rest water. Simmer as gently as possible for about an hour – check one piece of the meat to see that it's tender.

While the veal is cooking, prepare your roux. From the time of Carême until the advent of nouvelle cuisine, the roux was an essential component of a French sauce. You make it by melting some butter, then whisking in the same quantity of flour. Let it cool and then whisk in your hot stock and, *voilà*, you have a smooth, tasty, thickened sauce which will coat the back of a spoon and add body and richness to your dish. How long you cook the roux depends on the type of sauce you are aiming for. For this dish, you need only cook it for two to four minutes so that the raw flour flavour is cooked out and the roux thickens smoothly. If you want a darker sauce, you can cook it for around twice as long.

Meanwhile, you have plenty of time to prepare your garnish. A classic *blanquette de veau* is garnished with button mushrooms and pearl onions (cooked separately), along with the, by now excessively cooked, vegetables from the pot, usually sliced prettily at an angle to distract the diner from their mushiness. I still can't abide cooked carrots, but I keep the pearl onions because they are one of my favourite garnishes, adding a crunchy acid-sweetness that virtually every dish can benefit from. To make them, simply peel and trim the top and most of the root of some pearl onions, place in a small pan with water up to their shoulders, a good dollop of butter and some salt and a pinch of sugar, bring to the boil and simmer until reasonably tender – you don't want them to disintegrate. Eight minutes or so ought to be enough, depending on how large they are. They can keep warm in their liquid until you need them, then strain or, if you want an extra flavour kick, put over a high heat to evaporate the rest of the liquid and gently caramelise them (this is why you don't want to cook them too much in the first instance – if you do, caramelising them will turn them to mush).

Instead of the button mushrooms I like to use shitakes, partly to keep with the vaguely Asian spin on this dish, and partly because they do bring a complex flavour to the dish that button mushrooms don't. Simply fry them in oil and butter, with salt, pepper and, at the end, a good squeeze of lemon juice.

When your veal is tender, ladle around 400-500ml of the cooking liquid into a new pan. You have a couple of options now. A classic *blanquette de veau* adds this liquid to the roux then a cream and egg yolk mix to thicken it. This is too gloopy for me. In my version you can either simply reduce the cooking liquid until it has a flavour you like, then serve the meat, onions and mushrooms in a bowl with the liquid strained over them like a kind of broth or, for a closer approximation of the traditional dish, reduce the liquid much more and strain it into the cold roux. Put it over a high-ish heat and whisk well until it reaches a reasonable thickness – enough so that it covers the back of a spoon and, if you wipe your finger through it, the path your finger has taken remains clear for a brief moment. Add a good spoonful of crème fraiche, stir well and pour over the meat and garnish.

Serve with whatever you fancy: perhaps a couscous with grilled, skinned, diced peppers and a lovely, tangy-salty vinaigrette dressing. Caramelised endives would be nice too – something with a bit of fight in it.

Between the exam and the graduation we would have our end-of-term party. It was held, for some reason best known to the school, in an English theme pub in Bercy, in the east of the city and by the time I arrived many of the younger students had been downing free drinks for a couple of hours. It was heartening to see the people I'd worked alongside for the last three months loosening up over cocktails and beer. Christine, from San Francisco, had grown in confidence during Basic Cuisine, becoming more outgoing with each week. She and Hayden had become particularly close although Sarah, a usually reliable and informative gossip, assured me they were just friends. Henrique had bounced back from Flavia-gate and was working his way through the more attractive girls on the course. Samantha, the English girl with an unfortunate nut allergy ('It's like I'm dying. I start puking; I can't breathe; I have to get to a hospital . . .'), had hooked up with Osgur, a handsome, laid-back Turk with a penchant for George Michael-style designer stubble. Dingbang continued his distant infatuation with Natalie the pretty receptionist, and spent the evening trying to pluck up the courage to talk to her. As a married man I was, naturally, not usually part of the flowering of romance at Le Cordon Bleu, but the night of the party turned out to be an exception.

I had met Akiko, a pretty Japanese woman in her late thirties who was studying Superior Pastry, the previous week when I had sat down in the Winter Garden at school to tuck in to some shop-bought sushi for lunch. Akiko didn't speak much English or French but that hadn't stopped her gaining something of a reputation as a maneater, rumour had it she was desperate to find a husband. That lunchtime there were clearly paltry pickings on offer and so she had sidled up to me. 'You like Japanese food?' she asked. 'Oh yes, sushi is my absolute favourite food,' I answered (although, truthfully, Milky Ways probably shade it). 'And what about Japanese women?' she laughed, batting her eyelashes. I flushed red and mumbled something about them being lovely too. At that moment another Basic student, Danielle from Miami, sat beside me. 'Watch her,' she whispered. 'She's after a donor, and I don't mean blood,' and promptly left, giggling. I made some feeble excuse about having to sharpen my knives before the practical session and left Akiko to trawl the room for other fish.

The night of the party, I left at around midnight to catch the last Metro home. Our babysitter had let us down at the last minute and so Lissen had had to remain at home with the kids. It didn't seem fair to stay out to the early hours and blow twenty euro on a cab home. As I left the pub I found Akiko at my side. 'You go early?' she said, tugging my sleeve. 'No, you stay!' 'Oh, no, really I must go, my wife you see . . .' I didn't finish the rest of the sentence as Akiko had flung her arms around my neck and planted her lips on mine. I backed away, holding her wrists firmly. 'I'm so sorry, I don't think you understand,' I blustered, and hastened away into the night.

I spent most of the morning of our graduation ceremony in a state of pre-crimson apprehension waiting for someone to say that they had seen the snog, but either no one had or they were too tactful to mention it.

And still Basic Cuisine had one last surprise in store for me.

The graduation took place in the Winter Garden, with the chefs arranged stiffly on a dais in front of the assembled students. After a lengthy speech in French from the director of the school, introducing each of the chefs we had known and worked with for the last three months, our names were called for us to approach Chef Bruno, receive our certificate and have our photograph taken. I was one of the first up and was astonished to hear the director announce, 'Michael Booth, Great Britain, fifth in Basic Cuisine.' Somehow, against all expectations, I had come fifth out of fifty-five students. My heart swooshed in my ears as I accepted Chef Bruno's congratulations, the applause of my fellow students echoing somewhere in the distant background. When I sat down I had to check several times with Sarah who was sitting next to me that I had understood it all properly.

Paul, the semi-pro chef from Texas, had come first ('I'd have been pissed if I hadn't won,' he told a crowd of admiring females). But that hardly mattered to me. Maybe I wasn't as bad as I thought I was. Perhaps I had it in me to be a chef after all.

I was doubly eager to discover what the Intermediate level of the course would bring after Christmas but, before that, I had a quick culinary detour to take. I was about to undergo an initiation into one of the darkest and most mysterious of all the culinary arts, an alchemy involving a substance whose origins lay in Aztec blood ceremonies, which boasts one of the most complex molecular structures in the world, a substance more cherished than gold itself.

Chapter 16

The man who calls himself a gourmand but eats like a glutton is not a gourmand. He is a glutton.

Antonin Carême

These days anyone who has the odd Mars Bar from the tea trolley or chooses the chocolate mousse for dessert in restaurants with a 'Would you look at me!' expression claims to be a 'chocoholic', but this is to grossly diminish the plight of those of us burdened with a genuine, debilitating dependency. What I have is not some fleeting caprice, it is the craving of a laboratory beagle for his cigarettes; the desperate frailty of the craven lush who douses his cornflakes in half a litre of vodka in the morning; or, well, it's like me with cakes. I can not pass a day without eating chocolate. I love the stuff. I need the stuff. I can easily eat a kilo over a period of twenty-four hours, washed down with uncut Nutella eaten straight from the jar with a few spoons of raw cocoa powder as a chaser. I have been known to gnaw away the outer crust of chocolate on liqueurs (tip: old people often have a box hidden away in their bureaux) even though I find their sugary, boozy filling repulsive. Sometimes, if there's nothing else around, I'll eat Nestlé.

I wanted to find out how to work with chocolate myself and save a good deal of money in the long term. They do teach some chocolate techniques as part of the pastry course at Le Cordon Bleu, but I fancied a change of scenery and enrolled instead at the Ecole Ritz Escoffier, in the basement kitchens of the Ritz Hotel, for a five-day course just before Christmas.

If that sounds like a self-indulgence, it pales in comparison to the most extravagant meal of my life, quite possibly the most extravagant thing I have ever done, which had taken place a couple of days earlier. To celebrate my shock fifth place in Basic Cuisine, Lissen and I, acting on rash impulse, decided to take ourselves off for lunch at one of the greatest restaurants in the world, a place renowned for its relentless pursuit of perfection and all-out lavishness: Alain Ducasse at the Hotel Plaza Athénée. This is also one of the most expensive restaurants in the world and, if we had known quite how parlous our finances would become in the New Year we would . . . honestly? We would have gone anyway, and packed for the poorhouse.

The Hotel Plaza Athénée is on Avenue Montaigne, Paris' most effortfully chic street; home to the super rich, their freeze-dried wives and their alopecia-plagued gerbil-dogs. It is flanked by the kind of clothing stores whose assistants would really rather you want elsewhere; it is also the only street I have ever visited where Havana cigars outnumber cigarette butts in the gutters. To tell the truth, it takes some courage to even venture onto Avenue Montaigne when most of your wardrobe is older than your children and has been used by them as a dishcloth for the last five years. We were awed further still by the imposing glassy marble lobby and gargantuan floral arrangements of the Plaza Athénée, one of the city's most opulent hotels. By the time we approached the entrance to ADPA (as it is known in the trade) – two engraved glass doors, behind which a wall teasingly conceals the high-rolling gourmets at play beyond – it took some nerve not to turn and flee.

But the front of house staff were warmly welcoming and not at all sniffy. Remarkably, they told us it would be no problem getting a table for lunch even though we had no reservation. More of an issue, apparently, was the fact that I had no jacket but the maître d' summoned a spare: a slightly oversized, heavily starched blazer. It was hardly the best camouflage in which to slip unnoticed into the rarefied society that awaited us, although, if I lifted both my arms up, the jacket entirely covered my head, which might come in useful when it came time for the bill.

We were led into the palatial dining room with its freshly gilded ceiling from which hung a stunning deconstructivist chandelier, its crystals seeming to explode across the room, each one suspended by an individual, invisible twine. We were shown to a linen-covered corner table, and seated on oval-backed chairs with small pull-out tables built into their bases, for ladies to rest their handbags on. The menu was presented but, before we had a chance to finish reading it, one of about twenty waiters working the room approached us baring a large wooden cigar box. Cigars before the dinner? What kind of a cockamamie, avant garde joint was this? But no, it wasn't cigars. We could smell the contents of the box before he opened it: white truffles from Alba, in Italy. He wafted the open box underneath my nose as if it were smelling salts, and its nutty-mouldy aroma began to have a curious effect on me. This was Ducasse's not especially subtle method of tempting diners to take his three-hundred-euro white truffle menu. It works. I commenced immediately trying to justify spending our monthly grocery bill on a fungus.

Alba truffles, or *tuber magnatum pico* (Rossini called them 'the Mozart of mushrooms'), are possibly the most sought after culinary ingredient in the world, I explained to Lissen. They only grow in the wild and, as with all truffles, are difficult and labour-intensive to find. 'Yes Michael,' she said, laying a steadying hand on mine, 'but children's clothes *don't* grow in the wild. One has to buy them. With money.'

I would have to content myself with the more routine Ducasse experience, which of course is routine only in the sense that Prince Charles is rumoured to have his staff prepare eight boiled eggs before he selects the one that is cooked just he way he likes it, is routine. These days Alain Ducasse is far more than a chef; he is more even than a mere culinary legend: he is a global phenomenon. The youngest man to win three Michelin stars (this was in 1990, Marco Pierre White was later to steal that title) and the first to have three restaurants, each with three Michelin stars, he now has restaurants, bakeries, delicatessens and bistros in Paris, Monte Carlo, Italy and New York. He leads the life and, judging by every picture I have seen of him, wears the suits of a high powered international lawyer. Although it is hard to imagine him tucking into a stale muffin and Pret a Manger wrap, he must spend half his life in airports as he allocates three weeks in rotation to each of his three-star restaurants on Casino Square in Monte Carlo, at the Plaza Athénée and in New York's Essex House. He has been called the man who detoxed French haute cuisine, thanks to his efforts to remove much of the butter and cream from his food and replace them with simple flavours and high quality olive oils – the latter his defining flavour. He vows he does it all in the service of the raw ingredients, his ultimate aim being to let their flavours sing clearly and vibrantly.

Of course, these days every chef on the planet from Gordon Ramsay to the grill chef on the A3 will repeat this same mantra when asked about their food philosophy: 'Food should taste of what it is,' they say. 'I like to keep my food simple; I only use the best, locally sourced, seasonal ingredients and keep the flavours pure and distinctive, blah, blah, blah.' I have tried to maintain a fascinated expression while interviewing several chefs who have all said precisely this but, not only is it an insufferable platitude, akin to the 'It's a game of two halves' employed by footballers but, actually, I rather like it when a restaurant does something clever and unexpected with food. I like to eat food that I wouldn't or couldn't make at home, or to be presented with a plate on which the various elements work together to create a different or new flavour.

But Ducasse, at least, walks the talk and, anyway, I suspected that his 'respect the ingredients' code was slightly misleading; after all, Michelin doesn't give three stars for gently poached chicken and a lightly dressed salad. I knew also that his obsessive drive to indulge his guests' every whim has been known to reach absurd heights – offering a choice of pens for diners to sign their cheques with at the end of the meal, for instance, or his most famous extravagance:

waiters clipping tea leaves from live bushes while wearing white gloves.

We ordered and before we had time to gird our loins (or what-ever the pre-dinner equivalent may be) two *amuse bouche* arrived: one a puff pastry and spinach arrangement, the other a cocktail glass with an arresting truffle and lobster foam – intensely salty and mush-roomy – that blitzed our palates and caused the first of many raised eyebrows of delight. I should say here that years of disappointment, envy and fights over who gets to taste each other's food have taught me to always order exactly what Lissen chooses. She has an uncanny knack of picking the best from a menu and I long ago learned simply to shadow her choices. I wasn't going to take any chances with the most expensive meal of my life so we both started with what was described enigmatically on the menu as 'vegetables and fruits cooked/raw, tomato marmalade/cèpes' and which turned out to be a technicolour firework display featuring the freshest, most efferves-cent vegetables and fruits – carrot, courgette, fennel, beetroot – each finely and precisely prepared: diced, sliced, frilled, *ciselé* and, in the case of the beetroot, deep fried into fragile, crazy spirals, by an obvi-ously accomplished, anally retentive *commis chef*. Within this explo-sion of vegetables lay perfectly placed, immaculately *brunoised* lobster. It was sweet, tart and invigorating.

We sat back and took in the hushed and reverent atmosphere, casting furtive glances at our fellow diners. There were only a dozen, mostly Asian and power-dressed. We sipped our *coupes de champagne*, and tasted the twin, conical butters – one salt, one unsalted – embossed with the Ducasse logo, slathering them on our chewy, crusty sourdough pointy rolls – rolls so pointy they would be confis-cated if you tried to get them into a football ground.

Our *turbot de Bretagne en matelote* arrived, carried aloft on a silver surfboard serving tray on the shoulder of our waiter, the fish just barely cooked enough to have moved beyond the sashimi stage; ethe-really translucent, yet firm and warm. It came with, essentially, the same garnish as a *coq au vin*, right down to the deep, dark, sticky, reduced red wine sauce. There were lardons; lightly caramelised onions; and turned mushrooms just like the ones we had made in Basic Cuisine, the whole scene set with a fringe of vivid green herb sauce delicately drizzled around the rim of the plate. We had matched red wine sauces with white fish at school, so it wasn't a surprise to see it here, the delicacy of the fish supported by and contrasted with the weighty, rich acidity of the sauce.

Venison with juniper and another red wine sauce – this time accompanied by apples, quince, pear, pumpkin, chestnut and fennel – followed, almost overpowering us with a flurry of meaty sweetness. Lissen and I had vowed not to drink during the lunch, both to save money and to focus more on the food, but the sommelier promised us he had the perfect red wine to go with the venison, and it seemed rude to say no; the glass of 1985 Château Magdelaine he brought us was one of the most memorable wines I have ever tasted.

A pre-dessert featured a pyramid of chocolate and coffee *macarons*; a tiny sugar tart; and soft cloud-like pastry puffs of hot pineapple and ginger. The real dessert was a caramel *parfait* with a fromage blanc made from goat's cheese, speckled with ground black pepper and a quenelle of fragrant honey ice cream. Then came the candy trolley with toffees, nougats and caramels and long marshmallow snakes. I have quite an infantile taste in sweets and always go for the foamy, spongy, multi-coloured stuff at the pick and mix, so I was keen to try Ducasse's take on the marshmallow. It was foamy-light and delicately flavoured with orange blossom. Fabulous.

'What's French for "doggy bag"?' I hissed to Lissen. She didn't know. Overhearing us, the waiter helped us out. 'It is doggy bag,' he smiled. 'Would you like one?' By now the sweet trolley had departed, and a plate of chocolates had been left on our table. But we had reached the 'Mr Creosote' stage and could not stuff another morsel into our mouths, so agreed.

'Does Mr Ducasse come here very often,' I asked the waiter. 'Yes,' replied the waiter, 'He's here today.' Alain Ducasse! Here! As we were eating! The back of my neck prickled with goosebumps. As we left, having been relieved of a sum of money greater than I paid for my first car, we were each handed – in a carefully choreographed flurry of waiters and hostesses – a bag with a copy of the menu, our doggy bag of chocolates and a fresh baked loaf of bread. My jacket was removed, our coats offered and we were wafted away, bloated but content, onto Avenue Montaigne.

Chapter 17

Look, there's no metaphysics on earth like chocolates.

Fernando Pessoa, Portuguese poet

The next morning, still satiated enough to skip breakfast, I set off eagerly – more eagerly perhaps than I have ever set off from home before – for the Ritz Hotel, and a date with perhaps my most abiding infatuation.

The Ecole Ritz Escoffier is, of course, named after Auguste Escoffier, the man who revolutionised restaurant cooking in the late nineteenth and early twentieth centuries and whose fiendishly complex cookery books had caused me so much distress in the past. The school is rather different from Le Cordon Bleu, as I discovered when I arrived at the tradesman's entrance to the Ritz Hotel on rue Cambon. Following protracted negotiation with the small wizened doorman I was allowed to pass and was formally greeted by the school's dark-suited director, Bruno Sagne. I followed him down into the bowels of the hotel, along an endless, functional corridor. On the right-hand side I caught a glimpse into the vast and gleaming hotel kitchens, its walls and floors lined with Portuguese tiling, and silently teeming with chefs in paper toques. The school – two kitchens: one large cuisine kitchen, one smaller room for patisserie – plus a couple of administrative rooms, lay on the left-hand side, but first Sagne took me down one level further beneath the school to pick up my uniform from the hotel laundry. We stood in a short queue of hotel staff, each dressed like an extra from a dance routine in *Oliver!* in black aprons, pinstripe trousers, double-breasted, gold buttoned jackets, and top hats.

In the changing rooms I discovered that I had been given a uniform at least one size too small (they obviously had me down as an urchin), so by the time I found my way back to the laundry, changed and arrived in the patisserie kitchen, my fellow students – six bashful Japanese women of varying ages – were already in place, standing around a large, marble worktop. At the stove end stood Christian Forais, a short, jolly-looking chef, with a pronounced pot belly and a bushy moustache. He bore an uncanny resemblance to the picture of *Le Compte de Saint-Germain, Célèbre Alchimiste* hanging in our living room.

Naturally, I was wary of entering a room full of Japanese women, aware as I now was of the powerful sexual magnetism I exerted over them, but these ones were too busy separating caramelised nuts, like the diligent squirrels in *Charlie and the Chocolate Factory*, to notice me. I joined them as the chef began to explain our first lesson: how to make a *ganache*.

Before coming to live in Paris the *ganache* had made only a peripheral impact on my life, but within a week this had all changed and the affect could be measured in kilos on the scales. A *ganache* is simply a mixture of chocolate and hot cream, typically 50:50, which can be flavoured in countless ways. The word originally meant 'cushion' and these soft, creamy chocolates are quite possibly my favourite thing in the entire world. I couldn't believe I could just walk in off the street and be told how to do this, to learn this alchemy, and then create more complicated confections by enriching them with butter or adding fruit pulps and infusions.

Simple Yet Awfully
Time-Consuming Chocolate *Ganache*

Ingredients (Serves 4-5)
400g couverture chocolate – I like to blend something mild with something darker and more malevolent, even 99 per cent – you can play around to find a blend that works for you. I have tried with ordinary cooking chocolate, thinking that it

didn't really matter because I was going to cover it later with couverture, but it didn't set very well and I had to put it in the freezer so that I could cut it up into pieces before coating it.

225g double cream

Around another 150g *couverture* chocolate for the coating

Bring the cream to the boil. If you want a flavoured *ganache*, now is the time to add the ingredient – for example, a large bunch of chopped mint leaves or the zest of two lemons or oranges. If you are doing this, leave it to infuse for a couple of minutes after it has boiled. Strain the cream over the chocolate in another bowl off the heat and stir until it melts and mixes.

This is the slightly tricky part because you will now need a mould. After scouring the cooking supply stores of Paris, I still couldn't find the type of mould they used at the Ritz school, so I got a local metalworker to knock a couple up out of stainless steel. What you are after is a very simple frame, like a picture frame with the glass and backing removed, around 200mm x100mm and 10mm deep. Cover a chopping board with clingfilm, place the frame on top and pour in the cream and chocolate mixture, trying to keep the top as smooth and level as possible. Cover with cling-film and leave it to set in a cool cupboard for at least a day.

This is a *ganache*. You can scoop it out and form it into quenelles as an accompaniment to ice cream or other desserts, or just wolf the lot down before anyone in your family discovers you have made it. Alternatively, to turn it into posh little choco-lates with which to astound your friends, remove the frame from the *ganache* (cut around the edge with a sharp knife to release it). Melt some more chocolate over a bain-marie, and paint it over the top of the *ganache* with a pastry brush. Leave it to set, then turn the *ganache* over and paint the underside too, leaving that to set also. You may have to give it two coats. What you want it a soft *ganache* sandwiched between crisp chocolate. With your sharpest, longest knife, carefully cut the *ganache* into bite-sized squares, 10mm x 10mm x 10mm, or larger if you don't care what people think. Place your knife in hot water and then wipe it dry once in a while as you do this.

Now comes the tricky part: tempering the *couverture* chocolate so that you can cover your *ganache* sandwich in glossy, snappy coating. Melt two-thirds of the chocolate you have set aside for this ever so gently over a bain-marie (Valrhona recommend taking a day or so to do this, which is plainly ridiculous) until it reaches the prescribed temperature (see the bit about tempering later in this chapter). Then remove it from the heat and mix in the other third, stirring to form a well in the centre until its temperature comes down. Then place it briefly back over the bain-marie to bring it up to the final temperature and remove it from the bain-marie.

Using a couple of forks – you can get special ones for this, but you don't really need them – gently drop your *ganache* squares into the tempered chocolate and roll them until sufficiently coated. Place on a clingfilm-covered chopping board to rest. Leave to dry and then trim the excess melted chocolate that will have oozed around the base of each chocolate with a dry, sharp knife and store in a sealed container in a cool place, with minimal humidity – not the fridge.

It soon became clear that the pace and the methods of Ecole Escoffier were different from those at Le Cordon Bleu. Instead of students themselves making a dish or, in this case, a type of chocolate, from start to finish, we would all muck in to help prepare several different types of chocolate at the same time. It took a while to adjust and I spent the first day flustering around, offering help where it wasn't needed as my fellow students – who had been at the school for some weeks following other courses – set about following Chef Forais' instructions. It was fast-moving, confusing and, as the only male student, not a little intimidating. Trying to be helpful, I would hand one student a sugar thermometer to help her assess the temperature of some jam she was making, for instance. She would take it with a polite smile, and then quietly set it aside – it would be some minutes before it was needed. She had everything in hand.

Out of the corner of my eye I saw the chef melting some chocolate over a bain-marie. He removed the bowl from the heat and tipped a quantity of solid chocolate pellets into the melted chocolate. I knew enough to know that he was tempering the chocolate – heating it then cooling it according to strict temperature guidelines – but I had no idea why, and it all happened too quickly for me to follow.

I tried to ask Chef Forais about it, but he had already launched into an explanation of his unique jam-making technique. His secret? Less sugar. Apparently, the classic proportion for making jam is to cook one kilo of fruit with one kilo of sugar, but Chef Forais used half the quantity of sugar to reduce the unpleasant sugar burn in your throat you can get from jam, and to increase the pure fruit flavour. He did the same with nougat and fruit jellies too. The downside is it won't last as long because the sugar acts as a preservative, but it is unlikely to linger in the larder long enough to go off anyway. I never thought I could make these kind of products taste better than the ones you can buy in the shops, but even the nougat we made was an improvement.

And but still, I couldn't shake my thoughts from the chocolate and the mysteries of tempering. Why was it necessary to play with the temperatures in this way? How did the *couverture* chocolate that Chef Forais was using differ from the bars of cooking chocolate you buy in the supermarket? I was determined to pay more attention the next morning, and press Chef Forais for answers.

The next day I busied myself stirring more jam and making whisky truffles as, like timid forest creatures, my fellow students began to approach me, asking where I was from and what I did for a living. There was a murmur of excitement when Mariko translated the news that I was studying at Le Cordon Bleu. As with all of the students at the Ritz Escoffier who I told this to, their response made me feel like a traveller bringing news from some Elysian paradise. 'Is it . . . is it *better*?' they would ask me tentatively. I explained how, at Le Cordon Bleu, each student made a dish from start to finish, which drew gasps of wonderment, but I had to concede that the Ritz school was posher, better kept, and the way it worked was more analogous to working in a restaurant where chefs often complete elements of a dish rather than the whole thing. ('Yes, but all we do is chop vegetables,' one young, English male student moaned to me in the locker one morning. I explained that we did a fair bit of that at our school, but a few months later I ran in to him after he had jumped ship from the Ritz and crossed Paris to Le Cordon Bleu where he seemed much happier.)

By the third day I had begun to learn a little more about my fellow students – one was a dental hygienist, another a hairdresser from Kyoto. One of the eldest was an accomplished cake maker who proudly showed me her scrapbook filled with photographs of elaborate cakes she had made. Mirako, the youngest student, had been to England, she told me. Did I know a big house called 'Sha-woo'? No, I couldn't say that I did. She tried again. 'Shats-wo?' Nope, sorry. She wrote it down on my pad: 'Chatsworth!' Another of my Japanese cohorts plucked up the courage to tell me that patisserie chefs didn't wear the neckerchiefs that cuisine chefs wore, which I had been wearing since I arrived. There were polite giggles all round as I took it off. 'What? Patisserie chefs don't sweat?' I asked Chef Forais. He shook his head, smiling, and held up the palms of his hands as if to say, 'Haven't you noticed how cold it is in here?' It was true: the patisserie kitchen was cooler than the cuisine kitchen – all the better to work with chocolate.

Which, at last, we did. 'This is my MacGyver solution!' the chef said proudly, as he began to wrap the entire marble worktop with plastic-wrap in the manner of a Cristo art installation. It was an excellent way to keep everything easy to clean once the chocolate began to flow, he explained, and flow it did, brothers and sisters, oh yes, praise the Lord, it done flowed like the River Jordan!

We began by filling pre-made chocolate spheres with raspberry *ganache*, which we then dipped in melted *couverture* chocolate and rolled on a round wire rack used for cooling cakes in order to give them a rough, spiky outer texture. We took another *ganache* filling we had made the day before and which had been setting in the chiller overnight, cut it into squares, dipped them in tempered chocolate and placed them on a piece of stiff, transparent plastic sheeting. The chef then gave us a pile of smaller plastic squares with delicate gold stars laser etched on to them, which we placed on top. After they had cooled, we removed the plastic covers leaving the gold stars on top. So, this was how the *chocolatiers* produced those perfect, flat, glossy *ganache* chocolate squares with the different decorations.

Next came a tasting. The chef brought out several bags of *couverture* chocolate pastilles and invited us to taste each, advising us to place the pastilles in the side of our mouths and pay particular attention to the after-taste. 'Chocolate has more than six hundred different kinds of volatile molecules and almost as many flavours as wine,' he said. 'She is very complicated, like a woman!' A Caraïbe (sixty-six per cent cocoa solids) was strong, dark and acidic compared to a lighter Equatoriale (fifty-five per cent), but the Guanaja (seventy per cent) had the longest lingering flavour – quite intoxicating in fact. Chocolate was similar to olive oil and wine, the chef explained, in that the earth, the direction of the sun and the humidity where the cocoa beans were grown all played their part in creating its flavour profile. This explains the current fad for single – estate chocolates, produced from beans grown in the same plantation, or *Les Grands Crus de Chocolat*, a French categorisation inspired by wines. 'The best chocolate you should let breathe, just like wine,' the chef said. A minimum of eighty per cent humidity is needed to grow cocoa beans, although humidity is the enemy of finished chocolate, which is why the school used special, dehumidified fridges for storage. Generally, the best beans are used to make *couverture* chocolate, but, the chef raised his finger to stress, the quality of chocolate is not all about the percentage of cocoa solids. Buying chocolate just because it has a higher percentage leads you inevitably to the ninety-nine per cent bars you can sometimes find which, though I find them strangely addictive, are a difficult taste to acquire. Buying chocolate according to its percentage is like buying wine according to its alcohol content. The way the beans are grilled plays just as important a role in flavour, for instance, as of course does the blend of beans.

There are three main types: Forestero, which accounts for around eighty per cent of the chocolate we consume and, unsurprisingly, is the lowest quality, most bland of the three; Trinitario, from Trinidad, which is better but still not as good as the third type, Criollo, which is grown mostly in Venezuela and takes five to six years to mature, the trees being grown in the shade of banana trees (although there is some dispute as to whether genetically pure Criollo still exists). Generally, the cheaper quality beans come from Brazil, Mexico and India, where genetically modified beans are common.

Cheap chocolate is made with vegetable oil, the chef warned. 'Belgian chocolate is made with vegetable oil,' he sniffed. 'In France all chocolate is made from only cocoa butter. If it has over thirty-two per cent cocoa butter it is technically *couverture* or 'confectioner's' chocolate. Less than thirty per cent is *chocolat de cuisine* – cooking chocolate.' He pronounced 'cooking chocolate' with evident distaste. This is the sandy, cloying stuff you buy in the supermarket to make cakes and brownies. Because it lacks the cocoa butter content it will always remain thick when you heat it; *couverture* chocolate, meanwhile, thins out beautifully and remains glossy once it cools. You can't temper cooking chocolate as it never really becomes liquid enough, which is why homemade chocolates usually look lumpen and have an unappealing matt finish. What's more, tempered *couverture* chocolate has a higher melting point, so it melts in your mouth not on your hands and will snap with a satisfying crack, rather than a dull, clay-like 'plap'.

I keep using this word 'tempering' as if simply through sheer repetition I will come to understand it, but it is a complex procedure fraught with pitfalls. Those in the know refer to it as a crystallisation instead of tempering, for a start, and, once you have indicated even so much as a passing interest in the subject, they will bore you – to the extent that you will plead for a short and painless end to your life – with talk about beta, leique, palmatique and searique crystals. We did have a lecture on all this but my mind drifted to the raspberry *ganaches* we had made earlier; what they might taste like, how many I could eat there and then without drawing attention to myself, and how many I could get away with taking home.

In fact, tempering simply means heating chocolate to a specific temperature (depending on the type of chocolate, this is usually around 40°C for white chocolate, 45° for milk chocolate and 55°C for dark) then cooling it (to 26, 27 and 28° respectively) and heating it again slightly (to 28-29° for white, 29-30° for milk, and 31-32° for dark). (Most *couverture* chocolate comes with a graph on the side of the packet showing the target temperatures at each of the three stages.) You heat the chocolate in a clean, dry bowl over a bain-marie with the water at the barest of simmers. Resist all temptation to stir the melting chocolate at this point and, beware, if you heat the chocolate too much those ugly white streaks will form when it cools. To temper the chocolate, you remove it from the heat, add around half the quantity of solid chocolate again to the melted chocolate in the bowl (i.e., if you have melted 200g, add 100g solid), and stir until the solid chocolate has melted. Finally, bring the temperature of the chocolate back up to the required target over the bain-marie and, *voilà*, you have perfectly tempered chocolate, ready for dipping. Fortunately, if things do go wrong it is a fairly forgiving substance: you can simply start the process all over again by melting the chocolate once more.

This is how you or I might temper chocolate, but Chef Forais had another, more theatrical method. Eschewing thermometers, he heated the chocolate until he could tell it was ready by dabbing a blob on his lip, then he poured the whole lot out onto the cold, plastic-covered marble to bring the temperature down, mixing it with a spatula in elegant, sweeping movements to cool it further to a little above room temperature, before sweeping it all back into the bowl and heating it over a bain-marie until he could judge by sight that it had reached the final temperature. He invited us to try the same method, but it was like juggling with ectoplasm, and I ended up with more on my trousers than in the bowl.

We used this chocolate to make our own bespoke chocolate bars laden with thyme and candied orange zest and nuts, and then made chocolate eggs by brushing the chocolate around the inside of some moulds, letting one layer cool before brushing on second, third and fourth layers to build up the required thickness. After they had cooled completely we removed the egg halves from the moulds and stuck them together by melting their edges slightly on the hot plate and pressing them together, which was deeply satisfying. The chef then let us loose on a machine which turned dyed cocoa butter into spray paint to decorate the eggs. By the time we finished the session we were covered from feet to the top of our toques with chocolate.

On the last day there were group photos, exchanges of email addresses and even the odd tear at our parting. We'd worked well as a team, my Japanese friends quietly, studiously preparing the chocolates, while I interfered, messed things up a bit and was gently sidelined as they got on with it.

Chapter 18

We cook today the way people cooked in the Middle Ages ... this
at a time when space probes are being sent to Mars.

Hervé This

Back home I filled our *garde manger* – the cool cupboard built into
the wall in our kitchen – with the chocolates I snuck home from
the Ritz in preparation for Christmas and an influx of guests.
Though the French are admirably low key when it comes to their
Christmas celebrations, our family is more inclined to obscene over-
indulgence. Not since the decline of the Roman Empire had Europe
witnessed such scenes as Christmas at our apartment that year –
not just on account of the quantities of chocolate we gorged on,
we also ate foie gras until we could justifiably empathise with the
geese that had produced them.

Foie gras is an essential part of a Parisian Christmas. At this time
of year the shops are full of these *mi-cuit*, or partially-cooked, duck
or goose livers which are vacuum packed or sealed in jars and sold
for around thirty euro a kilo. Whole livers usually weigh around a
kilo and are unfeasibly large. 'That's why ducks waddle!' Chef Terrien
had joked as he held one up to show us during a demo earlier on
towards the end of Basic Cuisine. Of course, many right-minded
people – as well as animal activists – are horrified by the *gavage* method
by which the geese are force fed, and concerned by the health conse-
quences of eating foie gras, but farmers maintain that their birds
enjoy being fed this way. Stressed animals make for bad produce, so
why would they do anything to harm them, they say? As for the
health issue, I have convinced myself that as foie gras is full of non-

saturated fatty acids it is virtually a health food. For better or worse, foie gras remains one of the star ingredients of French cuisine and there were dozens of questions during Terrien's demo. Stephan asked where the best foie gras came from and Chef Terrien told us that Perigord foie gras was famous but that he always bought his from Alsace. Someone else wondered why *foie gras d'oie* – goose livers – cost more than duck (or, *foie gras de canard*). 'Goose liver is more elegant than duck liver, it has a more subtle flavour,' he said, adding that less than ten per cent of livers sold come from geese.

Taste foie gras in its raw state and you might wonder what all the fuss is about: there's not much flavour and what flavour there is not terribly pleasant and somewhat like clay. You need to apply heat to pure foie gras to get the best from it. You can make foie gras mousse, use it as a stuffing for poultry or add it to a sauce. We were even shown how to make a foie gras crème brûlée by mixing it with eggs, cream and milk and topping with the usual caramel crust (sounds revolting, and it was) – but my two preferred methods were these: the first is simply to slice it on the diagonal – to give as great a surface area as possible – to a thickness of about two centimetres, and fry the slices in a dry, hot pan until the exterior is lusciously caramelised. Cheap foie gras melts more quickly than the better sort because it has a higher fat content, so should be avoided if you are frying. That was one reason my fried foie gras had always melted back home in England; the other had been that I had added oil to the pan before frying. Foie gras contains enough oil to fry itself, you don't need any more. It is great served with something sweetly acidic such as *confit* of onions – very long, slow-cooked onions in butter and a little oil with a little sugar – peaches stewed with vanilla, or a fig or tomato jam, perhaps with a sprinkling of *pain d'epices* (dried, ground gingerbread) over the top, and a simply dressed salad. Warmed through, foie gras tastes richer and more savoury and it melts like hot butter in your mouth . . . before dispersing quickly through your bloodstream and blocking your arteries as effectively as putty seals a draughty window.

Alternatively, you can go for broke and make a foie gras terrine. I tried this for the first time at New Year. We had a friend, Lars, and his family visiting us from Denmark. Denmark is not the ideal place to live if you are a food lover, like Lars. So he tends to go a little crazy when he travels to more enlightened countries. Caught up in his whirlwind of gastronomic enthusiasm I agreed that the best thing he and I could do to mark the end of one year and the beginning of another was to make our own foie gras terrine. Neither of us had any experience of how to do this, nor did we have any recipe, but Lars had a hunch that it involved cognac and slow cooking in the oven. Sadly, hunches only really work if you are Detective Columbo and, after carefully pressing our costly liver into a cheap terrine hastily bought from Dehillerin on New Year's Eve, and then putting it in a medium oven for a while, we were, essentially, left with foie gras and cognac soup. Foie gras, it seems, requires careful handling. This is how to do it properly.

Foie Gras Terrine

Ingredients

1 duck or goose liver – it really has to be good quality, not the tinned stuff

30ml cognac

30ml port (white is best because it doesn't colour the terrine, but ordinary red port is fine)

30ml dessert wine

Salt, pepper, perhaps some nutmeg

Before you start, you need to bring the liver up to room temperature, otherwise it will be like trying to work with chilled clay; some even advise soaking the liver overnight in lightly salted water to draw out moisture and blood but I can never be bothered. First, de-vein the liver. This is rather like removing the veins from an oak leaf – you break the liver up and pull out any stringy bits. Try to keep the pieces of liver as large as possible because it will look better when you come to slice the terrine. Place the pieces of liver in iced water as you do this to prevent them melting. Also cut out any unpleasantly discoloured or bloody bits. This is a costly ingredient, so Terrien showed us a clever trick – press the more appetisingly coloured 'waste' from this process through a drum sieve to recuperate any foie gras that has clung to the veins.

Place the liver, by now a substance hard to reconcile with a functioning animal organ, in a baking tray or dish and sprinkle over a little cognac, port and dessert wine (a Jurançon or Muscat is good), around 30ml of each, a little fine salt (just one or two per cent of the weight of liver), nutmeg if you are a nutmeg fan, and finely ground white pepper. Leave in the fridge for the rest of the morning – at least three hours, or overnight.

Heat your oven to 130-150°C. Heat some water for a bain-marie. Place the liver in a terrine dish – an enamelled, cast iron one is preferable to plain porcelain as it conducts heat better – and press down well. You can add fresh truffle, finely sliced, in with the liver now if you like (arrange it so that it'll look pretty when you slice the terrine – I can never manage this, but you might have better luck), just don't fill the terrine all the way to the top. Drizzle over a little of the remaining marinade. Wrap the terrine in several layers of oven-proof clingfilm. Place it in the warm bain-marie on a couple of pieces of kitchen paper to keep it in place when you move it – the water should reach to about three-quarters of the way up the sides of the terrine – and put it into the oven for thirty to forty minutes.

Remove the terrine from the oven. Some oil will have risen to the surface so carefully pour this off and keep it to one side. Leave the terrine to rest for an hour until completely cool, then unwrap. Cut a piece of cardboard to fit snugly within the terrine to protect the surface of the pâté and place a couple of tins of tomatoes – or some other handy weight – on top of it to compress the foie gras below. Leave to settle in the fridge overnight – or at least a good few hours. If you are planning to store it for a couple of days, remove the pâté from the terrine. Clean the terrine, pour in the fat you saved from the top and grease the sides well, put the pâté back in and cover with more of the fat. It will keep for up to a week in the fridge like this. Traditionally foie gras is eaten with sweet white wines but it is excellent with dry white Alsatians too – wines, that is.

We returned to the familiar smells of Le Cordon Bleu in the first week of the New Year. I was slightly more confident than on my first day back in August, buoyed, of course, by my shock fifth-place finish at the end of Basic Cuisine (did I mention that already?). Some friends had left us – Hermann the Austrian was avoiding winter completely by sailing around the world with his oil tanker, for instance, and allergic Samantha had left to work in London – but several new students joined Intermediate Cuisine having completed an intensive Basic Cuisine course in the weeks before Christmas. In fact, there were more students than ever at the school which made the changing rooms yet more cramped. As I changed that first day I heard one student quip: 'I had to go outside to change my mind.' Moments later, he was crushed beneath the mob and never seen again.

We had a new allergic to replace Samantha: I overheard the familiar, almost proud litany of symptoms from behind me as I took my place in the demonstration room for our first lesson. 'It's not just mushrooms, it's shellfish too. I get hives, I faint, it can be quite serious. I have to wear plastic gloves if I even touch the things.' This was Alison, a tiny, bookish Canadian, with frizzy brown hair and freckles. She was attending Le Cordon Bleu en route to a creative writing course back in Toronto and, over the coming months, would show possibly the least aptitude for kitchen work of any life form, something she would explain – often, and to anyone who showed a passing interest – by citing a rare neurological condition she suffered from that affected her spatial awareness. As if this wasn't enough, Alison had a bit of an issue with knives: she was petrified of them. 'So what the fuck are you doing at a cooking school?' Paul had asked her one day, after patiently listening to her various neuroses. Alison looked dismayed for moment, then launched into Part One of her life story. Paul simply turned away and started telling the person seated next to him about his time working in a leading New York restaurant, where he claimed to have met Anthony Bourdain. Apparently, he so impressed the celebrity chef with his knowledge of French cooking that Bourdain offered him a job. 'I told him thanks, but no thanks. I'm looking to open my own place,' said Paul.

The two chefs in charge of Intermediate Cuisine were Patrick Terrien and Marc Thivet. Though both in their fifties, they could not have been more different. Terrien was dapper and precise, with immaculate silver hair, a perma-tan and laughter lines that set his eyes to permanent twinkle. It was easy to imagine Terrien cruising the beaches of St Tropez in a pair of those eye-wateringly brief trunks that French men tend to favour, pausing by a group of young ladies to lower his sunglasses and flash that dazzling smile, or welcoming over-dressed widows to his captain's table on a cruise liner. He was an incorrigible flirt in the grand French tradition and kept himself in fine physical shape with regular tennis matches against the younger patisserie chefs. 'Cooking is all about love,' he explained while showing us how to make a *tian d'agneau* (a kind of multi-layered lamb 'cake') in the first demonstration of the new term. 'You need to touch meat to see how well it is done, like an Italian touching a woman.' He gave the Japanese women in the front row a fruity wink.

During demonstrations Terrien was prone to whipping off his apron and retying it in order, we suspected, to exhibit his stomach which, though hardly a washboard, was, in the context of the other Cordon Bleu chefs, a finely contoured specimen. 'Why does he keep doing that?' whispered Tessa during one demonstration. 'I think it's some kind of mating ritual,' I whispered back. 'It's for all the Asian ladies in the front rows.' Terrien was known to have a soft spot for Asian women, a fondness that was to cause a fair deal of bitterness among other female students during the course when, as they saw it, he was prone to doling out high marks to certain flirtatious Japanese females.

Though perfectly amicable, of all the chefs Terrien was the most authoritarian. He wasn't slow to make it known when someone had disappointed him and, on a bad day when we were all making a royal mess of things, he would storm through the kitchens shouting, 'Terrorists! You're all terrorists!'

'I want you to be calm, studious and conscientious,' he had told us in that first demonstration, but I fell foul of his meticulous eye in the first practical session when he borrowed my paring knife to show me, yet again, how to turn a potato perfectly. The knife was blunt. He tried a couple of times to peel the potato. He looked intently at the knife blade, then turned to face me, his eyes searching my face for an explanation for such unconscionable sloppiness. He lowered his chin into his chest and raised his eyebrows. He didn't say anything; he didn't need to. My knives were never blunt again.

It was hard to imagine Terrien's knives ever being anything less than razor sharp. He was supremely confident in his abilities, a proud man. He walked with a shoulders-back swagger, but even when he said something brazenly boastful, such as, 'Do you know the difference between my apple tart and a pastry chef's apple tart? Mine is better,' it was always with a wink and a twinkle. Terrien, who was from the Touraine region of France, had clearly seen all there was to see in the restaurant world. Uniquely among the Cordon Bleu chefs, he had actually had his own restaurant, in Tours, and had won a Michelin star there. He claimed that the highlight of his career had been working as *sous chef* for Joël Robuchon, but he had also worked with Pierre Gagnaire during the molecular wizard's early career at the Intercontinental Hotel. Perhaps understandably, Terrien took on a world-weary air when talking about the business of running a restaurant: 'The trouble with restaurants these days is not enough people pay with cash,' he told us one day. 'You just can't fiddle the books like you used to.'

In contrast to Terrien, Chef Thivet's flirting days were long behind him. Thivet, born and bred in the Champagne region, was short with a trimmed grey beard, a barrel belly and pink cheeks. He might tenderly caress a rack of lamb or a nice fillet of sole, or occasionally let out an involuntary whinny of pleasure when tasting one of his sauces, but that was, thankfully, the limit as far as any overt sensuality was concerned. Where Terrien was controlled and authoritative, the keen snail-hunter Thivet, was a touch slapdash; on more than one occasion he looked as if he had slept on the couch the night before; and we would often have to yell out 'Chef!' during a demonstration to alert him to a pot that was boiling over.

There was no doubting his prowess and experience – he was heavily decorated by many of France's top culinary organisations and had been head chef at the Hilton in Paris – but the work of a professional chef has much in common with the professional sportsman and Thivet was something of an old stager. He made mistakes, spilled things, forgot ingredients, cut his fingers (twice while demonstrating a celery flan) and burned meringues – although, with the latter, he steadfastly claimed that he *meant* them to have turned a very dark brown and to *prefer* the bitter taste. While making a *salmon farci en feuille de chou vert* (savoy cabbage filled with salmon) he forgot to add the mushrooms to the stuffing; melted a plastic plate on the hob; added the red wine too early; and burned the crêpe that was to go with dessert. Largely because of this kind of thing, both the students and his fellow chefs mocked Thivet mercilessly, imitating his nasal voice whenever they wanted to raise a cheap laugh. It didn't help that he would occasionally refer to himself in the third person, and even impersonate himself. In truth though, Thivet had forgotten more than most students would ever know about cooking, and what remained was still more than we would probably ever learn.

Thivet considered himself something of a raconteur-performer in the Peter Ustinov mould. There was the – sadly one-off – mime about a *charcutier*'s dog stealing a string of sausages that he performed during a sausage-making demonstration, and his Napoleon impression, which essentially involved him turning his hat sideways and sticking one hand in his jacket. Thivet had a catchphrase too: 'Do you want to know a story?' he would ask mid-way through a demonstration, looking up from his chopping board. The first few times he asked this, we all answered enthusiastically, '*Oui*, chef!' Soon, though, we came to realise that Chef Thivet's idea of a good tale obeyed few narrative conventions.

'Do you want to hear a story?'

'*Oui*, chef!'

'For lunch you have got to get clients sat down, fed and a bill on the table within one hour or you're out of business. Even if you have two Michelin stars. [Pause for punch line.] Which is why company dining rooms boomed in the 1980s!'

'Do you want to hear a story?'

'Mmurmurggergngh.'

'I was chef de cuisine at Le Dôme, a one-star restaurant with a hundred and twenty covers. One Saturday we turned the covers three times. That was three hundred and sixty covers. That was in the rooms where Napoleon married Josephine.'

'Do you want to hear a story?'

'. . .'

'There used to be a diner who kept a fly in a bottle and would put it in his consommé to get a free dinner. Eventually all the chefs got together and banned him.'

We might not have shown Thivet quite the respect he deserved. Perhaps sensing this, one day he passed round an old photo album. It was filled with photos of himself as a chef in the 1970s, working in the grand hotel kitchens of the Côte d'Azur – in Loews and the Grand Hotel and Casino in Monaco, among others. It was strange to see the young, smiling man in the pictures, standing proudly, chest puffed and with a defiant smile, beside elaborate buffets and ornate sugar sculptures. He looked like Harvey Keitel, fresh from the set of *Mean Streets*, in flares and pennant-collared, patterned nylon shirts.

Equally touching was the image he himself evoked on occasion of an even younger Thivet standing on a box his grandfather had made especially so that he could watch his grandmother cook. As with many French chefs – from Ducasse and Robuchon down – Thivet often cited his grandmother as the ultimate culinary authority. 'It was she who told me that if you put a used oyster shell in water it will attract the chalk,' he said, stopping halfway through grating some carrot to stare into the middle distance for a minute or so, and we dutifully noted this tip down in our books as if it were the wisdom of Athena herself. Perhaps because of his grandmother's influence, Thivet was very much a traditionalist in the kitchen; his heroes were Escoffier and the great post-war hotel chefs. One of his most treasured memories was the time he had breakfasted with Paul Bocuse at the market in Lyon ('We drank some wine, I can tell you! I couldn't remember the lunch service after that!' he said). He preferred the old ways, and would go glassy eyed at the recollection of silver service and carving trolleys. He reserved his greatest scorn for the new wave of molecular gastronomers. 'Did you see the cooking show on TV last night?' he asked us one Monday morning. 'It was terrible. There was a restaurant where the chef took a whole egg, removed the yolk and white through a small hole and filled it with crème anglais. He then broke it at the table in front of the customer into nitrous oxide so that it made instant ice cream on the plate! Can you believe it?' He shook his head as if he had literally watched the world go to hell in a handcart. To us students, meanwhile, it sounded thrilling.

This difference of opinion between chefs and students wasn't unusual. The last decade has seen a schism in the highest levels of the global restaurant scene: a split between the pioneers and the purists, if you like. Leaving aside classical French cuisine, for which there will always be an audience, in terms of contemporary restaurant cooking we now have two distinct factions: there is the 'things should look likc and taste of what they are' brigade, who dedicate their kitchens to the service of the ingredient, respecting the seasons, preparing usually locally-sourccd food without undue fuss or interference. The constituent elements of every plate will be instantly clear and recognisable. Their carrots will look and taste of carrot; their legs of lamb will taste of lamb, and so on. Done well, this is probably the most difficult cooking to pull off. As with any art that purports to be the simplest expression of its form, there is very little to hide behind with this kind of cooking; there are no complex sauces, little melding of flavours, no smoke-and-mirrors presentation. The purist's technique is exposed entirely; it demands the very highest quality of ingredients, of course, and an exacting precision in its preparation.

Then we have the molecular mob, who employ a barrage of often scientifically-sourced techniques and equipment to transform ingredients beyond recognition. They fill balloons with scented air, released by the waiter at the table; turn anything from chocolate to Jerusalem artichokes into ethereal foam; or reduce an entire course to a bubble on a spoon. Molecular chefs blur the boundaries between technology and art in a high-wire act in which flavour can often seem of secondary importance to the effect a dish makes upon its entrance. It is astronaut food. Heston Blumenthal has created one course in which diners wear headphones with microphones relaying their own munching back to them, for instance; Wily Dufresne at WD-50 in New York is famed for his smoked mash potatoes; while the Spanish chef, Ferran Adrià, the acknowledged king of molecular cuisine, jellifies everything: a chef friend of mine once calculated that he had eaten around half a kilo of gelatine when he dined at El Bulli. Needless to say, the waiters spend a good deal of time explaining what diners are eating.

Early in the New Year Christine and Hayden were lucky enough to get a reservation at El Bulli, Adrià's restaurant on the Costa Brava in Spain, and returned with photographs of each of the thirty courses they had eaten, along with wide-eyed tales of liquid nitrogen *caipirinhas*; smoked foams; a caramel encased egg yolk; melon caviar and the like. I'll admit that molecular cooking sometimes confuses me. Though its theatricality and humour are exhilarating, it often raises more questions than it answers, not least: 'how on earth did they do that?' I try every year to get a reservation at El Bulli in the hope of finding some answers but it is always fully booked for its six-month season as soon as the reservations book opens.

For the article on the Paris food scene mentioned earlier I had made an appointment with one of the founding fathers of molecular gastronomy, the *physio-chimiste* Hervé This, at his small, surprisingly dingy office-cum-laboratory in the Collège de France on the Left Bank. This promptly relegated most of my questions to the rubbish bin at the start of our interview by announcing baldly that 'molecular cooking was dead'.

'I have been pushing for international acceptance of molecular gastronomy for twenty years. My aim has been to change the way people cook,' he said as he made space for me to sit amid the chaos of the Professor Branestawm spiralling glass tubes, Bunsen burners, olive oils, and bags of sugar and flour in his office. 'The older people were resistant, of course, but the younger chefs have taken up my ideas. The step has been taken, this is why I say that molecular cooking is dead.' What was going to replace it? I asked. 'Well,' he continued, without taking breath, his crazy, Einstein-grey scientist's hair bouncing energetically as he spoke. 'There is still a lot to be discovered, of course. We can send a probe to Mars but we still don't really know what happens to a carrot when we cook it! Right now my assistants and I are looking at what happens to green vegetables when you boil them, and whether you should shake or whisk butter into a sauce. Beyond that, there are two directions we can go in with food in the future. The first is artificial meat and vegetables. Synthesised food. It is a new continent! But please be careful.' He raised his finger in warning. 'Just as when they discovered Australia or America, it will be dangerous. People will die! So I propose something else.' He relaxed back into his chair. 'We are on the verge of an exciting new field: the building of food. And this is my work now: I call it, Culinary Constructivism!'

He gave me an example of what he meant. Pierre Gagnaire wanted to show This a new dish he had created in which grape jelly was layered with smoked salmon. But there was something wrong, This felt. 'He had put the grape jelly on *top* of the smoked salmon so that you tasted the grape jelly first but its flavour was immediately replaced by the stronger taste of smoked salmon.' He pulled a face. 'I suggested that the smoked salmon should go on top so that the flavour of grape jelly would have more of a chance. This is what Culinary Constructivism is about: building a dish to its best advantage. No one has ever formalised this before, no one. Not Ducasse, not Robuchon. Show me anywhere in print where this has been discussed! For me this is like discovering America!'

I thought about this. But our chefs at school are always talking about how a plate is arranged and the way we combine the textures of our food, I ventured. 'Yes, but this is not the same. I am taking it much, much further than that,' he boomed.

He gave me another example, turning to his computer, as he did frequently during our discussion, to call up a photograph of a simple dish of gnocchi in a wild mushroom sauce which he had sampled at a restaurant a few weeks earlier. It looked appetising enough to me, but This had other ideas. 'It looks flat, boring, doesn't it?' He showed me a diagram of how he would turn the dish into what he calls a 'three-dimensional chessboard', made up of alternate cubes of gnocchi and mushroom — like a kind of edible Rubik's cube: 'And the sauce will be in the centre of the cube! Imagine how that would feel to eat!'

But this was not the only new area of investigation for This. He was compelled by the notion of love, he told me in a conspiratorial whisper, and how it manifested itself in the food we make. But surely love is an intangible, immeasurable thing. How can science investigate it? I asked.

'Imagine that you are from the town where they make Stilton,' he said. 'You live in Paris now and I invite you to dinner. Before you come, I go to the trouble of finding some real Stilton and then I make a soufflé with it. I have put love into that, and you would taste the love, I am sure of it.' He then continued seamlessly, to a brief lecture on the social habits of gorillas. 'If you take a gorilla away from its friends and isolate it, it dies. That is why people congregate in cities, why they all go to the Champs-Elysées on Saturday. For love, to be together. And you *can* test this with food and dining: you can give the same dish to people and have them either eat it together, sociably, or eat it alone in a room. The food tastes better eaten together. Dutch scientists have already done this experiment. But I propose an experiment in which there are four people at a table. One has the sauce, one has the meat, one has the wine and one has the vegetables. I am sure that, because they have to share and socialise in order to eat, the food will taste better. Ultimately,' he said, softly, 'what we give to eat is love.'

Chapter 19

Many sins have been committed in the name of haute cuisine.

Elizabeth David

Despite hearing the language spoken every day, my French remained rudimentary. It had shown few signs of improvement over the five months we had been living in Paris, despite the fact that I never left the house without an iPod playing Michel Thomas' *French for Beginners* in my ears. 'Love me, I'm stupid' is a common ploy of the memoir or travel writer, but in this respect I genuinely was rather backward. My command of French was roughly comparable to that of a well-funded African child. Perhaps because of this, any progress towards my better integration in French society – no matter how trivial it might have appeared to others – became a source of great personal pride. I was especially satisfied when I figured out how to buy the monthly Metro pass: for some reason it made me feel like a real Parisian. But my pride was short-lived and painfully pricked.

One day, coming home from school, I was caught in an ambush by French transport police as I changed lines at Pasteur. The risk of being caught cheating is as integral a part of French life as the abuse of farm animals or bizarre beauty treatments. Whether it is income tax, building regulations or Metro fares, the French habitually dodge and cheat, safe in the knowledge that the odds of being caught, though high enough to warrant some caution, are mostly in their favour. Though their cheating is targeted primarily at their government, is endemic throughout all levels of French society: exams of any kind, the return of rent deposits, queue dodging of course, and jumping the barriers at the Metro are all perfectly acceptable transgressions for otherwise respectable members of French society. I, however, am an Englishman and as such, the fear of being publicly embarrassed by being caught *just* shades the advantages of circumventing the rules and regulations.

Upon being approached by the police I thought I was in the clear, and with the irritated 'Tut!' of a habitual Metro traveller, I reached for my wallet to show the guard my ticket and continued to walk past in a theatrically weary way.

'*Arrêt, monsieur, s'il vous plaît*,' said the guard. 'Can I see your identity card?'

'I don't have an identity card,' I answered, puzzled.

'If you have one of these tickets, you must have a photo ID.' I frowned. But I had a *ticket*!

'You have two choices. We can call the police, they will take you to the station, charge you and you will have to pay sixty euro, or you can give me thirty euro.'

'But I had no idea I had to have a picture ID with this ticket! I bought it from a machine and at no point did it tell me I needed photo ID,' I said.

'You are expected to know. If you had bought it from the ticket office they would have told you. Are you going to give me the money or shall I call the police?'

'Bbbut . . .' I stammered.

'How do we know you bought this ticket? You could be borrowing someone else's.'

'What if I promise to get an ID card?' I said.

'Yes, but you must still pay me the money. Let's make it twenty-five euro and be finished.'

We weren't haggling over a pound of cherries, surely a fine was fixed.

'I'm not paying that.'

He sighed. He had probably endured this conversation thirty times that day and I could sense his will was waning.

'Do you have a passport, any ID with your address on it, a driving licence?'

I had none of these. In a last desperate roll of the dice, I pulled my Cordon Bleu recipe folder out of my bag. It was the only thing I had with my name on it.

'This is all I've got. I am going to a school here to learn about French cooking.'

At the sight of the folder the guard's demeanour changed entirely. It was as if a shining beacon of civilisation had beamed from my satchel, accompanied by a choir of angels.

'You are going here?' he asked.

'Yes, French cooking is the best in the world!' I exclaimed, sensing the tide might be turning.

He paused and took me aside from the place where he had already taken me aside to.

'Listen,' he said, handing me a blank ID card, 'take this and put your photograph in it and make sure you travel with it in future.'

'Thank you, thank you so much,' I gushed, and hurried on my way.

Clearly the power of Le Cordon Bleu worked in mystical ways. Could this be the answer to all my troubles with French bureaucracy?

I had occasion to test this some days later. I had borrowed a very expensive Maserati with a very long bonnet from the UK for an article I was writing for an English newspaper, and was gingerly edging it out into the traffic on Avenue Marceau. A car had stopped to let me out but as I slowly pulled into the road I hit a man on a moped who, having noticed the slowing traffic, had taken his chance to overtake about five cars without wondering why they had stopped. Fortunately it was the slightest of glances. He stopped, looked at me, paused, and fell to the ground. But he was determined to make a meal of it, assuming that a man in such a car would simply stuff a bundle of notes into his coat pocket and leave it at that. I think he was as dismayed as I when the police arrived and, again, I found myself without any ID, passport or driving licence (I had only gone out to move the car to a different parking spot on my way to catching the Metro to school).

'Ah, but I do have this!' I said, pulling my Cordon Bleu recipe folder from my satchel.

I was arrested, held at the station for two hours, fined an apparently arbitrary one hundred and fifty euro, and ordered to return with my licence within a week.

Chapter 20

To consume food we have to destroy it.

Priscilla Parkhurst Ferguson

Accounting for Taste: The Triumph of French Cuisine

Looking on the noticeboard after our first demonstration in the first week of the New Year, I saw that Intermediate Cuisine Group E had four new members. Max — male or female, wasn't clear — and Andy were from the States, Ingrid was from Costa Rica, and Hortense was from Slovakia. Max and I were to be the practical assistants in the first week, but when I went down to the *sous sol* to collect our baskets of ingredients for the first practical (*coquelets rôtis persillés aux légumes primeurs*), he/she was nowhere to be seen.

I loaded the baskets into the dumb waiter myself, cursing this Max character under my breath, and rushed up to the practical kitchen to divide everything up between the nine students in the group. Already waiting in the kitchen were a tall, beautiful black woman, who looked like an extra from a Tarantino movie as she sharpened her knives with a professional swish; a short, sweet-faced, girl with blonde hair and porcelain skin; and a slender young Japanese man with an impressive kit of Global knives rolled out on the worktop.

'Are you Max? Are you Max?' I blathered to the black woman, sweating and out of breath.

'Do I look like a Max?' she answered curtly. 'Max is a boy's name. I'm Ingrid.'

I tried hurriedly to think of some female Maxes, but couldn't (of course, much later, I came up with a great long list of them, all of

187

which I have now forgotten again). 'Are you Max?' I said to the other two.

They weren't. Sarah, Christine and the others arrived and started helping me apportion the ingredients. Chef Thivet arrived to supervise the class and, finally, in ambled a short, dishevelled man in his early twenties. He looked like a character from a Bukowski novel, with dense, matted brown hair, three-day stubble, stained chef's jacket and a large scab on the bridge of his nose, presumably from a recent brawl.

'Are you Max?' I asked.

'U-huh,' he said.

'Do you realise you're supposed to be the assistant with me?'

He answered neither aggressively nor apologetically, but simply, with a sigh, in a weary West Coast accent, 'Yeah.' And started to unpack his knives.

Both Max and Ingrid had completed the Intensive Basic course before Christmas and alarmed us with their speed and accomplished knife skills. The originals of Group E had been out of the kitchen for a couple of weeks but these two were match fit and raring to go – Max especially. Both he and Ingrid left us for dead, offering their plates to the chef for marking while we were still sweating our *mirepoix*. I was willing my potatoes to cook more quickly, poking them with a knife every few seconds as Max washed up and got ready to leave. I worked at the other end of the kitchen so had no chance to see how he could be so quick. He was an enigma.

In contrast Hortense, the porcelain doll, was struggling from the start. It was almost as if she had never been in a kitchen before, which as far as the Cordon Bleu's were concerned was true. Having transferred from a hotel management college in Switzerland, Hortense had somehow been allowed to skip Basic Cuisine and join us straight at Intermediate level. The problem was, she barely knew how to chop a carrot and for weeks she would struggle in the practical sessions, usually only starting to cook as the rest of us were cleaning up with impatient chefs, watching their precious lunch hours disappear, breathing down her neck. Hortense was a reminder of just how much we had all learned during Basic Cuisine.

Andy was from Hawaii but had Japanese parents, and was rather more experienced. He had worked in professional kitchens both in Hawaii and in New York, where he was doing a business degree at university, and had completed Basic Cuisine at the London Cordon Bleu. He was attending Le Cordon Bleu as part of his degree on a scholarship and, though he wasn't quite the kitchen natural that Max was, he soon found his feet. Like many American youths, Andy had a boundless, puppyish confidence and was rarely troubled by self-doubt. If he hadn't been so good natured and enthusiastic, you might have mistaken this for arrogance but we soon hit it off. Andy taught us a trick or two, the best one being his method for cleaning the cast-iron frying pans which were not supposed to be washed with detergent, and which he would fill with salt and leave to stand on a hot plate for ten minutes or so. This degreased them so that they were virtually like new, although the method did have the unfortunate side effect of filling the kitchen with acrid sodium smoke.

After our first, brusque encounter, I thought I ought to apologise to Ingrid. We got talking later that first week in the Winter Garden. 'So you are from Costa Rica?' I asked. 'All over, honey,' she answered. 'Costa Rica, Germany, France, New York, I'm a citizen of the world!' Ingrid was a former model turned jazz singer and possibly the coolest person I have ever met. She was flirtatious, funny and warm. Often during practical sessions she would burst into song while she chopped onions – 'La Vie En Rose', being a favourite. She had a dream of opening her own restaurant in New York, where she currently lived, and it turned out that she and I were the same age. She had a teenage son who lived in New York with his father to whom she would return after Intermediate finished at the end of March.

As we talked I remembered that I was still an assistant and that a special guest ingredient was waiting for me in the basement. We would be making a dish that I had been looking forward to with equal measures of fascination and dread: *homard Américaine* – made with live lobsters.

There had been gasps from the students during the demonstration as Chef Thivet unveiled his victims: medium sized Brittany lobsters sitting, mostly still, except for the odd, disconsolately twitching antenna, their powerful claws bound with thick, blue rubber bands. Thivet had then proceeded with a preposterous rigmarole – devised I suspect, to assuage the delicate sensibilities of the Americans in the audience – whereby he brought some water to the boil in a large pot and gently dipped only the lobsters' heads into the water. 'This stuns them,' he explained. 'They don't feel a thing. Then we can kill them.'

This wasn't terribly convincing as the head-dipping merely served to wake the lobsters up, after which they started to writhe, obviously in some discomfort. Thivet carried on regardless, and then held each one down as he plunged a large knife into the top of their heads, cutting them lengthways through their bodies and tails, though all the evidence clearly indicated they were still very much in the land of the living. But why go to these extraordinary lengths? Why not just buy lobsters already killed or frozen? The answer was partly that the flesh tasted better cooked from fresh, but also that we needed to retrieve an oozing brown-green gunk from the lobster's head – the chef called it lobster mayonnaise, but its proper name is the hepatopancreas: Kind of the lobster version of foie gras. As soon as the lobster is killed this 'liver' begins to degenerate, but though it looks like the contents of a Gruffalo's handkerchief, it is bursting with lobster flavour and a key ingredient for our sauce.

Face to face in the upstairs kitchen, dispatching my lobster was turning out to be more difficult than I had expected. It didn't help that Ingrid gave each of our lobsters a name as she handed them out from the basket. 'Bye bye Alice, look after her, Michael!' she chuckled. I turned my lobster over: she was pregnant. There was no way I could look this thing in the eye (they were eyes, weren't they?) and end its/her life without the aid of anaesthetic, or at the very least, soothing whale song. Christine came to the rescue, surprising – and faintly appalling – us all with her blood lust. 'Give it to me,' she said. 'I'll do this if you do my flambé. Deal?' 'Deal,' I said, too relieved that the death of a crustacean would be absolved from my conscience to worry about setting light to myself. She took my lobster by the head and was about to do the deed when, without warning, the electricity went out. As we were in the second-floor kitchen with no natural light, we were now in complete darkness surrounded by death-row crustaceans who had nothing to lose. We all froze. The only sound was the clatter of claws in metal trays as our key ingredients perhaps sensed their last chance for escape.

'What the fuck?' said Max. 'Nobody move!' said Sarah. 'Everyone put your knives down.'

We did as we were told, happy that someone had taken charge of the situation. The lights came back on again. I looked at Christine to discover that she had already wrenched Alice in half, severing her tail from her body. She smiled and handed the two parts to me, the tail and antenna still twitching in blissful ignorance of their recent divorce.

A while later, after we had fried the lobster tails, claws and heads with finely chopped onions and shallots, it was time for me to fulfil my part of the bargain. I warmed the cognac and poured it into Christine's pan, lit the match and, stretching from as far away as I could, tried to ignite the pan. Nothing happened. I edged closer, shielding my face with my free hand. Still nothing. Then, in the spirit of Wile E. Coyote looking down the barrel of his rifle to check it is working, I bent over the pan and stuck the match right into the vapours. Whoomph! My vision was momentarily blurred by a giant petroleum-coloured cloud. I stepped back and instinctively felt for my eyebrows which were now slightly crusty. Only inherited male pattern baldness – something I had hitherto only had reason to curse – had saved me from the full Arthur Brown flaming-hair routine. So traumatised was I by this that I took no chances with my own flambéing and as a result managed merely to set fire to a piece of lobster claw, then my tea towel.

This wasn't the end of the crustacean carnage as, a couple of weeks later, in early February, we made *quenelles de sandre sauce Nantua*, a traditional Lyonnaise dish of pike-perch quenelles (a kind of very fine, fish mousse which you form into mini Zeppelins using two spoons, and gently poach), with a spectacular, vivid red sauce. This time the unfortunate victims were crayfish, prehistoric-looking green prawn-type things. My excitement at learning how to make one of the grand staples of haute cuisine was tempered by the fact that the making of *sauce Nantua* requires a series of acts that would make the lobster homicide look like a moment of childish spite and which, were they to show up on a serial killer's profile, would send any psychoanalyst's bells ringing.

First, the chef told us, we must take the crayfish and locate the middle 'fan' of its three-fanned tale. This was the key to unlocking the inner workings of the crayfish. And what does one do with a key? One twists it. The key is attached to the poor creature's intestinal tract which you can then pull out in one swift movement. The crayfish did not take this very well, curling up and writhing in what I would have called dire agony if I hadn't convinced myself that crustaceans are insensible to pain.

Again, Christine stepped into the breach during the practical session – opening them with relish, like so many cans of Coke, before passing them to me for the next stage of our crayfish massacre, which involved ripping the backs of their heads off, bashing their brains to a pulp with one end of a rolling pin and frying them in hot oil.

Still, if they could have tasted the rich, sweet sauce, I'm sure even the crayfish would have agreed it was worth the sacrifice.

Chapter 21

You're such an asshole, Michael.

Jamie Sparks

Where do you stand on the whole 'chocolate with strawberries' issue? I'll tell you where you stand, you're violently opposed to the whole notion of serving the two together, that's where, just as any right thinking person should be. But, sadly, not everyone is as discerning as you or I. Believe it or not, despite quite clear scientific evidence to the contrary, not to mention the indisputable dictates of good taste, there are some people for whom chocolate and strawberry gateaux, say, or strawberry Quality Streets or – the essence of culinary evil – chocolate-covered strawberries, represent the ultimate indulgence. Me? I'd rather eat chocolate-coated soil.

You would expect students at a culinary school to have more refined palates, not to be the types to have their heads turned by gaudy, suburban gimmickry, but this was sadly not the case. In fact, it turned out that some of my *best friends* at Le Cordon Bleu claimed that chocolate and strawberries were a *perfect* match, something that would fuel arguments into the night at the tabac around the corner from the school. Things finally came to a head when Christine made chocolate-covered strawberries as a Valentine's treat for Hayden, and proudly told us about it the next day.

Despite Sarah's claim that the two were just good friends, Christine and Hayden's relationship had blossomed over Christmas and the New Year and the two were now an item. When Christine told me about their Valentine's Day I could hardly contain my shock – not that they were together, but at the strawberry thing. I launched into my well-rehearsed tirade: yes, we all like chocolate, and we all like strawberries, and we *think* that these two things we really like ought to taste great together. But it has been proven (although I seem for now to have mislaid the evidence so you'll just have to trust me), that the molecular construction of strawberries is completely antithetical to that of chocolate. 'This is science,' I said, shaking my head ruefully. 'You can't argue with science. You only *think* they taste good together. Now, blue cheese and chocolate – now there's a molecular partnership made in heaven . . .'

It was a conclusive argument and I assumed that we could draw a line under the entire sorry episode but, though I could tell Christine had realised her error, she wasn't about to admit it. 'Michael, you are wrong. I really liked them and so did Hayden. Everyone likes strawberries and chocolate.' Jamie, a freckle-faced girl with waffle-wavy brown hair and a permanently sceptical look on her face, was passing at that moment and had a more robust response, one I'd grown used to hearing over recent weeks: 'You're such an asshole, Michael.'

Jamie and I often sat next to each other during demonstrations, sniggering when the chefs made sausages, or at the more stupid questions asked by some of the Korean students. Jamie was from Salt Lake City, but always denied this, claiming instead that she was from Costa Rica. It's true that she had lived in Costa Rica for some years but there was far too much mileage, as far as I was concerned, in taunting her about her Mormon upbringing to let it rest at that – which is perhaps why so many of our conversations would end with Jamie calling me an 'asshole'. (Jamie tells a great story about how she once tried to explain the Mormon church to a group of teenage Australian girls she met backpacking in Thailand: 'I was telling them about the Church, about what they do and so on, and they were looking at me kind of funny. In the end, one of them said, "So, like, they can go on *land*? For real?" It turned out they'd thought I'd been talking about *mermen*!') In fact, Jamie had not been brought up a Mormon although I didn't let that get in my way:

194

'What would the Mormon brothers say about that, Jamie?' I would ask disapprovingly, when she would tell me about the number of tequilas she'd drunk the night before, or the men she'd flirted with at Buddha Bar. To retaliate, Jamie started a rumour that I had excessive ear wax; as a rumour-monger she was highly effective and for weeks afterwards I would catch sight of other students straining to check my ears when they thought I wasn't looking. Inevitably the dispute escalated. At the next practical, I invited her to imagine Chef Thivet wearing Speedos, and she had to leave to room to get water.

Jamie and Christine ganged up against me in the great Strawberry Chocolate debate together with, to my lasting shock, about half the class. But I wasn't giving up without a fight. Clearly I needed allies from higher levels. During one demonstration, which involved a chocolate fondant garnished with raspberries, I asked Chef Terrien if he'd recommend using strawberries instead. He pulled a face. 'Why would one use strawberries?' he answered, genuinely puzzled. 'Raspberries are much better with chocolate. I've never used strawberries, no.' I flashed a look of smug triumph in Christine's direction. She scowled back. Jamie nudged me hard in the ribs. As far as I was concerned that sealed my argument, but I was wrong.

About a week later I arrived in the locker room to change into my uniform. As I went to open my locker, I could see a paper plate on top of it. I raised myself on tiptoe to discover a single, large strawberry, covered in thick, glossy, dark chocolate. I looked around to see who might have placed it there but saw only an assortment of stretching underpants, as other students bent over to pull on their chef's trousers. I took the plate down and looked at the strawberry. No one else seemed to be claiming it. Who would know if I took a nibble of the chocolate? After all, chocolate is chocolate. I didn't have to eat the strawberry.

After I had cleared the strawberry of its coating, there was the issue of what to do with the fruit itself. I liked strawberries, and this was a large one. So I popped it into my mouth.

Outside, as usual, a crowd of students was gathering in the Winter Garden before entering the demo room. I sat at one of the tables to go through my recipe file to see what the chef would be showing us that day. When I looked up a few moments later, another small paper plate with a chocolate-covered strawberry had materialised in front of me. Had that been there before? I couldn't be sure. In the crowded room it was impossible to see who had put it there. Perhaps they had made them in the Patisserie class that morning. It was quite usual for cakes and pastries to be left lying around unwanted in the Winter Garden in this way. No one seemed to be claiming owner-ship of this one either. I was surrounded by a wall of backs and the bags of other students in conversation, so, again, I popped the whole thing in my mouth.

I took my place in the demonstration kitchen. Jamie had sat elsewhere, near the front with the Koreans. She had taken Chan Woo Park's place and he sat next to me in a grumpy huff. Chan Woo suffered from an intriguing form of cooking-induced narcolepsy; he literally fell asleep during *every* single demonstration he attended during the entire nine months of the course, often within twenty minutes of them beginning (we used to take bets on when his head would begin to nod and, during the slower demos, flick chewed paper at him).

Halfway through the demo, I reached under my seat for the bottle of water I usually placed there. My hand instead came across another plate with another chocolate-covered strawberry. Okay, this was starting to seem a little spooky, but by this time I was in the midst of a kind of eating frenzy; like the lion that first tastes human flesh and henceforth will only eat people, I was developing an immunity to – perhaps even a taste for – this forbidden combination. I pulled the plate up off the floor. I looked around: the other students were busy taking notes and watching the chef. Chan Woo was fast asleep, a dribble of drool glistening in the corner of his mouth, his pen teetering on the edge of his desk. Christine was right behind me, earnestly scribbling in her notebook. The chef disappeared for a moment to the small washing-up room behind the demo kitchen and I took the chance to have a surreptitious nibble.

'AHA!' About twenty students – some of whom I had up to that point considered friends – stood up and pointed at me. Having just stuffed the rest of the strawberry in my mouth, I was unable to speak and so was forced to sit and soak up the shame. 'Bbgbh-mooo,' I protested, but there was little point. I had been caught red-chinned. 'Still think they don't go together, huh Michael?' said Jamie, an unattractive note of triumphalism in her voice. The chef returned, frowned quizzically to see half his class standing and laughing at another student, and carried on with the demonstration. They all sat down and I wiped the strawberry-chocolate spittle from my face.

This dispute added an extra twinge of competitiveness between Christine and me. We always worked side by side in the kitchen and often shared the chopping and preparation of ingredients at the start of practicals, but over the three hours, as the deadline loomed to present our plates, the camaraderie would usually give way to an underlying note of rivalry. Often I would be on my way to the chef with my finished plate and Christine would get there just before me, shouting 'Chef!' to grab his attention. The tension was turned up a notch halfway through Intermediate when we were given our half-term grades and Christine was shown to be ahead of me. I had dropped out of the top five. In fact, a nonchalant glance at other students' marks showed that there were now at least twenty others ranking higher than me.

This was disappointing, although hardly surprising. I still had the lingering suspicion that my fifth place had been the result of a clerical error. Perhaps it had been caused by the new Palm Pilots issued to the chefs to record their marks, but which they barely knew how to operate, frequently wiping their memories and ascribing one student's score to another. They regarded their new mini-computers with bewilderment and suspicion born of what I suspect was a terror of any new technology.

Not everyone took their mid-term marks as stoically as I did. Ingrid was furious and raged at the staff of the administration office, while Jamie, peeved that the female Japanese students appeared to be getting significantly and – to her mind – undeservedly high scores, also made her feelings known. My excuse for my low grades, one I made widely known through the school, was that I had been suffering from a month-long bout of flu. At one point I had a temperature – I am not a little proud to record – of over 40°. Most gratifying was the reaction of the doctor whom I insisted Lissen call to my bedside: 'Ooh, yes, you are hot,' she had said. I made a 'See?' face at Lissen, who is used to my baseless hypochondria and was genuinely surprised that after all these years I actually was ill. Later, in my feverish state, I believe I might even have compared my suffering to that of a woman during childbirth. Lissen pointed out that women giving birth didn't spend days moping in bed listening to Radio 4 on the Internet and reading food magazines. But my flu hell had taken its toll on my cooking and, to my surprise, I found that my fifth place from Basic Cuisine had come to mean a great deal to me.

A hitherto dormant competitive streak was revealing itself deep within me. There was some catching up to be done.

Chapter 22

Rome is feminine. So is Odessa. London is a teenager, an urchin, and, in this hasn't changed since the time of Dickens. Paris, I believe, is a man in his twenties in love with an older woman.

John Berger

There can be few more auspicious venues in which to make one's professional catering debut than the Musée d'Orsay, the majestic steam-age railway station, turned nineteenth-century art museum on the Left Bank. Le Cordon Bleu had asked for volunteers to man a buffet to be held there to mark the fortieth anniversary of the Alliance Française language school. I and about twenty other students had put our names forward and, one chilly Wednesday afternoon in February, we found ourselves huddled like sheep against the wind outside the museum's back door. On offer was a free tour, with a guide, of what is one of my favourite museums in Paris. Also 'free' happens to be one of my favourite words. If it meant I might have to hand out a couple of canapés, it seemed a fair trade.

Unfortunately, the payback for the twenty-minute tour was five hours of shifting furniture and shovelling food into the open mouths of posh, elderly French people. And, I tell you, despite all this 'French women don't get fat' nonsense (hang out in the Les Halles shopping centre on a Saturday morning and you will swiftly be disavowed of that notion), the French upper classes, women included, can't half put it away.

After we had changed into our uniforms we were instructed to clear the banqueting room of all its furniture. I suggested I might be better employed tidying the flower displays and was heading in that direction when a museum employee thrust a stack of chairs into my chest. So we moved furniture for an hour or so. After this we were handed over to the professional caterers who would be supplying the food and organising us for the rest of the evening. We were told to get cracking, production-line style, assembling myriad miniscule, fussy hors d'oeuvres. We stood for another hour around trestle tables, assembling tiny foie gras tartlets, miniature smoked salmon crêpes, wee little toasted sandwiches and sweets that looked like eyeballs, commanded by a scary woman in spiky glasses and a hairy man with a monobrow.

It seemed I wasn't the only one lured by the siren word 'free': the museum's majestic banqueting room, overlooking the Seine, was packed to its gilded rafters with guests hell bent on celebrating the not-particularly-milestone anniversary of a language school. Once we began emerging with the nibbles on silver trays, it took just a few minutes for a small herd of them to figure out the source of the food by following the trail of Cordon Bleu-uniformed ants: a door to the rear of the banqueting hall. They followed us here – elderly ladies no higher than our hips with hair like lacquered candyfloss, and tall, rickety men in blazers and brogues – and waited like stray dogs by the butcher's back door, pouncing on us as we left the kitchen with our newly-loaded trays and stuffing their bulging cheeks with our fiddly fare. It became a mark of honour among the students to see how far we could get across the room without our trays being cleared. Andy made a courageous run for the windows on the other side of the room, but was halted in his tracks almost immediately by a short-bearded man who grabbed his elbow. Soon he was surrounded by a gang of them. He stood no chance. While so many of the guests were distracted, I made my own assault on the far wall, but was ambushed by a flock of blue rinses which sprang from behind an urn. They stripped me clean in seconds. We returned to the kitchen where Monobrow loaded us up and sent us back out like cannon fodder from the trenches of the Somme.

Monobrow was not what one would call a people person and the students soon began to tire of his commands. Resentment was brewing and there were murmurs of a walk-out. 'You know, in English we have a special word,' I said to him after he had thrust a bottle of Evian into my hand and ordered me to take it to the bar. 'It's called "please".' 'Huh?' he answered. 'Take some wine too.' He piled three bottles into my arms and pushed me out of the door. By the end of the evening, Hayden, for whom this kind of manual labour was clearly alien, appeared in a state of shock. It had been a salutary lesson for all of us about how to treat waiting staff, not to mention the perils of plastic surgery. Ingrid, accosted by a Botox experiment in an Issy Miyake dress that, Ingrid said, made her look like 'a Chinese lantern filled with potatoes', had finally lost her temper. 'She told me to go and get some more water!' she recounted, still fuming. 'I told her to friggin' get it herself.' Only Andy, with his boundless energy, continued, and virtually served the room single-handedly.

Looking out at the guests during one of my time-outs behind a pot plant, it struck me that the average age of the guests must have been in the high fifties. This wasn't all that surprising. To me, Paris always seems like an older person's city. John Berger might think of it as a man in his twenties, but I think it's more a slightly bitter, posh lady in her early sixties. Though it has this image of up-to-the-season fashionability (you'd expect Parisians to be contemptuous if they caught you wearing last season's knickers, for instance), in truth the city doesn't have the relentless faddishness of London or Barcelona. Though I'm perhaps not the best judge – left to my own devices, and given an unlimited budget, I would dress exactly like Patrick McGoohan in *The Prisoner*, all the time – I don't think Paris is terribly fashionable at all. It is more a city of rigid social uniforms: there's the casual chic of the sixteenth arrondissement, where the men wear pastel jumpers and loafers; the corduroy chic of St Germain, where corduroy jackets, black turtlenecks and jeans have been compulsory since the 1950s; and the shabby chic of the tenth, where the pastel jumpers have holes and the loafers are worn. And in the breeding grounds of the fifteenth, they all wear whatever Monoprix tells them to.

Everywhere you go, at least west of the Bastille, you are struck by how sedate Paris is, how conservatively dressed everyone is, how, away from the Champs-Elysées' barbarian hordes, everyone is so very well behaved. There are pharmacies on every corner, their windows dressed with orthopaedic supports and a bewildering array of suppositories. Florists outnumber record stores by ten to one, and shoe shops sell proper leather footwear, rather than gym pumps. As we discovered, it is not a city for young children; pregnant women are notable by their absence; and even the teenagers seem sophisticated beyond their years. It is as if their education system hothouses their growth to such an extent that French kids skip adolescence and go straight to the dinner party and mortgage stage, letting rip from time to time when their parents are away, by inviting their friends round for cigarettes and playing 50 Cent at full volume.

As I reel in the years at the speed of big-game fisherman, I'm not sure any of this is a bad thing – I love London and Barcelona, but could no longer live in either city. I just don't think I'd fit in. I like living in a city where I wouldn't feel awkward asking people to turn their iPods down on the Metro or telling youths to take their feet off the seats. I like the fact that the shops generally don't play loud music and people won't look askance if I wear a hat. In Paris you are never more than twenty metres from a dry cleaners.

Amid the wrinkly throng, which included some of the Cordon Bleu chefs looking stiff and awkward in their uniforms, I spied Monsieur Cointreau, the owner of Le Cordon Bleu. He was giving a speech in French about the school's partnership with Alliance Française. He was small and surprisingly knackered looking for one so rich and powerful; his speech was greeted with muffled munching. I attempted to approach him through the crowd and introduce myself as his fifth-best student, but was cut off by Monobrow, who wanted to know why I was circulating with an empty tray. 'So that they get the message there's no more food and go,' I answered. He pulled me out of the room – I believe he would have used my ear lobes if he'd thought he could get away with it. 'Do you have a problem here?' he asked. As always, looking back, one can think of any number of devastatingly witty and clever comebacks for these kinds of situations. 'Yes,' would have been good, for instance. Instead I looked down at my shoes and mumbled something about being 'a bit tired'. 'Take this,' he said, thrusting a tray of tiny tartlets at me.

Reflecting over a beer in a Left Bank bar afterwards, though few of us had found the experience instructive in terms of food preparation, we had learned some important life lessons.

'There is no way I am ever serving a French person again as long as I live,' said Louisa, with a weary shake of her head.

'Man, they were like animals!' said another student.

'We keep pigs back home, but I've never seen a feeding frenzy like that. I mean, they were *splattering* me with food, they couldn't wait to shovel it down!'

'I got my ass felt up so many times. I felt like a lap dancer.'

'If one more of those fucking frogs had clicked their fingers at me, I would have bitten them off.'

'Did you see how fat that old sow was who was waiting at the door for us? It was like feeding time at the farm! I couldn't believe it.'

And so on . . .

I had a chance to make a direct comparison the next day. Lissen, Asger, Emil and I took the Metro south, past the school, to the exhibition halls at the Porte de Versailles. This was where we had come the previous autumn for the Salon du Chocolate; this time round it was hosting the Salon International de l'Agriculture, a gigantic, defiantly *non*-international celebration of *La France Profonde*, the mythical rural homeland to which most French people claim an umbilical link. Country Mouse comes to visit City Mouse and brings his sheep, if you like. We have farm shows in the UK, of course; they take place in fields with animals, tombolas, tractor races and chutney competitions. But the Salon was more like a motor show, held entirely under cover in the vast exhibition halls, with various breeds of immaculately presented pedigree cows, sheep, goats and pigs on display like the latest Ford or Chrysler beneath hot spotlights.

Unlike us British, of who would probably rather not be troubled by thoughts of where their produce has come from prior to arriving sealed in plastic in the aisles of Sainsbury's, the French aren't at all squeamish about acknowledging the link between the living livestock and the stuff we eat, so it seemed perfectly natural that the Salon was accompanied by a giant food show. (Similarly, no one in Paris batted an eyelid when the new aquarium that opened beneath the Trocadero chose a sushi restaurant as its in-house caterer even though, to me, it was like going to the zoo and dining on elephant.)

There were some extraordinary, over-bred animals here: pinky white cows which were shaved like poodles; massive buffalo-like Partlenanse from Gascony; Swiss Herens fighting bulls; and luscious Blondes d'Aquitaine. There were sheep so immaculate they looked like cuddly toys, and unusually fragrant pigs. But mostly there were cows, lined up in their open stalls, tethered through their noses, passive and serene despite the relentless prodding of curious children. If we had taken Asger and Emil to Batman's cave where he'd given them sticks and let them fire water pistols indoors, they could not have been more excited.

After wandering for an hour or so looking at cows' backsides and trying to explain the concept of insemination to Asger and Emil we all took a seat in the arena and watched as men in leather boots and feathered hats coaxed animals the size of delivery vans around the woodchip-strewn parade ground. Once the cows were cajoled into position, other men wearing plus fours would drape them with mayoral ribbons. Everyone applauded and cameras flashed and I thought to myself how heartening it was to see a people with so much pride and interest in their food that they are more concerned with chickens and tractors than the latest BMW or wide-screen television. That's a lazy generalisation, of course, the French are just as keen on wide-screen TVs as the rest of us (although they treat their cars with admirable indifference), it is just that they seem to have a far closer affinity to the produce they eat and the countryside that raises it. It is one reason, I suspect, why the organic movement has never really grabbed the French public's imagination in the way that it has in Britain and the States. The French have an almost subliminal conviction, almost entirely misguided, that their agriculture is already of the highest organic standard. To a Frenchman every tomato is an 'heirloom' tomato and, because they still have independent butchers and fishmongers, they take it for granted that every chicken is free-range and every sea bass line caught. The truth is that the French use just as many pesticides on their crops (more, actually); have their own GM test sites; eat battery chickens; and buy prawns from dodgy farms in Madagascar, but as I think we have already established, they are never ones to let the truth get in the way of a potent myth.

As I was saying to Lady Penelope Holmes, the wife of the British ambassador to France, recently, I do so detest name droppers. We also talked about the French and organic food (the subject of an article I was writing at the time). 'The French have just been very slow to cotton on to organic food,' she said, as we wandered around the vast, immaculate kitchens of the ambassador's residence on rue Faubourg Saint-Honoré. 'The British are much better at it. Part of the reason is that the French do have such good normal produce, but I think a lot of the reason is to do with the Internet. Someone recommended me some smoked salmon from the Outer Hebrides and I was able to find the supplier online and order some by mail. You would never get that from, say, an organic foie gras farmer in Perigord.'

After I interviewed Lady Holmes, she invited Lissen and me to an evening of British cheese tasting at the residence. It was intended to offer French cheese producers and food writers a chance to taste the cheese of these upstart *rosbifs* and talk to their producers, in a formal event to be held in the dining room of the magnificent eighteenth-century mansion. The residence was bought by the Duke of Wellington from Napoleon's sister and became the first permanent British embassy abroad; it is, as you would expect, intimidatingly grand. Lissen and I mingled self-consciously with the rest of the guests in the drawing room, the pungent barnyard smells of stiltons and cheddars wafting in from the banqueting hall.

After a while we snuck out into the conservatory overlooking the garden. The walls were incongruously hung with contemporary British art, including a Damien Hirst spot painting. As we looked at it, a short, grey haired man wandered over and we started chatting.

'It's an amazing place, isn't it?' said Lissen.

'Yes, it is rather lovely,' said the man.

'Look,' I whispered. 'That's the ambassador's wife over there.'

'I wonder who she had to sleep with to get to live here,' joked Lissen.

'I don't think we have been introduced,' said the grey-haired man. 'I'm John, the ambassador.'

Chapter 23

At the table of a gentleman living in the Chausée d'Antin was served up an Arles sausage of enormous size. 'Will you accept a slice?' the host asked the lady who was sitting next to him; 'You see it has come from the right factory.' – 'It is really very large,' said the lady, casting on it a roguish glance. 'What a pity it is unlike anything.'

Brillat-Savarin

The Physiology of Taste

The recipes of Intermediate Cuisine were to be themed around the regional cooking of France. One week we were in Provence, the next in Normandy, and then the Isle de France and so on. As far as the students were concerned, this was an excellent way to get a feel for the rich variety of French cooking, while for the chefs, most of whom had grown up outside of Paris, it offered another chance for them to get slightly emotional about their grandmothers' cooking.

The recipes had become more complex and tended more towards the traditional. Often we were shown dishes rarely found these days other than in those 'restaurants that time forgot' you sometimes come across in gritty provincial French towns (sepia-coloured net curtains are usually a good sign, I find). There were terrines galore and a duck *pot au feu*; we learned how to clarify stock to make aspic (and never to bother again); and were shown a *coq au vin*; but if anything typified the recipes of Intermediate it was the concealing of things within other things, the Russian doll approach to cooking. The most obvious example of this was sausage making – the closest cooking comes to a sex act. More challenging was a salmon we filled with a *farce* (stuffing) of brunoised, sautéed vegetables and diced, smoked bacon, which was then wrapped in a blanched savoy cabbage leaf and rolled in plastic wrap. This fish-cabbage 'log' was then poached in boiling water and served sliced – its plastic wrapping removed – with a reduced veal stock and red wine sauce. It was, actually, a wondrous thing to behold with its vivid green layer of cabbage spiralling around a multi-coloured filling, all framed with a dense, winey, mouth-puckering sauce.

We were shown how to fillet and stuff a trout with a *duxelle* of finely chopped morel mushrooms and shallots, and then a bream which we stuffed with minced prawn, shallots, ginger, olives and breadcrumbs, held together with an egg white and, this time, wrapped in a blanched lettuce leaf. Again, rather wonderful, and, with the addition of ginger, verging on the exotic (at least as far as Cordon Bleu recipes were concerned). Then there were the dishes that involved a meat *farce*, which was usually made from pork fatback – a slab of waxy, white fat – ground with some of the 'host' meat (if we were stuffing veal, there would be some minced veal, for example), plus some chopped mushrooms, breadcrumbs, herbs, onions and perhaps an egg to bind it. This tasty, coarse cement would be stuffed into yet more meat or a blanched cabbage leaf, and then the whole shebang would then be wrapped in *crépine*, or caul fat.

Caul fat – the lacy abdominal membrane from a pig or sheep – is an unsung hero of traditional French cooking, holding its contents together in the pan or the oven and then modestly melting into the background when it is cooked. It was interesting to learn how to use it and to try these ancient recipes, but towards the end of Inter-mediate Cuisine the use of cabbage and caul fat began to pall. 'I'm just waiting for them to figure out a way of using it in dessert,' Maria, a student from Madrid, whispered to me as Chef Thivet launched into the explanation of another instalment of culinary pass-the-parcel: guinea fowl and chicken liver, stuffed into guinea fowl breast and wrapped in shortcrust pastry. In fact, he did go on to show us a stuffed dessert that day although, thankfully, it was a delicate dish that layered ultra thin slices of pineapple with a mint, coriander and mascarpone filling, served with a pineapple sorbet and orange and honey sauce.

Perhaps the ultimate 'things stuffed into other things' dish was the *ballotine*, or the 'There was an old lady who swallowed a fly,' of French cooking. Chef Terrien showed us how to make a chicken *ballotine* stuffed with ham, pork shoulder, pork fatback, foie gras mousse, egg and pistachios. Jamie, who is a vegetarian, visibly blanched at the sheer quantity of meat involved and refused to taste it. The rest of us watched goggle-eyed as, swiftly, Terrien de-boned the chicken – the first step.

De-boning a chicken is one of those 'rites of passage' techniques for a cook. It can seem daunting, but it is a simple enough process: you cut along the length of the chicken's spine, and scrape the meat away to the left and right. The secret is to scrape the meat keeping as close to the bones as possible, then break the leg and wing bones away from the body. The tricky thing is not puncturing the skin, particularly at the top of the crown where the breasts meet but, again, with practice it is easy. People look at me strangely and back away when I do it, but it makes an excellent party trick.

After stuffing and then poaching the chicken in stock, Terrien tested the *ballotine* see if it was done by sticking a trussing needle deep within it, counting to ten, then removing the needle and placing it against his lips. If the tip of the needle was hot, the inside of the *ballotine* was cooked. No need for thermometer probes.

Though another interesting technical challenge, the *ballotine* was one of many Intermediate main courses that I wouldn't care to encounter late at night in a dark alley. The recollection of a piece of cod fried in lard and served on a bed of vinegary-sweet red cabbage with parsley potatoes and a beer sauce (supposedly popular in Flanders) still sends a shudder down my spine, for instance, as does the Easter pâté we made – a terrine of pork jowl, veal, fatback and onions with whole boiled eggs running through the middle. Pigs' trotters, which I expected to be repellent were, on the other hand, tasty and satisfying – *über* pork, if you like – especially served on sourdough *pain de campagne* with foie gras and walnuts.

The Intermediate desserts were as heavyweight as the main courses, often featuring caramelised apples and spirits like Calvados and Armagnac. A horrendous strawberry soup made with red wine, and a prune flan that could have sunk the *Bismarck* are two troubling dessert nightmares from this period.

The *coq au vin*, a dish so important to the French that its recipe has been protected by government decree since 1967, was something of an anti-climax. It is a revered relic of French cooking – one of those dishes, like cassoulet or pot au feu – that brings out the pedant in the French cook, each of whom thinks they the definitive recipe. A couple of weeks earlier, back in early February, I had eaten what is supposed to be the most authentic *coq au vin* in Paris, at Chez René, an old-fashioned bistro on Boulevard St Germain. I'd had *coq au vin* before, of course, but only made with chicken. That was fine enough but not really in keeping with the spirit of a dish that was originally created to slow cook a tough old bird so that it fell from the bone.

In the pedantic spirit of the dish, I wanted to make sure Chez René served the real deal.

'Is this really a male bird?' I asked the waiter – actually René's son – when he bought the dish to the table.

'Oh yes, it's a real cock, A GREAT BIG COCK,' he shouted across the packed dining room as he walked back to the kitchen.

As it turned out, I found the real thing a little too gothic. Chez René don't use any stock when they make their *coq au vin*, just red wine, butter and blood. The blood is the key to thickening the sauce of a genuine *coq au vin*. Ideally it is supposed to be the rooster's own, but veal or pig's blood is often substituted. (The blood turned out to be a key prop in one of Terrien's favourite tricks too. When trussing a chicken for another dish, he suddenly let out a yelp of pain, bent down behind the work surface, hastily doused his hand in some of the chickens blood and then stood up with the trussing needle sticking between his fingers. The front row Korean girls squealed). The trouble is blood doesn't taste very good. It has a harsh, metallic kick and can give the sauce a grainy texture. I could hardly finish mine.

Coq au Vin

Proper, authentic, genuine, traditional *coq au vin*, but without the blood. And with some stock. And you don't really need a rooster.

Ingredients

1 big chicken or, yes, a big old cock, portioned

1 litre of red wine, or a full-bodied white will do just as well

3 carrots, sliced

2 sticks of celery, sliced

Bouquet garni

10 peppercorns

150g bacon

Butter, oil, or, if you have some, duck or goose fat is good and not at all unhealthy

Salt

4 or 5 dessertspoons of flour

Hot stock – chicken or veal (optional)

200g pearl onions

200g button mushrooms

Blood – if you really must but I wouldn't if I were you

When we came to make the Cordon Bleu version of *coq au vin* in the practical session, time constraints meant that we weren't able to use a real rooster as this required marinating in red wine overnight, but we did get to use veal blood, which the chefs talked about in hushed tones as if it were contraband. 'It's not illegal as such, let's just say the authorities tolerate it,' Terrien whispered out of the corner of his mouth. In fact, if you have a good Chinatown near you, you should be able to source fresh blood without difficulty, but I really don't think it is worth it. For me, it is far more important to marinate the chicken.

To do this, first reduce the wine by a third to burn off the harsh alcohol flavour, cool it thoroughly, and pour over the chicken pieces. Add the sliced carrots and celery, the bouquet garni and peppercorns and leave covered in the fridge overnight.

The next day, remove the chicken and vegetables from the marinade, and drain well for at least half an hour, then pat the chicken dry. One key to a good *coq au vin* is to roast the flour, which you do by simply spreading it evenly on a baking tray and leaving it in the oven at around 200°C for ten minutes or until it starts to turn brown. Now, cut the bacon into thick matchsticks and fry for a couple of minutes in a casserole. Remove and set aside on kitchen paper to drain. Season and roll the chicken pieces in some of the flour, and brown them in the same casserole. Remove the chicken, and fry the marinated vegetables for about five minutes until they start to colour. Pour the vegetables into a *chinois* to strain, and dab any excess oil from the casserole with kitchen paper. Return the vegetables and bacon to the casserole, add a couple of dessertspoons of the roasted flour, and cook while stirring well for a minute or so.

Strain the wine over the vegetables and whisk thoroughly to incorporate the flour, then bring to a boil. Reduce the heat and skim any nasty stuff that rises to the surface. Add the chicken pieces, bring to the boil again, and reduce to a gentle simmer. If the chicken isn't properly covered, add some hot chicken or veal stock (I like to have some stock in a *coq au vin* to temper the acidity of the wine). Place the casserole, covered, in the oven at around 160°C and cook for thirty minutes or so.

Meanwhile, peel the pearl onions, and lightly trim the root.

Cook in a small pan with a little water, a dollop of butter and salt until they caramelise lightly. Fry the mushrooms until soft and add them to the casserole, with the onions, at the end.

After thirty minutes the sauce should be fairly thick. If you want it thicker, strain the chicken and vegetables and pour the sauce into a new pan. If you are using blood, you can whisk it in now with a teaspoonful of white wine vinegar, but under no circumstances allow the sauce to boil as the blood will go grainy. Alternatively, you could simply reduce the sauce as it is over a high heat, then pour it back over the chicken, bacon, onions and mushrooms. Serve with rice or potatoes, and some large croutons, fried – if you can be bothered – in clarified butter and dipped in chopped parsley.

As the members of Cuisine Group E got to know each other better, our usual courtesy in the kitchen had been replaced with a more efficient brusqueness. Andy, who never missed an opportunity to remind us that he had worked in professional kitchens, introduced us to the practice of yelling 'KNIFE! KNIFE!' or 'HOT POT! HOT POT!' when passing through the kitchen on the way to the washing-up sink. As we approached the end of Intermediate term exams in early March the 'Would you mind awfullys' and 'Do excuse mes' of Basic Cuisine had become a thing of the past.

I flew through our final practical – *mignons de porc aux châtaignes en cocotte* (pork tenderloin with chestnuts cooked in a casserole that is sealed with an inedible dough around the outside and served in that manner at the table). Our supervising chef was a new part-timer whom we had nicknamed Pirate Chef on account of his goatee beard, earring and general piratey demeanour. Unlike the other chefs, Pirate Chef was quite happy for students to see the marks he was giving – usually we had to sneak a look over the chefs' shoulders. He had given me four and a half out of five across the board, my highest score ever and considerably higher than my disappointing mid-term marks. '*Pas mal pour un Anglais!*' he said, and slapped me on the back.

Again, the written exam was simple enough, but the practical exam would take the same format as in Basic: we would have to learn ten recipes from Intermediate, and we wouldn't discover which one we were going to make until we were in the kitchen. Cock it up and you risked failing and having to repeat the course. The build-up was a period of some stress for all involved. Jamie told me she had dreamed she took the practical exam on roller skates with all fifty-five of students working together making five dishes. More helpfully, Christine kindly made photocopies of her notes and the photographs she had taken of each of the chefs' demonstration dishes and gave them to all of us as revision notes. Ingrid hosted a revision session at her apartment close to the Opera Garnier, but a few too many bottles of wine meant that we soon descended into gossip about our favourite topic: the sex lives of the chefs.

Once again rumours about the exam dishes spread like measles through an Amazon tribe. During the revision session Ingrid let slip that Terrien had let slip to *her* that we would be doing the trout or the guinea fowl recipes we had been shown. Well, I'd fallen for that kind of talk before. As a failsafe, I had asked one of the kitchen assistants to text me as soon as he heard anything, but three days later, with two days to go, his text had not materialised. After my *blanquette de veau* farrago I could take no risks: there was nothing for it, I would have to learn the ten recipes.

My memory is not what it was. It is a rare day that I don't find myself in a room without the faintest idea why I am there; I spend so much time retracing my movements in the hope of sparking some flicker of a memory that I sometimes wonder if I couldn't just hire one of those off-duty policewomen they use for crime reconstructions. PIN numbers are a constant source of distress, and I have genuinely forgotten how to spell my middle name. So the learning by rote of ten complex recipes was not a task to be taken lightly. For five nights in a row I sat by the light of my desk lamp repeating my arcane culinary mantras: 'Never roast a guinea fowl'. 'Eggs must be at room temperature before making hollandaise'. 'Always sniff the blender before using it', and so on, before waking Lissen in the early hours of the morning and asking her to ask me how to make a soufflé or truss a quail. She didn't know how to do these things, of course, and was unable to decipher my appalling handwriting, so we had no way of knowing if I was right or wrong. I could have been reading out the solution to the Schleswig-Holstein problem for all she knew. So, as the day of the exam approached, I resigned myself to another *blanquette de veau* fiasco.

My stomach churned like an ice-cream machine as we stood outside the exam kitchen, waiting for Chef Chantefort to finish setting out the ingredients. Ingrid was singing quietly to herself while rocking backwards and forwards; Andy was pacing the corridors like an expectant father; Christine's face was buried in her notes; and I was talking to anyone who would listen about nothing of any consequence. All we needed was a giant Native American and we could have put on *One Flew Over the Cuckoo's Nest* right there in the hallway.

We were told to enter the kitchen and choose a coloured token from a mixing bowl – red or blue. I chose blue and took my place before a metal tray containing a whole trout which I would have to fillet and stuff with mushrooms and shallots, using its bones to first make a *fumet* and then a sauce with Riesling and crème fraiche. It was one of my favourite Intermediate dishes and I thought I knew it well but still, for the second time in an exam, I forgot a crucial ingredient – in this case the onion that should have gone in the stuffing. I only discovered this *after* I had made the stuffing using all the other ingredients and packed it between the fish fillets. With the clock ticking, and other students beginning to plate around me, I had to unstuff the fish, mix the onion – which I had fortunately already diced and sweated, but then put 'somewhere safe' and forgotten about it – into the stuffing and spoon it back into the trout. By now royally freaked out, I over-cooked the fish, thickened the sauce too much and was the last to complete my plate. I didn't have time to taste my hollandaise sauce – which, because of the delay, had taken on the consistency of ripe camembert – before it was sent out to the jury for tasting.

I had never set out to be the best at the school; my aim was merely to survive the nine months, learn as much as I could, and graduate. But then they had gone and given me fifth place and that competitive streak had reared its ugly head. In the days leading up to graduation I replayed the exam, step-by-step, over and over. I bored everyone with the tale of the missing onions, the frantic race to complete the dish and how I wished I'd tasted my hollandaise before I'd sent it up to the mystery judging panel.

'Michael, does it really matter so much?' Lissen asked me, the night before graduation, after yet another analysis of where I thought I'd gone wrong. 'Aren't you getting all this a little out of perspective?'

'Perspective!' I sobbed, my face in my hands. 'Don't you understand, this is the most important thing that I have ever done in my life!'

Chapter 24

Seventy per cent of success in life is showing up.

Woody Allen

Unlike the Basic Cuisine graduation which was held in the school's Winter Garden, the Intermediate graduation would take place, together with the Superior students' passing-out, at Monsieur Cointreau's private members' club next door to the British Embassy on the rue Faubourg Saint-Honoré. I invited Intermediate Group E and some others for a glass of champagne and nibbles (dried figs, quartered, then wrapped together with diced mozzarella in strips of prosciutto, and drizzled with a dressing of wholegrain mustard, olive oil and honey) at our place before we took the Metro from George V to the Place de la Concorde. From there it was a five-minute walk to what turned out to be an impossibly grandiose building with a cobbled forecourt and a glamorous, swooping staircase.

We assembled upstairs in the glittering banqueting hall dressed in everything from jeans and T-shirts to dinner suits and ballgowns. Some of the Korean women came in national costume – fabulous – bell-shaped dresses in candyfloss pink and scarlet that made them look like giant tea cosies – while the Japanese women wore kimonos. The chefs had made an effort too; they sat on the stage dressed in their uniforms.

The Intermediate Patisserie students were to receive their awards first, which gave me time to reflect on the weeks that had passed, the things I had learned, and the crustaceans I had mutilated. A rumour was spreading, and was confirmed during the announcements, that a Mexican student, previously only notable for his

217

dependable tardiness and high-pitched voice, had failed Intermediate Patisserie. He had forgotten to add gelatine to a dessert which
had collapsed into an oozing chocolate puddle as a result. They had
at least told him in advance and he had not turned up.

I was thinking about this, about how close I had come to failure
on two occasions now, and how, really I was happy still to be sitting
here having at least been assured of passing through to Superior
Cuisine, when the school administrator made the following, earth-
shattering announcement: 'Michael Booth, Great Britain, first place
Cuisine Intermediate'. I was out of my seat and making for the
stage with unseemly haste before she had pronounced the first
syllable of 'Cuisine'. I accepted my certificate from Chef Terrien
and from there on, well, it all went a bit foggy. I remember Chef
Chalopin pumping my hand, putting a medal round my neck and
congratulating me. For some reason best left to neuroscientists
versed in the freak synapse responses of the bewildered, I replied:
'*Quelle surprise!*' (In the photograph of Chalopin and me taken at
that very second, he looks utterly foxed by this and it was only
later that I discovered that this favourite French phrase of the
British is, in fact, meaningless in French.) In the background I
could hear Sarah shout: 'Go Michael!' and the cheers of my friends.
It was like an Oscar win without the orchestra. I didn't stop grinning for hours.

I had attended my wedding and witnessed the birth of my two
children, but my input during these events had been mostly restricted
to looking keen and trying not to faint. As for my achievements at
school and university, these had been middling at best. It wasn't that
I was particularly feckless, more that I just couldn't give a feck. This,
then, was without rival as the most magnificent achievement of my
entire life.

During the cocktail party afterwards, held in an upstairs room
overlooking the club's gardens with views to the glass dome of the
Grande Palais, I graciously accepted the congratulations of my fellow
students, all except for Paul, whom I had relegated to second place.

He avoided eye contact with me throughout the afternoon, standing seething in a corner with his usual coterie of young ladies.

That evening we celebrated my success – although, looking back, I think the initial pretext was something to do with Hayden's birthday – with dinner at Mon Vielle Ami on the Isle St Louis. Mon Vielle Ami opened a couple of years ago as one of the new breed of Parisian bistros cited by many as a sign of hope for the city's culinary scene, with funky, stylish interiors and hearty, lightly reworked bourgeois bistro food. So good was the food that I was concerned that it would overshadow the events of the day, but I did my best to steer the conversation round to my first place every time it veered off course. The others, however, wanted to talk about what we might expect from the final leg of the course: Superior – the Jedi level. There was an air of mystique surrounding Superior, partly because translators weren't involved (everything would be in French only), and partly because the students who finished Superior left the school straight afterwards to do their *stages* (internship) so there was no one to report from the 'other side'.

'They say we get to create our own recipes,' said Christine, with wide eyes. 'And the chefs are much tougher on us.' 'Yes,' added Hayden. 'And we even get to use the Paco Jet.' 'This is when it really starts to get tough,' added Henrique. 'I was told the chefs start to treat it like we are working in a real restaurant.'

'Hmm, yes, yes,' I wondered. 'But more importantly, do you think they will treat me differently now I'm number one?'

Chapter 25

On n'arrive à rien quand tout le monde s'en mêle. (Nothing gets done when everyone gets involved)

French proverbial equivalent of 'Too many cooks . . .'

Imagine a writing course where Philip Roth pops by to help with your punctuation or a painting class where David Hockney gives tips on doing swimming pools. This is the kind of treat the students of Le Cordon Bleu savoured on a weekly basis when some of Paris' leading chefs dropped by to reveal the secrets of Michelin-starred cooking. These '*Chef Invitée*' sessions were one of the highlights of the week. During Intermediate Cuisine especially they were a welcome relief from the onslaught of nineteenth-century pork fat and cabbage dishes, and they brought us face to face with 'real life' chefs: men and women fresh from the trenches – intense, often battle scarred, usually highly strung and invariably brilliant cooks. They gave us a glimpse of a working environment to which many of us aspired, a gruelling world of eighteen-hour days in subterranean kitchens where chefs pushed themselves to the cusp of insanity to win or maintain stars.

The first chef to visit, back in the early days of Basic, had been Chef Vangort from Jean-Georges Vongerichten's restaurant Market, a slick, contemporary fusion place on avenue Matignon just off the Champs-Elysées. The young, handsome Vangort and his assistants were surprisingly laid-back as they demonstrated three dishes from their menu, offering occasional, shyly mumbled explanations. 'We don't shout and scream in our kitchen,' Vangort told us. 'We're pretty cool, a young kitchen.' He was the antithesis of the histrionic grand French chef.

Vangort had assembled what he called a 'crunchy' themed menu starting with tuna coated in puffed rice – as in Rice Krispies – with an emulsified sauce of egg yolks, orange and lemon juice and spicy Sriracha chilli sauce. It was a fresh and playful pairing – the sauce tart and acidic, the fish meaty and metallic. That was followed by a saddle of rabbit – an underrated cut of meat, in the UK at least, which, when cooked well, is juicy and more flavoursome than chicken – stuffed with Kanzuri paste, made from chilli, salt and malt. The rabbit was de-boned, Swiss-rolled in plastic wrap, poached, then breaded and fried and served with a soya bean purée and *jus* made from the rabbit bones. Dessert was a chestnut soufflé with nutmeg sauce and caramel ice cream. Inspirational.

Some of Vangort's ingredients might have been tricky to source in Paris – they used *dashi*, the Japanese stock made from seaweed and flakes of dried fish; and *panko*, a kind of chunky Japanese bread-crumb – and Chef Boucheret looked a little bewildered at times, but none of the techniques were especially daunting.

So inspired was I by this first *Chef Invitée* session that Lissen and I went to Market that weekend. This is a sleek, unusually spacious place for central Paris, designed in a chilly-cool New York-style combining – improbably – modern Scandinavian with a hint of Poly-nesian beach bar. When it opened Market was famous for its luxury pizzas, topped with black truffle and raw tuna. It was instantly deemed the hottest place in town, mostly because of a reservation system that excluded anyone who wasn't personally acquainted with the joint owner, film director Luc Besson. But we had no problem bagging a table the same night, sampling the celebrated 'Black Plate' of raw tuna and lobster with *daikon* radish, prawn *brochettes*, crab parcels and the most deliciously herby, sweet and sour dipping sauces I have ever tasted, along with some spoon-tender veal cheek and a forget-table dessert that I have forgotten about.

Perhaps the most intimidating of all our *chefs invité* was Philippe Bodier from the three-star restaurant Ledoyen. The restaurant was housed in a classical pavilion built in 1848, in the middle of a former duelling ground on the southern side of the Champs-Elysées (telling, isn't it, that during one of the most tumultuous years in French history, they found time to build a restaurant?). It is one of the grandest and most venerable of all Paris' restaurants; the kind of place where everything arrives at your table beneath a silver dome and the desserts are topped with gold leaf. Chef Boucheret, who before coming to Le Cordon Bleu had worked at Ledoyen for fifteen years, introduced this short, neat man with the kind of rimless, oval glasses beloved of so many French chefs and the Nazi hierarchy. Prior to working at Ledoyen, Boucheret told us, Bodier had worked at the Ritz, the Louis XIII, and for Ducasse in Monte Carlo. A chef's CV doesn't get much more impressive than that.

Bodier kicked off with *truffe et fin macaroni en timbale cremée* (truffle and fine macaroni timbale with a cream sauce). Usually at this point the students would all raise their pens and begin taking notes, and this time was no different. Chef Bodier began by explaining how he cooked the extra fine macaroni, then drained it, cut each strand to the length required and used it to form a little, oblong casket within a steel mould lined with buttered paper – the culinary version of building the Houses of Parliament out of matches. He then filled the macaroni box with a chicken and cream mousse, diced ham, truffle and a reduced truffle cream, made a lid with more of the macaroni, and baked it, sprinkled with parmesan, before serving it with a Perigord sauce (more truffles, port and veal stock) and a turbot emulsion. It was the most complex, finicky and impossible to replicate cooking demonstration any of us had ever seen. After about half an hour, in which Bodier had only managed to build up one side of the macaroni coffin, I looked around to see that pens were slowly starting to drop. It made for hypnotic viewing though, like watching one of those stop-frame animators at work.

The main course featured another coffin (not the most obvious menu gimmick, granted), this time with sea bass as the filling and a casket made from rice paper. As a list of thirty-five ingredients might suggest, this was rather more complicated than your average dim sum. Other ingredients included porphyry, which is a type of seaweed; eel trimmings; sea lettuce (another type of seaweed); salmon roe; caviar; agar agar (which is a kind of gelatine made from seaweed); squid ink; Brittany kombu (seaweed); sea spaghetti (yep, seaweed); and pearl tapioca (which, confusingly for someone like me who spent his schooldays in mortal dread of the stuff, is trendy in Parisian restaurants right now). If Stanley Unwin had entered and begun reading *Finnegans Wake* in Mandarin, I think we would have stood a better chance of understanding, but the resulting dish had a poetic, ethereal beauty, with the rice paper decorated like a Miro painting and surrounded by a luxuriant sauce.

By the time Bodier's assistant wheeled out his nitrous oxide gun to make some kind of milk foam – part of Ledoyen's contemporary take on a *millefeuille* using a chocolate puff pastry with each sheet of the pastry 'paper' individually separated – he was faced with a sea of gawping mouth-breathers. Nevertheless, we all sprang from our seats when it came to the end-of-session tasting. It's not every day you get to taste three-star food, least of all, three-star food this intriguing, but the disappointed muttering began with the macaroni truffle, which tasted almost completely of its parmesan topping, and grew to a crescendo of underawed grunts with the sea bass, which didn't taste of anything much.

This was not to be our last encounter with the food of Ledoyen. The students got a chance to dine there when the restaurant's private dining room hosted our Superior student dinner much later in April. This turned out to be the first day of spring – the day of my neighbour's Kama Sutra display in fact – and the air was warm as we gathered over cocktails in the restaurant's small terrace for drinks. This time round the food was comparatively simple and, I thought, really quite lovely. A starter called *saveurs 'terre and riviere' fumées et acidulées* blended beetroot and smoked fish to unexpectedly delicate effect; there was a tender oblong of veal probably cooked *sous vide* with a herb and rocket-filled cannelloni for the main course; and various chocolate desserts, *caneles* – sugary, chewy mini rhum babas – *macarons* and marshmallows for dessert.

But of all the *chefs invitée* the one whose cooking really had me on the edge of my seat me was Gaël Orieux, a thirty-three-year-old with a CV that included stints working for the grand old man of French cooking, Paul Bocuse, as well as Phillippe Legendre at the George V Hotel and for the renowned Yannick Alleno at the Hotel Meurice's Les Ambassadeurs. Orieux is tipped for greatness and his then quite new restaurant, Auguste – named after Escoffier and in the seventh arrondissement – was quietly making a name for itself among the cognoscenti of the Paris food scene.

As I've said, chefs and food critics bang on about simplicity in cooking to the point where they sound like they are intoning some meaningless Buddhist mantra, but Orieux's cooking, for me, defined what simple, modern haute cuisine should be. He started with pan-fried foie gras, which was straightforward enough, but served it in a consommé made from shrimp, lemon grass, ginger and galangal; an inspired pairing of fish and fowl, rich and sweet, meaty and fragrant. He loves to mix earth and sea, he said, and uses a lot of Asian ingredients. But the real brilliance of this dish was the method he used to clarify the consommé.

Clarification – ridding a stock of its solid particles – is one of those complicated and involved rituals of French cooking that has become so freighted by cooking lore and the burden of generations of cumulative wisdom that it verges on the mythological. We had been shown how to do this the classic way by making a mixture of ground beef, tomatoes, *mirepoix* and egg whites and simmering it in the stock so that it would self-filter. Slowly – at about the rate that long shore drift transforms a coastline – the mixture forms a crust which rises to the top of the surface. But Orieux dismissed this method. He clarified his consommé without any entrapment by protein, without fuss or bother, simply by cooking the stock slowly and *extremely* gently for about an hour. 'It works as well for chicken stock as fish stock,' he told us, and created the most subtle, pure soup I think I have ever tasted. He placed the seared foie gras and a garnish of cooked asparagus, pak choi, pearl onions, baby turnips and shitake mushrooms in the consommé to create a breathtaking starter.

Orieux turned several rules, rules which we had been taught were indisputable, on their head. He didn't believe in searing fish in a hot pan, for instance, so for the main course he started cooking a fillet of sea bass in a pan from cold, and then placed it in a low-temperature oven until it started to ooze with white albumen, which indicated it was done. The fish was still opaque in the centre, almost raw in fact, but he wanted it to stay moist and fresh, he explained, he didn't want to brown it. Neither did he want to brown the onion and leeks that went into the delicate, light cream sauce with water-cress that accompanied it so they, too, were cooked using only the barest of heat, slowly and gently. It was anti-Maillard cooking.

Using a machine called a *roué* he turned a potato into one long shoe-string, which he wrapped around a metal ring mould and deep fried to a crisp, golden brown nest. Served with a cress purée it combined to make a kind of very posh, French fish and chips.

Dessert was equally astounding: a white chocolate *ganache* which included yoghurt and gelatine served with a peach jelly and a deli-cate tea and cardamom sorbet. Orieux's food was everything I dreamed of making myself: subtle, wise, modern, gentle and poetic.

Chapter 26

Look me! Is byowteefool!

Chef Didier Chantefort

I hardly had time to alienate most of my friends and family by gloating over my first place in Intermediate before Superior Cuisine began, just four days after the epochal events of the graduation. Our initiation kicked off with what was, by Cordon Bleu standards, a startlingly modern demonstration by the course head, Chef Didier Chantefort, with three dishes featuring such hitherto unseen exotic ingredients as puréed passion fruit, lime juice, dried hibiscus flowers, tandoori spices, papaya and turmeric. The starter was scallops with a passion fruit, lime and honey sauce ('The marriage of acidity and sugar is superb!' the chef beamed); followed by John Dory fillets pan-fried with a tandoori spice rub, served with a fish fumet-based sauce enlivened by papaya and mango, and rounded off with a quite shockingly vulgar baked banana dessert. It was just what we needed to energise our spirits following the long slow trudge through the cabbage and caul fat of Intermediate. It seemed like everything we had heard about Superior might just be true. Could we be about to go fusion-molecular?

Up until now a fringe figure in our Shavian transformation from food urchins to culinary aristocrats, Chef Chantefort would at last take centre stage during Superior Cuisine. It was no less than the grand showman of Le Cordon Bleu deserved. I first encountered Chantefort in the early days of Basic Cuisine. This bulky, fleshy-faced man with close-cropped, light hair had dazzled us all with his levitating tea towel trick and offbeat humour. One minute he would be pretending a nest of spun sugar was underarm hair, the next he'd pause to rub his back up and down against the corner of the wall like an old grizzly. He was a joker, but one sensed that Chantefort had a hinterland, an intellectual depth that some of the other chefs perhaps lacked. He spoke Japanese, for instance, a legacy of his time at the Tokyo branch of the school, and would always use chopsticks to arrange decoration on a plate. He often broke off during a demonstration to joke with the female Japanese students or blow one of them a kiss, to which they would respond by giggling behind their hands. His English, meanwhile, was virtually non-existent. 'Oh my *good*,' he would suddenly swoon after tasting one of his sauces. 'Look me! Is byowteefool!'

As a young man, Chantefort, from Issoudun in central France, had been awarded the *Meilleur Apprenti de France* (Best Apprentice in France) and during his career he had worked in several Michelin-starred restaurants, eventually becoming *chef de cuisine* at Le Grand Cercle. Rumour had it he was friends with both Ducasse and Robuchon. As with many men of power, he had the faux humble habit of calling everyone else 'Sir' but, like all chefs, he had a temper too – something I first witnessed when a Superior Cuisine student brought him a dish twenty minutes late: 'If this was a restaurant you would be fired!' he yelled at the cowering boy. There was the constant feeling that, though he claimed to be 'sensitive, like a courgette blossom', Chantefort might at any time explode in the most fearful and decisive manner (it was Chantefort who had so memorably described Dingbang's sauce as 'shit water', you'll recall). He had an unnerving habit of punching the countertop with his fist, knuckles first, as if pounding air into imaginary dough. He would bash out uneven roasting trays using the same, raw-knuckle method; he even cracked lobster claws with his fists. So he was physical, but also passionate: the percussion of a whisk blending a hollandaise sauce in a metal bowl would send him into a syncopated reverie: and he ate while he cooked, not just tasting, but *eating* the stuff he was making.

Chantefort had his poetic moments – '*La cuisine est une sensibilité*' – but he was generally honest about the realities of being a chef. 'I completely understand why some of you who are lawyers and professionals want to change careers,' he told us one day as he rolled out some dough. 'You tell me you love to cook and I understand that but . . .' his expression changed, as it often did, from a twinkling smile to deadpan. 'It takes longer to become a good chef than any of your professions. It takes fifteen years. And then the hours are endless, the work is killing, there is no prestige and no money. Imagine you have four customers come in and order four different things. Imagine how much stuff you use to present one dish, multiply that by four, then by a whole restaurant. Lots of chefs are crazy because of this pressure.'

He was equally frank in responding to our criticisms of the school. Yes, it was true, we should have separate chopping boards for meat and vegetables, he admitted when I asked him if it was a good idea to use one board for both, but the school simply didn't have the space. And yes, it was also true that turning vegetables was 'the biggest load of bullshit in French cooking, learn it, then go home and forget it,' he said. As for kitchen hygiene, he had an unorthodox approach to that too: 'Really, we should paint everything black so you can't see the shit.'

Where Bruno was precise and measured, Chantefort was cavalier and spontaneous – dipping fingers in boiling sauces, throwing pots around and taking a more freestyle approach to the recipes. He was fearless. I once saw him taste the seasoning in a stuffing made from raw quail and a raw egg with his bare hands, and he loved goading students by ostentatiously licking spatulas and then using them in a sauce. He once spat on a lemon balm leaf to make it stick to the board so that he could chop it more easily. But for me all this was merely a symptom of his enthusiasm for food, which, as with all great teachers, was infectious. While some chefs would never express an opinion about the food they were making, Didier would always let us know what he thought, both positive and negative. '*Ooh la, la, que de bonheur!*' he said, kissing his fingers after tasting the passion fruit sauce he made for the scallops during the first session. '*Regardez la belle couleur.*' He was less enthusiastic about the wild rice that accompanied the John Dory, making his displeasure clear with a rousing raspberry trumpet.

Sometimes, for no apparent reason, he would break off from a demo to wave like a shy stage debutant to an imaginary lover in the back row, or would make trumpeting noises by blowing through his thumb and forefinger to announce the conclusion of a dish. Often he would end a demonstration by presenting his plates to the whistled accompaniment of Europe's 'The Final Countdown', bowing like a tenor at the curtain of *La Traviata*. The students adored him.

But Superior Cuisine would reveal a different Chantefort. He was more sombre, more business-like, partly because the school was now overcrowded, understaffed and ragged round the edges, and partly, I suspect, because it was his responsibility to prepare us for our first foray into a professional kitchen. 'It is tranquil here,' he began his welcoming speech on that first day of Superior Cuisine, 'but in a restaurant it will be very, very hard.' He demonstrated this with his uncompromising treatment of assistants: students who had either graduated from Superior Cuisine or were still in Intermediate and hoping to pay some of their course fees by helping the chefs during demonstrations. He was merciless with them, bringing demos to a halt to issue stern stares, or rolling his eyes in extravagant exasperation when they left the room to retrieve a piece of equipment they had forgotten. He thought nothing of dressing assistants down in front of the class: 'You do the preparation before the class, not during it!' he shouted at one unfortunate Greek girl who had forgotten to pre-shred some cabbage.

Chantefort was a master when it came to the presentation of a plate, and would load them up with all manner of extraneous foliage and frilly bits. He would never let the absence of vanilla or mint from a dessert prevent him from decorating it with a pod and some leaves, for instance, and would spend ages delicately placing spindly little sprigs of chervil on a main course. He had a particular weakness for 'high food', and would coax the components of his plates into phallic, gravity-defying towers. In the second week of Superior he showed us how to use a champagne flute, propped on its side in a tray so that it lay at a thirty-degree angle, as a mould for blancmange. When the blancmange set, he filled the other side of the flute with summer berries and a kiwi coulis. The result was a showbizzy dessert, the kind of thing you might imagine George Hamilton III ordering for a lady friend in a glamorous Côte d'Azur restaurant, circa 1976.

For the first few weeks of Superior I tried to copy Chantefort's decorative extravagances in practical sessions. Each time, Chef Chalopin or whoever was supervising us that day, would *tut* and dash the offending item – a tomato sculpted to look like a flower, or a bush of parsley atop a steak – from my plate, sighing 'Too much, too much!' 'But this is exactly what Chantefort did in the demo!' I would whine, but eventually I realised that Chantefort was simply giving us *all* of the decoration options on one plate. He didn't expect anyone to use them at the same time.

Aside from the introduction of bananas and tandoori spices, the most significant change with Superior Cuisine was that from now on everything would be in French. There were no translators in the demonstrations, so we would have to take notes directly from the chefs. Any questions we had, we would have to pose them ourselves, in French. The immediate effect of this was that we simply didn't ask any questions (apart from Tessa, whose French was almost as bad as mine although, to her credit, this never seemed to stop her), and at the start of the course in early April, there was an unseemly scramble to befriend a French speaker before each demo.

Another side effect was that Chef Thivet's 'little stories' became strangely soothing, giving us a few moments to relax amid his often frenetic demonstrations. Gradually though, the linguistic fog began to dissipate and, mysteriously, magically, I found that I could understand virtually everything they were saying. It helped, of course, that their words were accompanied by actions and that the language of the kitchen had been seeping into our brains for the previous six months. But, maybe, at last, I was beginning to get to grips with the French language.

Chapter 27

In England, there are sixty different religions – and only one sauce.

Voltaire

The tandoori fish and hibiscus flower melange of the first demon-stration proved to be something of a false dawn for those of us who had hoped that the recipes of Superior Cuisine might turn out to be a little more Blumenthal-esque than those of Intermediate. We were swiftly disavowed of this by another multi-layered recipe, prepared by Chef Thivet in mid-April that was to go down in Le Cordon Bleu legend as *Fish in an Overcoat*.

Its correct name was *petit bar en croûte façon Coulibiac*, consisting of a perfectly good sea bass, filleted and then stuffed with a mixture of rice, diced salmon, hard-boiled eggs, parsley, breadcrumbs and mushrooms. What was, essentially, now a gigantic fish sandwich was then encased in bread dough with the fish's head – its eyes removed – and tail put back in place sticking out at each end, before being baked in the oven for thirty minutes.

There was nervous laughter from the students when Thivet pulled this gaping-eyed monster from the oven. 'This is a classic dish! They used to serve this at all the grand hotels,' he said, genuinely hurt. Like several others I couldn't bring myself to taste it and, after spending three hours making it later that day at the end of which the supervising chef also refused to taste it, I took it home to show Asger and Emil. They thought it was one of the funniest things they had ever seen but, after a brief discussion between the two of them, also refused to try it. I looked at it and dumped the entire thing in the bin.

The arcane recipes didn't stop there. To Andy's outrage, during the next session we had to boil some tenderloin steaks for *filet de boeuf a la Ficelle, os de celeri a la moelle*, a kind of refined *pot au feu*. 'We should be frying steak this good, not boiling it!' he complained as we warmed the poaching liquid. 'But I thought it tasted fantastic in the demonstration,' I argued. 'The meat was so tender and it made a sensational sauce.' Andy's reply was the one he always used when we disagreed about food: 'Oh, you're so British. Why don't you just batter it and deep fry it?'

This was fairly typical of the other students' ideas about contemporary British cuisine. I was forever defending it, listing our great restaurants and acclaimed chefs, describing the remarkable renaissance that had taken place in British food in the last ten years (although, renaissance implies that there had been something of value there to begin with, which I'm not sure is true). They all knew Jamie Oliver, of course, and the Americans had a vague idea who Gordon Ramsay was, but the image persisted of the Brits as serial deep fryers. I grew used to taunts such as, 'Do you want chips with that?' and, 'More lard, Michael?'

This I could take but, for some reason, it really niggled me when Andy criticised the food I made. We usually cooked opposite each other in the practical kitchens. Students would chop and mix along either side of the central work station, and cook with hobs and ovens along the kitchen walls behind them. Ours was chatty group, fond of teasing, laughing, singing, and, in the case of Andy, the occasional tap-dance routine. It was a fun place to be but there was a competitive edge, particularly where Andy, Christine and I were concerned. We would each listen intently to the verdicts of the chefs on one another's cooking and I am not especially proud of this but, I would smile inwardly if Andy was reprimanded for adding too many spices or undercooking his fish. I would also quietly fume if he overheard a chef criticise *my* seasoning or clumsy plating skills. And I could barely contain my annoyance when Andy, having overheard a chef's critique of my food, would then wade in with his own opinion. This happened with a risotto we made in the first week of Superior in early April. The chef, quite rightly, gagged at the amount of garlic I had used. Another chef, in passing, tasted it and agreed. Sensing a wounded animal, Andy came in for the kill. 'Do you mind?' he said, as he leaned across and took a forkful. 'Ugh!' He pulled a face, and shook his head in mock sorrow. 'Way too much garlic, Michael. Too salty too.'

My increasing tension was, I'm afraid, a symptom of the pressure I was feeling as the new Number One. I was all too aware that things could only go downhill from here and, as Superior continued, I began to get more and more uptight about my cooking. And, as any sportsman will tell you, tension wrecks performances.

Midway through Superior, towards the end of April, we made yet another Russian-doll dish involving cabbage leaves stuffed with veal stuffed with foie gras, accompanied by stuffed tomatoes. This was one of my more notable disasters as, not only did I cut a corner of my finger off while slicing the veal, but my sauce was too salty and thin – more of a *jus* really – and my cabbage parcel fell apart when I tried to plate it. Andy had a field day with that, reminding me about it several times over the course of the following forty-eight hours until, finally, I snapped. 'What the fuck do you know about cooking?' I yelled. All the Winter Garden turned to look. 'You're only twelve years old and you've eaten fucking pineapples your whole life!' He graciously accepted my apology the next day.

While Andy spent much of the time complaining about the recipes and arguing with the chefs about their verdicts on his plates, Dingbang, who you'll recall had never set foot in a kitchen before coming to Paris, was steadily making progress with his cooking. As Superior continued the chefs grew more and more impressed by the plates he was presenting until, one fateful day, Chef Bruno advised me to taste Dingbang's pigeon wrapped in cabbage with a *jus* made from the carcass. 'Do you see the difference?' Bruno asked me. It tasted superb and was far better looking than mine, but there was something else: 'He let the meat rest properly, you didn't.' He was right.

When I cut into my pigeon breast it looked somehow more *tense* than Dingbang's, which was pink and juicy. I was furious with myself for continuing to let my impatience to plate scupper my grades. Dingbang, who, having only just recently discovered what my surname was, had taken to yelling 'Michael Boo!' every time he saw me, smirked cheekily. 'And look Michael Boo!' he said. 'You *jus* all greasy! Ha! Stress chef, stress pigeon!' I threatened never to help Dingbang fillet a fish ever again, but the truth was he didn't need my help any more. He had mastered the turning of vegetables better than any of us and could chop a carrot as fast as a seasoned professional due largely, I suspected, to having honed his motor skills through countless hours spent playing Pickachu Death Slasher.

Dingbang's precision skills came in useful for another bizarre fish dish we were shown in week two of Superior: a red mullet fillet with its scales and skin carefully removed and replaced with fake 'scales' made from potatoes, a haute cuisine classic. The scales were made by carefully turning a potato into a cylinder, then slicing it finely and then sticking the discs onto the fish with a clarified butter and egg yolk 'cement'. You then pan fried it to brown the potato scales and finished it in the oven for a couple of minutes. It actually looked rather magnificent when Chef Chantefort showed us his in the demo, a dish worthy of Vatel, but, inevitably, in the practical session things went awry as the 'scales' refused to adhere and slid from the fillets – all except Dingbang's, that is. Alone among us he had realised that the secret to making the potato scales stick was in having the thinnest, most precisely cut scales possible, and allowing the fish to rest in the fridge before frying so the cement could congeal.

The dish required gallons of clarified butter which, of course, entirely offset any health benefits of the fish, but healthy eating was never Le Cordon Bleu's objective. As I've mentioned, the chefs loved to goad the American students in particular with the huge quantities of butter they would dice and melt into sauces; we were encouraged to look on the fat in meat as a source of flavour rather than something to be trimmed and binned; and it is hard to think of a day that passed at the school in which less than a litre of full-fat cream was used. Early on in Basic Cuisine, back in September, I decided to trust my instinct, ignore that week's advice in the newspaper's health pages (which I knew all too well were written by journalists to a deadline, with a headline in mind), and decide that it is the fats you can't see in food – mostly processed food – rather than the fat on a piece of pork or some good, properly made butter, that will kill you.

That said, even I baulked at the menu prepared by Chantefort halfway through Superior Cuisine at the end of April. The starter on its own would have served as a perfectly adequate main course: sautéed asparagus (sautéing keeps the flavour of the asparagus much better than boiling, he explained), with fried langoustine, deep-fried beetroot chips and a beetroot vinaigrette made from a langoustine *jus*, sherry vinegar, garlic and puréed beetroot. But then came the main course: guinea fowl breasts, stuffed with an especially oily type of chorizo which had been finely diced, mixed with mascarpone (the fattiest dairy product in the world), breadcrumbs and olive oil to make a *farce*, and garnished with a cauliflower and satay spice purée. All of this was surrounded by a veal-stock-based sauce and topped with a long slice of crispy-fried chorizo. Assuming your dinner guests were still peckish – or breathing – Chantefort suggested that you might like to serve them chocolate *beignets*, or doughnuts, made by dipping cold chocolate *ganache* balls in a batter, deep frying them and serving them with two dipping sauces, one a semolina milk, the other a raspberry coulis. This being Chantefort, the presentation plate was fringed with mint leaves and, to ensure maximum diabetic risk, dusted with icing sugar. You gained weight just looking at it all, and I only managed to force down two or three helpings.

Chapter 28

I was making fast work of a crisp roast duck and a bottle of red bandol when my friend Michele called to inform me that profound interest in good food may be caused by a lesion in the anterior portion of the right cerebral hemisphere of one's brain.

Jeffrey Steingarten

I had always planned to give the skills I learned at Le Cordon Bleu a proper test by going to work in a restaurant and seeing if I could survive in a professional kitchen. As the end of my time at the school drew nearer what had been nothing more than a fuzzy, romantic whim began to draw into a more worryingly realistic focus.

Chef Chantefort organised the *stages*, or internships, in some of Paris' top restaurants for the students, and was well connected with many of the chefs in the city. Halfway through Superior, those of us interested in finding a place under one of them gathered in the demonstration room for a run through of how it would all work. It was a very different Chantefort who spoke to us that afternoon in late April: a weary, battle-hardened general briefing a new platoon whom he knew he would be sending to their early graves.

'You are all about to finish Superior Cuisine,' he said solemnly. 'You may have had a hard time here, it's not easy, but when you go to work in a restaurant it is another world. We are nice chefs. In a real kitchen you won't always find them to be as nice as us. It is not all, "Please very much" and "Thank you, sir" in a real kitchen. It is tough, tough work, and long, very long hours. You need to be disciplined and know how to take orders. You should not take it personally when someone shouts at you, you need to learn to think for yourselves and show proper respect. There will be people sitting waiting to eat the food you are preparing, they have paid for it – perhaps a lot of money – and they want it in good time and of the highest standard.'

He warned us that we might be taken advantage of by some kitchen staff. 'But if they ask you to clean floors, wash plates or carry rubbish all the time, that is wrong, you are there to learn and there to help with making food. If you have things like this happening, call me and I will talk to the chef. I have a good relationship with these restaurants and that is built on the fact that the students I send them are good, serious people. [At this moment two Koreans walked in late and looking confused. Chantefort sighed.] 'It is absolutely important that you turn up when you are supposed to, that you are always on time and that, if you are sick, you let them know. Don't just *not* turn up. That's bad for you, bad for me, bad for Le Cordon Bleu, bad for the restaurant and bad for the chef. They will not accept something like that more than one time.'

We all nodded intently, but it must have been difficult for Chef Chantefort to give that speech, as he did at the end of every three months to the graduating Superior students, knowing that a good number would let him down. I realised I might well be one of them. For all that I had learned I had no idea how I would cope in a professional kitchen. I hadn't had a proper job in over a decade.

Among the audience was Max, the twenty-three-year-old Buckowskian West Coaster whose dishevelled appearance belied an impressive speed and deft touch in the kitchen. Even so, he seemed to me to be one of the least equipped of us – along with the narcoleptic Chan Woo Park who, as usual, had fallen asleep during the meeting, and Alison, with her morbid fear of knives – to flourish in a professional kitchen. Max was a barfly, a drinker, a womaniser and, as he would freely admit to anyone who cared to listen, familiar with a whole bunch of non-prescription drugs. He was always late, never ironed his clothes or combed his hair, and usually looked as though he had crawled to sleep under a hedge in the Jardin du

Luxembourg. He lived life in a permanent haze but I liked him; he didn't have a malicious bone in his body and had a host of entertaining stories. He once told me a far-fetched, but I am sure entirely true, anecdote about a visit to a Uruguayan beach resort where he had 'lost it', woken up naked in a strange beach hut and, for reasons that I couldn't entirely fathom, decided to hitch-hike to Brazil wearing just a beach towel. 'Oh man, I have no idea how I ended up there, that was really some kind of shit,' he told me, shaking his head.

Le Cordon Bleu had a rule whereby if a student missed more than four demonstrations or practical sessions, they would fail the entire semester. Max missed four in Intermediate and only just escaped failing by claiming that he had missed the fifth demonstration in Superior because of visa issues (the only excuse the school would accept for missing a session). He was plagued by bad luck of his own making. I met him in the changing room on one of his less fortunate days.

'Oh man, I forgot to put on my underpants!' he moaned as he prepared to change into his chef's kit, 'I'll just change in this corner.'

He went and stood behind a row of lockers.

'I left my iPod in the taxi last night too, what a pisser; and someone stole my knife kit from my locker last night!'

'Wasn't it locked?' I asked.

'No, I lost the fuckin' key and we had to break it open!'

Max had hooked up with Alison early on in Intermediate. It seemed a fairly one-sided relationship. Alison did Max's laundry and trailed him like a Muslim bride. Max presumably had his wicked way with her and then treated her as if they had been married for forty years. At our various social get-togethers he would spend much of the evening chatting up Natalie – the school receptionist that Dingbang had taken a shine to – before inevitably giving up ('Those French girls are hard to crack'), and invariably left with Alison at the end of the evening. But, despite all this, Max was there for the *stage* meeting with the rest of us. The one thing he was serious about, it seemed, was cooking.

Our one-on-one *stage* meetings with Chef Chantefort took place

241

a couple of weeks after his introductory talk, towards the end of April. Didier Chantefort was an intimidating presence even when you were among an audience, and I was a little nervous about the interview. I had rehearsed several questions in French (he doesn't speak English) but Didier was a fast talker and there was no telling how things would pan out. Prior to the interview, I had thought long and hard about which restaurant I wanted to do my *stage* in. Ideally, it would be one that made the kind of food I wanted to eat and to learn how to make. That meant going to work somewhere with a more contemporary outlook than Le Cordon Bleu – a place where they didn't stuff cabbage leaves with foie gras and dress fish in pastry overcoats. Like everyone else I had nodded in wise agreement at Didier's advice that you learned more in smaller restaurants. I knew of one hapless *stagière* who had gone to work for Alain Ducasse at the Plaza Athénée and for the entire three months had only been allowed to lay the table for the staff meals, for instance. Nevertheless, I had decided it would be far cooler to work in the kitchen of a famous chef with a Michelin star or two under his toque. I had someone in mind, but did I dare ask?

I sat down beside Chantefort's desk. Pinned to the noticeboard beside me were notes and photographs of an elaborate new recipe involving mushrooms and scallops that he was obviously planning to introduce to the course. On his desk was a picture of his family. The rest was a chaos of paper.

'So do you have any ideas where you want to go?' he asked.

'Well, I, um . . .'

'Hotel kitchen? Restaurant? Bistro? Modern? *Classique?*'

'Well, probably not a hotel. A restaurant,' I paused. Cards on the table, or risk being placed in some dingy bistro in Montparnasse. 'I . . . I really like Joël Robuchon's food.'

This is like a mechanic saying he rather liked Enzo Ferrari's cars, or a footballer expressing a preference for playing for the teams of Alex Ferguson, and I blushed as I said it but, without saying a word, Didier picked up the phone and dialled.

'Chef Philippe Braun, please,' he said. 'Hello, this is Didier Chantefort from Le Cordon Bleu. I have a student here, very serious, very good student, who would like to come and do a *stage* with you. Would that be okay?'

He listened to the answer and covered the receiver.

'When can you start?'

'Umm, August,' I said, knowing that I would have to take a couple of months 'off' after Superior finished in early June to earn some money.

Chantefort repeated this down the phone, said a cursory goodbye and hung up. He continued, filling in my *stage* form as he spoke: 'Okay, you start at L'Atelier Joël Robuchon, August fourth. Your contact is Chef Philippe Braun. You know Michael,' he stopped writing and looked up, 'this is a very, very tough kitchen. When you find you've had enough, just call me and I can always find you somewhere else to work.'

I noted that he had said 'when', not 'if' and gave a nervous laugh. 'Oh don't worry, chef, I know all about hard work. I have two under-fives!' He looked doubtful but turned his attention to some paperwork, indicating that the meeting was over.

I went to meet Chef Braun at L'Atelier Joël Robuchon a week later to get his signature on the forms required by the French government for any *stagière*. I arrived at nine thirty in the morning. As I waited for the chef, other members of staff arrived for work, bleary eyed, slow and casual. As I watched the waiters flirting camply with each other, Chef Braun tapped me on the shoulder.

'So, you want to come and do a *stage* here, yes?' he asked. He was a little shorter than me, with precisely clipped, slightly receding brown hair. His eyes inspected me with laser intensity.

'Yes, very much,' I said.

'Right then, Chef Chantefort told me you were an excellent student. Where are you from, the USA?'

'No, England.'

'Okay, you start on August the fourth. We usually start at eight.

243

It is very tough.' He used the same pumping fist motion Didier had used to emphasise just how tough it would be.

'Yes, I've heard,' I said.

'You work three days on, three days off as part of the same team.' His eyes were now darting about the room as if, subconsciously, he had already moved on to the rest of the day's business. 'We will supply you with a jacket but you will need to bring your own trousers and they must be black. We have no lockers I'm afraid, so you'll just have to manage.'

'Where will I store my knife kit?'

'Oh, you won't need that. Just three knives: a paring knife, a kitchen knife and your *économe* [potato peeler].' He gave me a thin smile, shook my hand and left.

Chapter 29

'How can one be expected to govern a country that has 246 varieties of cheese?

President Charles de Gaulle

Superior Cuisine heralded the arrival of the 'fake chefs'. With Chef Terrien and Chef Thivet sent for short stints at the Cordon Bleu school in Costa Rica (one of the less arduous postings, I would imagine), Chef Boucheret now retired to the Auverne, and the student body swollen to a greater number than the school could really cope with – there was a dire shortage of chefs to supervise our practical sessions. To solve the problem, the school took to employing free-lancers – Hayden called them 'fake chefs', and the name stuck – from other restaurants and hotels in the city. In principle the idea behind this was sound: the more chefs we got to work with, the more we would learn, both in terms of new techniques and approaches to cooking, and how to cope with the eccentricities of these notoriously volatile professionals. Unfortunately, the fake chefs hadn't read the recipes. This drove us to the very brink of madness as we methodically followed Chef Chantefort's instructions, only to find ourselves caught in the crossfire for not doing things the way the fake chef preferred. Every chef has their own – usually sacred and inviolable – way of doing things, and they always seem to be different. More challenging still was trying to come to terms with their character quirks.

Rather than bother to learn their names – they certainly had no intention of trying to memorise ours – the students instead chose to give these rent-a-chefs nicknames. Thus we got to know Pirate

245

Chef, whom we have already met; Shagger Chef (a notorious woman-iser who, rumour had it, got a former student pregnant); Tight Pants Chef; and Angry Chef, who would fly into a rage every time he caught me peeling a carrot without having chopped its ends off first. Then there was Baby Chef, a tiny, twenty-one-year-old girl, who reduced many of us to emotional wrecks with her relentless, drill sergeant-style critiques, and Creepy Chef who was, well, just really creepy.

Of them all, Angry Chef was the most accomplished cook. A short, hounddog-faced Frenchman, AC had recently returned from living in Japan where, rumour had it, he had appeared on the legendary *Iron Chef* TV show (where guests chefs compete against a panel of regular chefs), and lost. From our first ever experience of him, in which he hypnotised a lobster, it was clear that Angry Chef, though not the most approachable member of staff, had a great deal he could teach us about cooking.

It happened to be my lobster. I had picked it up gingerly to examine it, hoping that it wasn't pregnant, when it suddenly began to writhe wildly. I dropped it on the worktop and, I'm afraid, I may have screamed, Dingbang told me later, in the manner of a twelve-year-old girl. The lobster scuttled across the marble but Angry Chef pounced and grabbed it behind its head. The lobster continued to flail like a knight with ants in his armour. 'Gather round everyone!' the chef shouted. The other students dropped what they were doing and walked over to my work station. 'Watch this.' To our collective bewilderment, AC started to stroke the hysterical crustacean behind its head, whispering '*Calme, calme*' into where presumably he supposed the creature's ear to be. Andy stifled a giggle. AC stared at him. 'Are you laughing?' Andy shook his head and looked down at his shoes. 'Just watch.' He placed the lobster face-down on the work surface with his tail up in the air and his claws spread out to either side as if miming a freestyle dive. The chef continued to stroke the back of its neck, whispering soothing words. Slowly, quietly, the lobster did indeed begin to quieten down. After a few more seconds of this the chef moved away entirely to leave it standing freely upon its nose, alone on the counter in a Dali-esque pose. Angry Chef tilted his chin upwards at us in triumph and walked away. It remains, to this day, one of the most remarkable things I have ever seen.

As well as a lobster wrangler, Angry Chef was a molecular gastronomy expert and claimed to be friends of both Hervé This and Pierre Gagnaire. Oddly, he was reluctant to share any of his secrets but would often hide himself in the corner of the kitchen and rustle up weird concoctions – such as the tiny orange balls, like salmon roe, that he once made from tomatoes – without ever showing us how he did it. An unfortunate trait for a teacher, I couldn't help think. When pressed to reveal how he had made these kind of things, he would instead offer us unfathomable demonstrations involving oil and water emulsions, then tap his nose conspiratorially – none of which left us any the wiser.

Around this time came our long-awaited trip to the mega market at Rungis, south-east of Paris. Since it took over the role of supplying produce to Paris from the original market at Les Halles in the seventies, Rungis has become the largest market in Europe – the French claim it's the largest in the world. It supplies most of the restaurants, hotels, market stalls and supermarkets in the city, and a large proportion of the rest of France. In fact, people come from all over northern Europe to buy fruit, vegetables, meat, fish and flowers here (when I lived in Denmark I knew of several restaurants and grocers who travelled to Rungis every week). It claims to feed over twenty million people, covers the same area as Monaco, and employs fifteen thousand workers. Like Monaco, it has its own shops, restaurants, banks and hairdressers although – and I can't help feeling it would be an enjoyable spectacle – it doesn't have its own royal family.

The action at Rungis starts at two in the morning and is usually all over by mid-morning. We gathered outside the school at five in the morning on the day of our visit to be driven by coach for about twenty-five minutes out of the city in the direction of Orly Airport.

You need a special pass to enter Rungis, and you can only get one of those if you represent a business that is somehow connected to catering. All of which lent our visit that added 'backstage' frisson.

Rungis is one of those things, like Angkor Wat or Brian Blessed, whose sheer scale is impossible to appreciate from close quarters. We started with a walk around the produce markets which, like everything in Rungis, is housed in vast, charmless single-storey warehouses. By the time we arrived the trading was winding down, but the porters and their trolleys were still on the move and we often had to jump out of their way. 'It reminds me of Costco,' sniffed Christine who, more used to the farmers markets of San Francisco, was not impressed by the stacks of polystyrene produce trays and the tell-tale waxy sheen on the peppers and apples. 'This is all intensively farmed stuff, isn't it?' said another student. 'Where are the heirloom tomatoes and the organic produce?'

We were too late to see the seafood market which starts earliest of all, but had a sniff in the cheese hall which more than confirmed the veracity of General de Gaulle's famous comment on the ungovernability of the French (although, never mind their cheeses – of which they actually have over three hundred varieties – surely their reluctance to obey simple traffic laws is more of a concern), and put on disposable white coats and hairnets for a tour of the meat market. Here hung row after row of cow, pig, lamb and horse carcasses, some of them with photographs of the subjects taken while still alive and, touchingly, pinned to their sides in death. It was unsettling to confront the morbid reality of meat production but at least, our guide explained, these animals were killed humanely, being stunned prior to death. I was, however, about to meet a man with a rather different approach to the slaughtering of animals.

Chapter 30

You should never get too friendly with a pig.

Gerard Depardieu

I am sitting in a garden in central Paris upon the throne of Obelix, wearing Obelix's pointed metal hat. Gerard Depardieu, who plays Obelix in the *Asterix* movies, is standing beside me in the voluminous orange T-shirt and blue stretch pants that I suspect he has spent the night in, having only recently awoken. Though about my height, Depardieu manages to tower over me, seemingly filling the entire patio of his cluttered, art-filled house deep in the sixteenth arrondissement. A Japanese chef from one of Depardieu's restaurants takes our photograph with my ancient Canon.

Sometime just after Christmas, Asger had discovered Asterix and Obelix. Even the previously hypnotic appeal of a good stick waned as Asger immersed himself in the culture of the pugnacious Gaul and his friends, his favourite, of course, being Obelix.

At around the same time, a magazine, knowing I was now living in Paris, commissioned me to interview Depardieu who had recently published a book, *Ma Cuisine*, featuring his favourite recipes. Towards the end of the interview I had mentioned how excited my eldest son would be to know that I had met Obelix in the flesh. Immediately Depardieu scuttled off to another room, returning with the hat he had worn in the last *Asterix* film, and led me out in the garden for a photo. (Asger was duly impressed and for weeks afterwards asked when Obelix would be coming to play.)

Ma Cuisine was co-written with the Laurent Audiot, the head chef at one of Depardieu's two Paris restaurants, La Fontaine de Gaillon.

249

To prepare for the interview, I treated myself to lunch there at the magazine's expense. The restaurant is grand and flowery and ranged over two floors of a seventeenth-century town house in a pretty square close to L'Opera. I was shown to a table on the first floor in a room with walls covered in romantic frescos depicting scenes from ancient Egypt. Unlike other culinary ventures owned by actors – Planet Hollywood, say, or Kenny Rogers' fried chicken chain – Depardieu's image is blessedly absent from the Fontaine de Gaillon. Unless you looked at the arty, black and white brochure, which has fuzzy action shots of Depardieu in a string vest and braces dashing about the restaurant's kitchen, you would assume this was just another of those places that Paris does so well – technically brilliant, poshed up yet still down to earth bourgeois cooking made with the highest quality, seasonal produce; the kind of place that should only really be visited at most twice a year, unless you are entirely at peace with your cholesterol levels.

'You had the rabbit!' Depardieu had said to me as I arrived at his house for the interview the next morning. 'I did,' I said, slightly disconcerted, yet flattered that he had taken the trouble to check. 'It was wonderful. The sauce was so rich, almost like a proper *coq au vin* sauce. Did the chef use blood to thicken it?' Depardieu's eyes widened in excitement, 'No! No! You want to know the secret? It's a just a little piece of chocolate! Just to thicken. I often use chocolate with dark meats like that. It is very good with game especially. I try to go back to cooking before the Revolution, before they started using so much cream and butter.'

This might lead you to believe that Depardieu's cuisine was in some way light and healthy. In fact there is still a fair bit of butter and pork fat in his recipes but, as we talked, the man who took himself off to hospital on his motorbike to have a quintuple heart bypass back in 2000, took a drag on a filterless Gitanes, looked me in the eye, and insisted that his favourite breakfast of *lapin en gelée* (rabbit in aspic) with a glass or two of wine, was 'very elthee'.

A great deal of Depardieu's food philosophy made perfect sense, however. The Americans, he said, were too preoccupied with fat and cholesterol and should worry more about their intake of sugar and the carcinogens in processed foods. In his book he writes eloquently about his connection with produce and the soil that bears it. 'I have felt at one with nature all my life ... My eye will roam with equal pleasure over the face of a beautiful woman as it will over the cuts of meat displayed in a butcher's shop window ... I prefer to eat with my fingers rather than to use a knife and fork.' He is equally passionate about the tastes and smells of nature; his must be the only cookery book to mention the smells of wild mint and the secretions of the anal glands of a fox as in the same sentence.

We talked some more and I told him that I was studying at Le Cordon Bleu. 'That's not very good, I don't think,' he frowned. 'The food they teach is so heavy. And you know, you cannot teach taste. I remember Berb De Niro came to my chateau [Depardieu's main home is the thirteenth-century Château de Tigné in the Loire valley, one of several vineyards he owns around the world in Argentina, Morocco, Portugal, the Languedoc and Spain] and I showed him my wine cellar. He tasted some of the wines and was so excited. "Gerard you must tell me where I can buy these wines!" he said, but I told him, "Berb, you cannot just buy a cellar like this, you need to build it up over the years, you need taste, a palate."'

It's true, I said, that Le Cordon Bleu teaches classic, heavy ways of cooking, but don't you need to learn the basic rules in order to break the rules and develop as a cook? Depardieu dismissed this out of hand. He preferred Italian cuisine, he told me. Gesturing to his small patio garden he said, 'Pasta is a great thing. I can make a great pasta dish just with the things I have growing in this garden. Everyone in Italy knows how to cook.'

He had little time for Michelin restaurants: 'There is not enough simplicity in French cooking. Starred restaurants get boring very quickly. You don't get any surprises with the *grandes tables*. Those chefs lose contact with humanity, they stop listening. Alain Ducasse is like a sect now, wherever he opens a restaurant it is the same, but he is never there!'

It is a measure of Depardieu's extraordinary social rise that the once virtually destitute boy from the grim provincial town of Châteauroux, 160 miles south of Paris, could now pronounce himself bored with posh restaurants. Depardieu, fifty-eight, left school at thirteen, famously drifting through his mid-teens in the company of prostitutes, pimps and thieves. At home, money was so short that they could rarely afford meat and – in an anecdote he has proudly retold on many of the world's chatshow couches – he recalled his father showing him how to prepare hedgehog by inflating the carcass with a bicycle pump via the unfortunate creature's anus to remove its spikes, then wrapping it in mud and throwing it on the fire. Depardieu claims it was delicious. Of course, since he became a movie star in the mid-1970s Depardieu has dined at the greatest restaurants in the world, from California to Barcelona and even London. 'I love to eat in England. Even through all that mad cow thing I was still eating British beef,' he enthused.

We talked about produce, which he claimed was one area at least where France continued to reign supreme. I disagreed, describing the waxy peppers from Holland and industrial tomatoes I had seen by the crateload at Rungis and how the French used more pesticides than any other country. Depardieu banged his meaty, fat palms down on the table top. 'No! we have good produce in France. If you go to a market in Brittany it will have different things than one in Provence – we respect the seasons here, and geography. In my cooking, before everything comes the produce. We don't buy at Rungis for my restaurants.'

So why were the French so tardy when it came to embracing the organic movement? Depardieu grasped both sides of the heavy, dark wood dining table as if he were about to lift it into the air and hurl it through the plate glass window before us. 'Pah! *Bio* [the French term for organic food] is a waste of time, it's just politics. *Bio* for me is obvious, I have been using *bio* before they even thought of the term. Chemicals kill *terroir*. In my vineyards we only use proper compost, no chemicals. You know, my grandmother who lived in Orly had an outside toilet and when we had a shit, we would put the shit onto the garden. It was magnificent compost!'

Often these impassioned speeches would be interrupted by an explosion of coughing from Depardieu, giving me a chance to look around the living/dining room where we sat. The walls were hung with original abstract artworks; the furniture an eclectic mix of Bauhaus and seventies' moulded plastic. The kitchen was state of the art though, in granite and stainless steel.

When his coughing subsided, we talked meat. 'When I first went to America in the 1970s I asked them, "Where are your chickens?" I couldn't believe it: they only ate the breast, their chickens didn't have legs! Things are better now. I have a very good butcher just outside of Salt Lake City. They even have cheese there now.'

I had heard that he killed his own pigs and sang to them as he slit their throats to minimise the stress to the animal and preserve the tenderness of the meat. 'Yes, but you must never get too close to them. Pigs are much more clever than dogs and you can too easily build a relationship with a pig – then it is impossible to kill them. A chicken or a rabbit is not the same, but you should never get too friendly with a pig.'

He gets up to indicate that the interview must end. Depardieu has to leave to catch a plane to the Ukraine where, he says, he is going to meet the president to discuss various wine and film projects. We go outside for the photograph and, as I am leaving, I ask Depardieu himself to put on the Obelix hat. I grab a picture of him. The picture, when developed, would capture the Greatest Living Frenchman™ in a characteristic blur of hair and nose and well-fed flesh.

Gerard Depardieu's Beef in White Wine
from *Ma Cuisine*

This tasty, tender beef dish is one my favourites from Depardieu's excellent book.

Ingredients (Serves 4)

75g fatty streaky bacon

1kg beef, such as rump or shoulder

60ml brandy, preferably cognac

200g streaky smoked bacon with rind

4 small carrots

4 shallots

2 garlic cloves

half a calf's foot, cut into slices by your butcher

1 onion, peeled and studded with 2-3 cloves

Bouquet garni

salt and freshly ground black pepper

400ml dry white wine

Freshly ground nutmeg

500ml veal stock

1 bunch parsley

Cut the fatty bacon into strips and briefly freeze. Using a sharp knife, make holes in the beef and insert the bacon strips into them. Place the meat in a bowl and pour over the brandy, then cover and leave to marinate in the refrigerator for about two hours, turning frequently.

Cut the rind from the streaky bacon and set aside. Finely dice the bacon, peel and slice the carrots and shallots. Peel and finely chop the garlic.

Brown the diced bacon in a large frying pan until crispy, without using additional fat. Remove the beef from the marinade, pat dry and add to the bacon with the calf's foot. Brown the meat well on all sides. Remove the pan from the heat and remove the contents of the pan.

Place the bacon rind at the base of the pan, then place the carrots on top. Return the diced bacon, beef and calf's foot to the pan, then add the shallots, garlic, onion studded with the cloves and the bouquet garni. Season with salt, pepper and a pinch of nutmeg. Pour over the wine and veal stock, then cover and simmer gently for four hours. Do not lift the lid during cooking.

Wash the parsley and shake dry, remove the leaves and chop finely. Before serving, remove the onion studded with cloves and the bouquet garni from the sauce, then take the beef and the slices of calf's foot out of the sauce. Cut the beef into slices and cut the meat from the calf's foot in slices. Arrange both kinds of meat with the vegetables on a warmed serving dish and sprinkle with the parsley. Skim any fat from the sauce, using a slotted spoon, then either pour over the meat or serve separately. Serve with a fresh baguette or potatoes boiled in their skins.

Chapter 31

Anyone who says they have invented a dish is just bullshitting.
Marco Pierre White

'Okay, so do you want to know the good news or the bad news about the exam?' It was rare that Paul the semi-pro chef from Texas made an effort to speak to me, although I had sensed a defrosting since Superior started back in early April, but he surprised me as I stood sharing a cigarette with Dingbang outside the school one hot May morning. 'The good news,' he continued, not waiting for an answer, 'is that we don't have to learn ten recipes from the course, so you won't be forgetting your onions this time, Michael. Ha-ha! They're going to give us a list of ingredients and we have to make something ourselves.

'I think it's great, it gives me a chance to *create* something for once. That's where my strength is, recipes are for slaves. But the bad news – for you all – is that we have to make four plates of it, all exactly the same and ready at the same time. If you're too early or too late, you fail.'

I pulled a face which I hoped conveyed how daunting this was. The worst thing, I had found, was to provoke Paul by implying you were as good a cook as he. Then he would feel compelled to rifle his mental Rolodex of improbable anecdotes about the famous chefs he had dazzled with his skill and ingenuity at the stove.

'That won't be a problem for me, I'm used to the pressure of a proper kitchen, but for people like you ...' he winced in mock-empathy, 'It's time to sort the men from the sheep.'

'The men from the *sheep*?'

'Yes.'

Chef Chantefort confirmed the format of the final Superior exam at that day's demonstration and presented us with the list of ingredients we would each receive. There were two lists, actually. The first featured all the standard store-cupboard items that would be available to us, including stock, wine, sugar, flour, gelatine, eggs, milk, onions, butter of course, the vegetables for a *mirepoix*, and tomatoes. The second list, *Ingrédients Principaux*, featured things like a single chicken breast, tomatoes, waxy potatoes, oyster mushrooms and caul fat that were optional, as well as four compulsory ingredients – things that *had* to appear on all four final plates in one form or another. These were 400g of peas; four *poivrade* artichokes (the small, purple variety); eight asparagus spears; 50g of foie gras mousse; and, the main ingredient, two, 500g pigeons.

In true Cordon Bleu style there were another two pages of rules. As well as the compulsory ingredients, each plate had to feature two *garnitures composé* and one *garniture simple*. The definition of the former was something involving two or more ingredients – a soufflé or a flan or a purée, for example; the latter was a single vegetable that required some technical expertise – clearly they had in mind the turning of vegetables. We were to give written versions of our recipes before the exam and would then have four hours to prepare the four identical plates. For every minute that we were late with presenting our plate, a point would be deducted from our final score out of a hundred.

The most obvious problem wasn't the combination of ingredients – peas and pigeon is a classic pairing – but the quantities. You usually get a whole pigeon when you order one in a restaurant, but here we had to spin out two of them over four plates. Four of those tiny artichokes weren't going to go far either; neither were eight asparagus spears. Who said nouvelle cuisine was dead?

As soon as the demonstration was over the discussions began among the students about what we were going to make, cautiously at first, as no one wanted to give away any ideas but then, as we all realised we had very different approaches, we became more open about our ideas.

'The curveball is obviously the foie gras mousse,' said Hayden.

'What's that? asked Dingbang.

'It's basically a cheap version of foie gras, but with most of the foie gras removed and replaced by milk,' said Paul. 'You can't do anything with it. You can't fry it, 'cos it'll fall apart. You can't apply any heat to it actually. It's absolute crap.'

'As far as I can see, there is only one thing you can do with peas,' I said to Christine, 'You can't just boil them and let them roll around the plate, they obviously want us to purée them.'

Andy joined in, 'No, no, no. You can boil them, fry them, make a soup, or a flan, or stuff the tomatoes with a purée. I've got more of a problem with the pigeon. I hate pigeons. Flying rats.'

There was a committed anti-pigeon consensus among the students, but I am rather fond of them. Pigeon, cooked well so that it stays pink and juicy, is a great foundation ingredient for a plate: it has a rich, bloody, gamey flavour which allows you to play around with other sweet and acidic flavours and crispier textures. But what exactly would the judging committee be looking for? Did they want innovation; something they hadn't seen before? Or did they want us to show them that we had digested all they had taught us over the previous nine months? This was the subject of more heated debate. Both Andy and Christine had decided to give the birds an Asian makeover; they each planned to deep fry the breasts with sesame seeds and accompany them with a sweet and sour sauce, but this seemed wrong to me. Why spend nine months learning about classical French cooking if all you really want is to do something completely different?

At the end of a long argument I said to Andy, 'So, what you're saying to the chefs is: "I've listened to you for the last nine months, but I think you're wrong and this is how I'm going to do it".' 'Yes, that's about it,' said Andy, whose simmering indifference to classical French cooking had developed into a raging antipathy during

Superior. He had had enough of being told his fish wasn't cooked enough, or that his sauces were too spicy and was planning a last, triumphant act of rebellion.

We had a trial run at school. This was the first time we had been allowed to create something of our own instead of reproducing what the chefs had shown us during the demonstrations, and some students flourished with this new freedom. I was forced to admit that Andy's deep-fried pigeon breast tasted sensational, although at the time I qualified this with a less than gracious: 'Yeah, but anything tastes great if you cover it with toasted sesame seeds.' Yeng Chan, one of the quieter students, from Taiwan, whipped up an impressive roulade of pigeon breast stuffed with a potato and a pea purée that wouldn't have looked out of place on the menu of one of the city's contemporary bistros. Conversely, the notably ill mannered, buck-toothed young Korean, Yim (famed for jumping the queue at the washing-up sink, 'borrowing' other people's equipment and even, on one occasion, stealing my hollandaise when hers split), clearly hadn't a clue what to do. Without her recipe notes to follow she cremated her pigeon and served it alone on the plate but for some boiled peas which she tried repeatedly to corral into shape. I enjoyed the confusion on her round, rabbity face enormously, of course, but fared little better myself. I stood around opening and closing my mouth for twenty minutes trying to think what to do, before eventually producing an unimaginative plate of pigeon breast stuffed with a *duxelle* (finely chopped onion and mushroom, to which, for no better reason that it seemed a waste to throw them in the bin, I added the bird's heart and liver). The breast looked rather lonely sitting on the plate with just a *jus* and some turned vegetables for company.

'There's something else you could do with that,' said Angry Chef, our supervisor that day. I looked at him blankly. 'Slice it and fan it out,' whispered Christine. She was right, it turned something paltry into something almost passable, but it still looked awfully, well, *brown*. As for the foie gras mousse, I had a grand vision of making some kind of foam, my token nod to the advance of molecular gastronomy.

With AC, the self-professed molecular insider supervising, it seemed an excellent opportunity to pick his brains but, after half an hour watching him trying and failing to whisk my mousse into anything more than gloop – a half hour which ended in him nodding sagely and advising me to *reflechir* on what he had shown me – I gave up on that altogether. Back to the drawing board.

It was clear I would have to experiment at home, but I couldn't find any pigeons in my local market, nor at the local butcher. Acting on a tip-off, I eventually found some at the poultry butcher on rue Montorgueil. I bought peas, artichokes and asparagus in the fruit and vegetable shop next door. That left only the unlovely foie gras mousse, which I tracked down at a foie gras specialist nearby. Back home, after several days in which my family grew royally sick of pigeon, I finally settled on a plan of action: I would make a stuffing for the breasts by blending the foie gras mousse, the chicken breast and a pea purée, then hollow out the breasts slightly for the stuffing – a delicate and bloody operation, I discovered – before frying them briefly and then roasting them for a few more minutes. I would serve the breast – sliced and fanned out prettily, as per Christine's instructions – on top of some chopped oyster mushrooms sautéed with cayenne and lemon juice to give them a little zing. The breast and mushrooms would in turn be placed on top of a delicate little *pommes dauphin*, a more refined Swiss rosti (not forgetting to put a blob of pea purée underneath the potato to make sure it all stayed cemented in the middle of the plate – a useful chef's trick that Chalopin had shown me). Around that I would pour a small moat of, hopefully bright green, asparagus purée, then a ring of perfectly turned and glazed carrots and onions and then, beyond that, a deep, yet pleasantly acidic reduction made from the pigeons bones, stock and wine. There weren't enough artichokes to go round, so I decided to slice them thinly on the mandolin and then deep fry them into artichoke chips. As if that didn't give me enough to do, I also planned to *confit* the pigeon legs with juniper, bay and garlic, and place one with the breast on the centre of the *pommes dauphin*.

It was an all or nothing plan involving techniques I had little experience of. I was far from confident that I could pull it off, particularly four plates all exactly the same, on time, but I would go down in flames trying.

Each student was to commence cooking at fifteen-minute intervals scheduled through the morning of May 23. As usual, I would be the first to start at eight in the morning. I arrived at seven forty-five to find Chef Chantefort flushed and rushing around the kitchen getting everything ready. His assistant had failed to show. I reckoned it wouldn't do my chances any harm to offer to help and so, together, we unloaded the dumb waiter and distributed the baskets of ingredients to the work stations.

Each exam group had been told to find a kitchen assistant: usually another student from Basic or Intermediate who was keen to see beyond the veil and find out what went on in the Superior exam. But instead of a Basic or Intermediate student, someone from our group had asked Paul to be our assistant. He turned up a few minutes later. 'But you're not scheduled to do the exam today,' I spluttered. 'No, I did it yesterday. Went really well actually. Couldn't have gone better. Phillipe [another student] asked me to be the assistant, he was our assistant yesterday.'

As an omen, vultures circling above as hooded men sharpened scythes by the ovens would have been preferable. 'Good luck,' said Paul, shaking my hand. It was almost as if he meant it.

I set to work, trying to block out his hovering presence as I removed the wishbone and then the breasts from the pigeons, and carefully cut away the legs for my *confit*, making sure to keep as much of the flesh on them as possible.

'Shall I get the deep fryer ready?' Paul asked.

Was he trying to distract me?

'No, thanks. I'm not going to be using it. But I do need the blender, do you know where it is?'

'Yep, it's over here in the cupboard, I'll set it up for you. Do you need anything else?'

'Urm,' I hesitated. 'Nooo, not right now.'

This was odd. He seemed genuinely to be trying to help, but there must be an ulterior motive. Was he going to rinse the blender with vinegar? I watched him carefully out of the corner of my eye. Nothing seemed amiss. He set up the blender and stood patiently to one side awaiting further instructions.

Max arrived 'fresh', he explained, from his brother's birthday party which had finished at just after six that morning (it was now eight thirty). 'Have you got a spare apron?' he asked. We would also be marked on our presentation during the final exam, so he could drop crucial marks if he was missing his. 'Here, take the key to my locker, there should be one in there,' I said. He took the key, stood swaying for a moment, and staggered back down the stairs to the locker room.

The *confit* was my priority. Even something as small as a pigeon leg still needed to be cured in salt for as long as possible and then cooked, in this case, in duck fat, for a good hour at a low temperature. We had four hours in total to complete our practical, which gave me just about enough time (a duck *confit* needs to be left in the salt overnight). I packed the delicate little legs in salt with a couple of bay leaves and garlic cloves. Paul scurried obligingly to the store cupboard to find me some juniper berries to add to the mix.

I shelled and boiled the fresh peas in salted water, puréed them, then pushed the purée through a drum sieve to make sure it was smooth, and mixed it with the foie gras mousse, finely diced, blanched lemon zest and shredded basil to make my stuffing. Meanwhile, I chopped up my pigeon carcasses and fried them to get some good brownings in the pan; degreased the pan; added a *mirepoix* of onions, garlic, carrot and shallots, cooked them a little, and then deglazed with cognac, before adding white wine, red wine, chicken stock and veal stock, and reducing.

I boiled the asparagus and, keeping the tips to one side for decoration, blended the rest of the stalks with a little cream, lemon juice, salt and pepper to make another purée which I kept warm in a bowl, covered with plastic wrap, over a bain-marie. Because purées kept warm in this way often start to congeal and thicken, I kept some of the cooking water – now a pale green and rich in asparagus flavour – to one side to thin it later if necessary. With my vegetables turned and now cooking things seemed to be going well. But there were still the oyster mushrooms to chop and sauté, and I had already forgotten something.

'What are these for?' asked Paul, picking up a couple of the potatoes I had set aside.

I had completely forgotten about the *pommes dauphin*.

I thanked him, peeled and grated the potatoes, then squeezed all the water I could from them by pressing them into a *chinois* with a ladle, and began frying them in clarified butter in the ring moulds which I had placed in the pan. But the first one started to burn and, when I removed it from the ring mould, it fell apart. I began to hyperventilate.

'Lower temperature, less oil, mix some potato flour in with the potato,' Paul whispered out of the corner of his mouth. I threw my first attempt in the bin, emptied some of the oil into my waste bowl on the countertop where it hissed with the potato peelings, and had another attempt at a lower heat with a teaspoon of potato flour mixed in as he had advised. Miraculously, the potato held together and browned perfectly into crispy cakes.

Having experimented with frying artichoke chips at home, I had decided that it was safer to fry them in a pan on the hob than risk them the fierce deep fryer – fry them for a second or two too long and, even if they didn't look too brown, they will have turned bitter. To guard their fragrant, artichokey flavour, they needed to be a pale, golden colour, and only just crisp. And that is just how they turned out. Things were looking up.

The next hour flashed by. It was time to plate. Hayden, who had done the exam the previous day, warned me to allow at least twenty minutes for this and he was right, it took ages. This was ample time, of course, for most of the food to go cold and congeal but, never mind; at least it made it all onto the plate, which was more than could be said for my previous exams. As I looked up from fussing over my final plate I saw Paul gently wiping the rim of each of them with a damp cloth to clear any sauce spills as if they were his very own. He placed them carefully on a tray to carry them up to the judging panel on the third floor. As he left the kitchen I let out a deep sigh of relief, tempered only by the lingering suspicion that he might yet sprinkle a pound of salt over my plates, and began to clear up. By now the kitchen was full with ten other students all rushing to finish their dishes, which made me feel all the more satisfied to be done. I took my pots down to the *plongeur* at the other end of the kitchen and started to tidy up.

I picked up some waste kitchen paper I'd left next to my chopping board. Something crunched. I unfolded the paper. MY ARTICHOKE CHIPS! I had left them to drain on the paper after I had taken them out of the oil, but forgotten to remove them. I grabbed them, stood for a moment torn between my natural instinct, which was to give up and resign myself to failure, or to fight to the death for my honour and ego. They were a compulsory ingredient. If they weren't on the plate, I would fail. I made a rush for the door and launched myself up the stairs, three at a time, scattering a half dozen Basic Patisserie students who were on their way down. I burst into the third floor conference room, but it was empty. Damn! They must be on the first floor. Down two flights of stairs I went, bowling through the patisserie students once again. I burst into the judging room – the first-floor patisserie demonstration room – passing Paul. He was on his way out but turned with some alarm to see me. '*I forgot the fucking artichokes,*' I hissed.

I turned to face the judges, three former Cordon Bleu chefs, now retired, each as grey haired and ancient as Methuselah, seated round a small dining table. Chef Chantefort stood behind them looking at a clipboard. Not one of them looked up as I swooped in and dumped a small fistful of artichoke chips on their plates, apologised, and hurried out backwards, nodding as though taking leave from a royal audience.

And that was it. My nine months at Le Cordon Bleu was over. I gathered all the equipment and clothing in my locker, went for a beer with some of the other students in the bar around the corner, and caught the Metro across the river and home to Lissen.

'So, that's it then. How does it feel now it's all over?' she asked me as I unpacked my blood-, sauce-, asparagus- and oil-stained uniform and knife kit in the hallway. Amid all the stress and tension of the exam preparation and the exam itself, it hadn't really occurred to me that I would not be returning to the school again. I would never see Didier's levitating ladle again, never feel that tingle of excitement when walking into the practical kitchen to cook, and never again have a Korean steal my pastry brush and not even bother to wash it. Though I planned to keep in touch with the friends I had made at the school, many of them were flying off almost immediately to their homelands and I would never see them again. I gulped, took a couple of deep breaths, and tried my best not to cry.

The Superior graduation would be as much a chance to say a final goodbye to old friends, to reminisce about the last nine months as to receive prizes and awards and partake of all that silly nonsense that no one really worries about. And, no, as you can probably guess, I did not, in the end, finish my time at Le Cordon Bleu on a high note. I came third. This was both devastating and remarkably fortunate bearing in mind my mid-term results – which placed me somewhere around twentieth – not to mention the four stone-cold plates of pigeon breast with their belated artichoke chips that I served up in the exam. Paul came second (a talented Israeli student came first) and he thoroughly deserved it. I congratulated him after the ceremony, which was held, as with the Intermediate graduation, in the gilded ball room of Monsieur Cointreau's private club on the rue Fabourg Saint-Honoré. He accepted my congratulations with an uncharacteristic humility. It seemed as if a weight had been lifted from his shoulders. We all said our farewells over champagne and canapés in the upstairs reception rooms overlooking the club's gardens with the Eiffel Tower sparkling in the distance.

Chapter 32

In this furnace, everyone acts promptly, not a breath is heard; the chef alone has the right to make himself heard, and everyone obeys his voice.

Antonin Carême

If we discount the self-mutilation, some never-fully-resolved seasoning issues, and the time I wore my trousers back to front, my time at Le Cordon Bleu had been one of the most joyous periods of my life. Spending nine months with like-minded, orally-fixated gluttons from around the world thinking, talking, arguing about and making food, had been a blast. I learned more at the school than all the cookery books in the world could have ever taught me, and by the end of the course I had achieved one of my two main goals. I could now walk through my local market, buy whatever was in season, on special offer or that just caught my eye, return home and create a coherent, harmonious meal without recourse to Delia, Jamie or Nigella.

I knew how to fillet fish; how to de-bone, prepare and truss any joint of meat that was thrown at me; what made a good marinade; when to use olive oil and sea salt, and when to use peanut oil and fine salt. I could win a fight with an artichoke; had learned to love offal; could spot a ripe camembert at thirty paces; and look a mullet in the eye and tell how long ago it had been caught. I knew how to maximise the yield from a lobster; open an oyster without giving myself stigmata; and what to do when an emulsion wouldn't emulsify (a quick blast with an immersion blender usually does the trick). I had cooked with blood, feet, intestines and the thymus glands of a young cow. I had committed unspeakable acts upon crustaceans, and cooked a Trafalgar Square's worth of pigeons. I had become privy to the mysteries of the *macaron* and the soufflé; learned how to make a truly transcendental veal stock; and I knew for sure that chocolate and strawberries don't go together. It had been the best of times, but it would lead promptly to the worst of times.

The omens prior to starting my internship, or *stage,* weren't great. The July break between graduation and my first day at L'Atelier Joël Robuchon, where I would be doing my work experience, seemed a good time to assess the physical toll of a prolonged proximity to classical French cooking. A cholesterol check produced figures that would not have looked out of place on Elvis' post-mortem report, figures that required immediate action. Cutting down my cake intake was one option, but I took the more challenging prescription medicine route. I try to avoid weighing scales because they are invariably fattening, but in the light of the cholesterol figures, I could avoid them no longer. More records tumbled. I was on a roll and, there were unfamiliar rolls on me too.

Chef Braun, head chef at L'Atelier, had told me that they would provide me with one of the restaurant's distinctive, black-with-red-piping chef's jackets – like a ninja warrior's I had thought when I first dined there – and a matching apron, but I would have to supply the black trousers myself. So I braved the apocalyptic inhumanity of the rue de Rivoli one hot Saturday in July to reach the Gap where I began to rifle the pile of black trousers for my usual size, a thirty-two-inch waist. An attractive female assistant came to help.

'You want what size, *monsieur?*'

'I'm trying to find a thirty-two, can you see one?'

She stood back and pulled a sceptical face, 'A thirty-two? I don't think so, *monsieur.* A thirty-four perhaps?'

'No, I take a thirty-two. Ah, found one!'

I tried the trousers on in the changing room, but could only pull them up as far as my knees. I returned to the rack where the assistant was waiting, eyebrows raised.

'Actually, I think you were right, ha, ha! I do need a thirty-four.'

'Or perhaps a thirty-six,' she said.

She was right. Oh, the shame. I left with two pairs of thirty-six-inch waist, black cotton trousers, the second to largest size in the shop. My humiliation was compounded by the fact that, it turned out, I had a thirty-inch inside leg, not a thirty-two. As a teenager one of my sartorial idols had been Don *'Miami Vice'* Johnson, but I had instead turned into Don *'It Ain't Half Hot Mum'* Estelle. I trudged home, walking all the way up the Champs-Elysées in an effort to shrug off some of my new, wobbly cladding. To heap injury upon insult, that night I burned my stomach with the iron while ironing without a shirt on. I was fatter, heavier and more unhealthy than I had ever been. So much for the French paradox, I thought to myself as I cooled my singed tummy with an ice cube. I suppose that if you are born to eat animal fat by the kilo and guzzle wine then your DNA has had centuries to adapt accordingly, hence the relatively low incidence of heart disease in rural France compared to the UK and USA. But if, like me, you are cursed with a finely-honed athlete's physique, well, beware the third helpings of cassoulet and crème brûlée.

The next morning, the first Friday in August, I left for my first day's work in a real restaurant; not only that, but a Michelin-starred restaurant with perhaps the most revered name in French cooking above the door.

I gave up all interest in participatory sport when I turned thirty and realised that, not only was the Olympic 400m gold I had long considered my destiny looking less likely, but that I would probably struggle to complete the distance on a bicycle. Up until then it had been a recurring fantasy of mine, as it is for most men, to imagine playing football for England – not as a skilled player who merited being there, you understand, but just as myself, with my limited ability. Friends and I would consider this scenario up the pub. 'How long do you think you could last without the crowd noticing you were an amateur?' someone would ask. 'If I could just keep running around, waving and shouting, I reckon I could probably see out a good eight minutes, ten if we were playing San Marino,' I claimed. Well, I was about to live out the culinary version of this fantasy. How long would it take the chefs of L'Atelier to figure out that I was an absolute beginner and begin to barrack? Eight minutes? Quite possibly.

I walked to the George V Metro station, took the train, changed at Concorde and walked from the Rue du Bac station (the great chef, Antonin Carême, was born somewhere near here – surely a good omen, I thought) to L'Atelier, my heart throbbing with nervous anxiety. I had never so much as set foot inside a real restaurant kitchen before and had little idea of what lay in store; my notions of restaurant life had been formed entirely from what I had seen on television and the movies. How well had Le Cordon Bleu prepared me for the real world of life in a top-level professional kitchen? I was about to find out.

I had dreamed about this moment for years, often imagining myself as a chef at home, creating little 'under pressure' narratives in my head as I chopped and fried. A large party of international gourmets has just arrived at the same time as Michael Winner and the Michelin inspector who has heard tell of a miraculous young cook working alone in a tiny local bistro, but I have run out of lamb, the waitress just dropped five plates and I'm down to just two hobs as the other two have broken. My reputation is on the line but, somehow, using just the store-cupboard ingredients I have to hand, and my own crazy genius, I manage to create a meal of such majesty and originality that it prompts joyous weeping – hysteria really – from the dining room. The waitress whispers that words like 'sublime' and 'unprecedented' are being bandied. They are discussing my cooking in terms of a whole new food movement, and begging me to whip up just one more fruit salad. Michael Winner sends a large suitcase filled with money round to the kitchen with a signed photograph and a note begging me to become his personal chef. After the meal all the diners come and thank me personally; the mood is reverent, as if I am granting an audience. The Michelin man awards me three stars, on the spot, in perpetuity. The gourmets invite me to oversee a new chain of restaurants in my name, and Michael Winner promises to introduce me to Roger Moore.

You will understand, then, that for me to be setting foot behind the scenes of a famous Paris restaurant was fantasy fulfilment enough in itself, but to be entering it with an apron, ready to participate in however insignificant a manner in the preparation of food that people would be paying good money to eat, would have been beyond imagining a year earlier.

It was almost a year ago that Lissen and I had eaten at L'Atelier and been entranced by the clarity and simplicity of its food and the theatricality of its open kitchen where the chefs worked within fat-spitting distance of the diners. At the time I had wondered aloud what it would be like to cook there in front of the diners in the open kitchen, as a core of the restaurant's chefs do during lunch and dinner service. Of course, I knew full well that elsewhere, probably in cramped, windowless rooms, dozens of other kitchen staff toiled to provide the front kitchen with the ingredients to create the dishes, and that would be where I would work for the duration of my *stage*. The chefs that the diners see preparing food front of house at L'Atelier are plucked from the highest echelon of the kitchen staff following years of experience and training. That night they had looked assured, calm and in control; masters of their métier.

Little did I know as I walked from the Metro station to the restaurant that morning, that within four hours of walking through the front door, I would be right there, in the front of the restaurant, myself, working alongside those chefs for all to see.

Walking through the front door was wrong for starters. The waiter who greeted me, still at that time of day dressed in his civilian clothes, rolled his eyes.

'Never use that door. There's a side door for staff,' he said. 'You want Chef Braun? He is in New York. Follow me'. If you remember the opening scene of *Goodfellas*, with that long, single take following

273

Ray Liotta through endless corridors and kitchens to reach his seat in the restaurant, imagine that in reverse and you are with me as I follow the waiter from the seating area, through the snazzy, low lit, open kitchen, with its frictionless black surfaces, hocks of Iberian ham hanging from the ceiling and glass shelves full with bottles of olives, garlic and red peppers. We pass a machine called a Nappy Jet; to this day, I do not know what it does. He prods a rubber foot button (like the brake pedal in a Citroen DS, for lack of a more broadly recognisable comparison) and the swing doors that lead to the backstage kitchens open electronically. More corridors. Faces glancing up, blankly, from chopping boards and sinks. I smile self-consciously as we bustle by.

We climb some stairs; a man in an office looks me up and down as if assessing livestock, picks up a file containing *stage* applications, cannot find mine, but doesn't seem too bothered. He throws a new uniform, still in its plastic wrapper, at me and the waiter leads me back down the stairs, past the washer-uppers, and through the heady aromas of the patisserie station where the chefs are primping a row of fruit tartlets that look more like jewellery than food. We come to the *viande*, or meat station.

The baton is passed here to Guillaume, a short, anxious-looking chef with close-cropped ginger hair and a tentative smile. He intro-duces me to six people working in a space no bigger than the in-terior of a camper van in rapid succession. 'Follow me,' he says, and I do, along more corridors, down more stairs and into the basement. All is impeccably clean and harshly lit. One after the other I am introduced to half a dozen walk-in fridges, though by this point I have little hope of recalling anything beyond basic autobiographical facts.

I am shown to a changing room, smaller even than the one at Le Cordon Bleu and, as its floor is covered with shoes and bags and clothes, clearly even more oversubscribed. 'No lockers I'm afraid,' says Guillaume. 'It's a bordello in here. Just see if you can find a spot to change.' He leaves me, which gives me a moment to gather myself, but also means that I now have no way of finding my way back to the meat kitchen. Eventually, having revisited most of the rooms, fridges, storage cupboards and kitchens that Guillaume has previously shown me, I find my way to the *viande* kitchen again.

'Where do you want to work?' he asks me. Stupidly, I hadn't given this any thought. I had assumed I would be told where to go. Before I have time to answer there is some mumbling and a consensus reached: 'For god's sake, don't let him work in here,' and I am bundled off to the *garde manger* next door.

They don't seem especially pleased to see me here either. The *garde manger* is where they prep the cold dishes, garnishes and some of the vegetable accompaniments for the main courses. It is a cramped, scalene triangle-shaped space lined on two sides with steel-topped work surfaces. Beneath the work surface on the left are three small fridges and one blast freezer, with a shelf above head height filled with plates and a large metal sink at the far end. Above the shorter, right-hand counter is a cupboard filled with wines, oils, dried herbs and other dry goods, and various machinery – a pasta roller, meat grinder, blender and mixer stored on a low shelf below the counter. The third wall, facing me as I enter, is taken up with a waist-high rubbish bin, a small hand basin, and shelving filled, mostly, with a giant meat slicer and what looks like a heavy duty photocopier.

As I am being introduced to the four people already crammed into this kitchen, a fifth enters with a see-through plastic bag filled with langoustines, opens the photocopier, places the bag inside it and presses a button. Its lid closes automatically, and it makes a sound like a submarine. Finally, it hisses and groans and the lid pops open. The langoustines are now vacuum packed. This is the *sous vide* – without air – machine. I have never seen one before and am strangely drawn to it.

Sous vide is one of the most fiercely guarded secrets of the restaurant kitchen. L'Atelier doesn't actually cook anything in vacuum packing, it only uses it for storage, but many restaurants do. Very gently simmering tough cuts of meat in the bags with herbs and seasoning creates intense flavours and unsurpassed tenderness; you can monitor and control the cooking better; the flavourings penetrate the meat better; and you can maintain a consistency when cooking the same dish for large numbers of people. The only real problem is that another name for this process is 'Boil in the Bag', with its troubling echoes of seventies cod in parsley sauce; people still think it sounds like a bit of a cheat. They would be surprised by how many restaurants use it.

The *garde manger* chef, a stony-faced Spaniard called Carlos, hands me a deep-sided metal tray filled with tomatoes and orders me to start chopping. A younger, taller French *commis chef* called Xavier, shows me how this is to be done – the tomatoes have already been blanched, so the skins fall off. I am to quarter them, scoop out the seeds, and dice them, exactly as we used to do at school (he even puts some soggy kitchen paper under the chopping board to stop it moving about, just as Chef Bruno had shown us all those months ago). This I can do, and for half an hour or so I am left alone to digest all I have seen so far.

I had squeezed in between two other cooks, a young Russian man called Yuri, and a young Korean woman called Ick Yong. Yuri is twenty-five, and from Moscow. He explains that the tomatoes I am chopping are to be served, very simply, on toast, seasoned and drizzled with some basil oil. Yuri claims to own a restaurant in Moscow, which seems improbable given his youth, although he later tells me that his father is an 'entrepreneur' which, I suppose, in Russia can mean anything. Yuri is also a *stagière*, in the middle of a course at another cooking school, where he will return to complete exams in September. He has been at L'Atelier for a month. He has a girlfriend and they are going to get married next year. As he tells me this he blushes from his neck up to his cheeks.

Ick Yong is the same age, but a paid *commis chef*. She also came here on work experience from Le Cordon Bleu, over a year ago. We reminisce – as much as two people with only very bad French between them can – about the chefs. 'Chalopin was here last week,' she tells me, and wrinkles her nose.

After I have finished with the tomatoes, asparagus, salad leaves and pigs' ears appear in front of me in quick succession for preparation. I have never handled a pig's ear before. Ick Yong shows me how to part the rubbery flesh from a triangle of cartilage within as if putting the ear on as a glove, and then rip the two apart. After I dice this porky latex, it is mixed with pre-packaged, shredded pig's foot; a quantity of *rillettes* (a fatty, shredded pork paste); mushrooms diced to the same dimensions as the ear; herbs; mustard; and seasoning, then made into quenelles, which I am shown how to form in the palms of my hands, before placing on a slender, ovoid crouton made by slicing the previous day's baguettes on the diagonal. When ordered, it is sprinkled with parmesan and toasted *à la minute*. It was another surprisingly straightforward dish, more an assembly of ingredients really, but I got to taste it later that day and it was meatily satisfying (though, obviously, not exactly what the doctor had ordered for me in terms of animal fat content).

Twice within three hours Carlos sticks his head around the corner of the kitchen wall and tells us to clean. The first time I begin to wipe down my work surface with a cloth. '*Non, non,*' said Xavier. '*Comme ça.*' He begins to clear every surface in the room; takes a bucket from under the sink and douses the entire kitchen, tiles, fridge doors and all, with soapy water. He then dries it off with one of those rubber scrapers window washers use, squirts it all again with disinfectant, and wipes that off. Yuri enters with a hose and washes the floor down, after which Ick Yong wipes it dry with a larger version of the rubber scraper. 'We do this between three and five times a day,' Yuri sighs. 'Depending on how many people are working here.'

As we are drying off the surfaces with paper towels the Chef de Cuisine, Eric Lecerf, walks past. '*Bonjour,*' he grunts, without looking at us. '*Bonjour, chef!*' everyone trills in reply. Lecerf has been Robuchon's right-hand man for years and is something of a legend on the Parisian restaurant scene. He is short and thick set, with a bulging stomach. He looks like a retired boxer.

The morning passes in a blur, but I am enjoying myself. I even make a reasonable fist of preparing some artichokes. And then Ick Yong asks me to make some mayonnaise: my first real challenge. I panic for a second, trying to recall the recipe but getting it confused with hollandaise. Ick Yong rattles off the ingredients in her garbled French accent: four egg yolks, 80g of mustard, 8g of salt, a bottle of oil and some Jerez sherry vinegar (in accordance with the Spanish influence of the food at L'Atelier). As she does this, she traces the outline of the relevant figures slowly with her finger on the counter top as if talking to a pre-schooler. I try to memorise the quantities but, as I leave to find the ingredients – an exercise which, of course, is doomed from the start as I have no idea where any of them are – the figures become jumbled so that, after ten minutes asking people where I can find eggs, mustard and weighing scales and so on, I return with eight eggs and measure 40g of salt. Off again, but upon returning to the kitchen there is no Ick Yong – the kitchen is empty. I wait for a few minutes. 'Come on, Michael, how difficult can this be?' I think to myself. 'You know how to make mayonnaise!' Having found a whisk and a bowl, I begin mixing the yolks, mustard and salt, then slowly trickling in the oil. As the oil emulsifies with the eggs the mixture stiffens, which is how it should be, except that the sheer scale of the operation means that my biceps just aren't up to the job of mixing it by hand.

Ick Yong returns. 'Oh, no! You should use the machine! We never do this by hand!' She might have told me, but I brush her concerns aside although by now I am huffing heavily as the mixture stiffens further. 'No, don't worry; you don't need a machine for this.' And I continue to churn, ever more slowly. After some considerable strain, the mayonnaise turns out fine, and I am enormously proud. I have made mayonnaise for Joël Robuchon.

I have little time to reflect on this achievement. It is midday, time for the lunch service. The other *commis chefs* begin to make their way through the electric swing doors into the show kitchen to start making lunch in front of the guests. Carlos turns and beckons me to follow. I look around, assuming he is signalling to someone else. He isn't.

Chapter 33

We perceived that we were not splendid inhabitants of a splendid world, but a crew of underpaid workmen grown squalidly and dismally drunk.

George Orwell on life in a Paris kitchen
Down and Out in Paris and London

Imagine you have been hanging round the back stage door of a West End musical hoping to get Elaine Paige's autograph. You take a few steps into the theatre to try and catch a glimpse of the world beyond but, suddenly, the stage manager hauls you backstage. A team of dressers envelop you with a Velcro-fixed costume, the lights go down, the curtain goes up and you find yourself thrust in front of a hushed, expectant audience. The orchestra starts up, your fellow cast begin singing and dancing but you don't know the lyrics, the tunes or the moves. You look around in a blind panic and try to follow what they are doing, but you keep bumping into them; you are constantly out of step, yet you can't get off the stage. Every time you try to leave, someone pushes you back on. The music never stops. You flounder, humiliated. The audience is casting confused glances, but there is no escape.

It is the stuff of nightmares, but it was about to become my reality.

The first customers, Japanese and American tourists, start to arrive, finding their places and settling in with an air of nervous, hushed anticipation. The low chatter and soft chinking of glasses wafts our way; the waiters take on their roles like actors; the chefs have lowered their voices. 'The most important thing is to listen carefully,' Carlos says. I nod, though I have no idea what he means. 'Welcome to Disneyland,' he adds.

Within a few minutes, Chef Lecerf, acting as expediter, checking each plate before the waiters take them from the pass to the customers, begins to call out the orders in a voice so soft that it is, to me, virtually inaudible. This is what Carlos meant by listening carefully.

Ick Yong, Carlos and Xavier begin to scuttle around, retrieving ingredients from the fridges around us, sprinkling seasonings, dressings, garnishes and herbs onto plates. Xavier pulls me over to a corner and shows me how to place the tomatoes I had chopped earlier on some toast, season them and drizzle it all with basil oil. He instructs me to put it on the pass, pluck a couple of the smallest leaves from the basil plant that grows there and place them in the centre of the toast. This seems simple enough, except the next time he asks me to do it, I have to prepare the toast as well. Suddenly, making toast is the most challenging task I have ever undertaken. I am to use a clamshell toaster. You need to keep an eye on it as there is no automatic function and, of course, I burn my first piece to a cinder. As I am contemplating this catastrophe, Carlos asks me to help him plate a sardine *amuse bouche*.

I shoot him a panicked look with accompanying upturned hands, as if to say 'I have no idea how to do that, I don't even know what that is!' More eye rolling. He shows me how to squirt two lines of yellow dressing on the plate like railway tracks, place a slither of toast between the tracks, squirt another line of sauce onto that, place a sardine fillet on top, season it with pepper, toss some rocket in a small bowl with some oil — I don't see which of the five different squeezy bottles he uses for this — place a little on top of the fillet, then take a plastic tub from one of the fridge drawers and from it remove two finely sliced, raw white onion rings. He places each, delicately balanced, on top of the rocket. This is one of the simpler dishes. There are about eight others, which though still just assembly jobs, involve a greater number of ingredients sourced from a variety of fridges, all of which have to be added in the right order. It soon becomes apparent that I am expected to learn how to plate all of the starters by some kind of kitchen osmosis; no one has the time or inclination to explain anything. It isn't so much a steep learning curve as a vertical learning ladder, and I am struggling to get my foot beyond the first rung.

Lecerf calls out more orders, for gazpacho; lobster carpaccio; tuna carpaccio; foie gras, a roasted vegetable stack with pesto dressing; and steak tartar, each of them involving another six or so components, and each of them required NOW.

I am trying to keep pace with these, watching the other chefs preparing them out of the corner of my eye as I work to assemble a gazpacho. I have just seen Xavier prepare one and reckon I can manage it. Having poured the cold soup from a teapot stored, I noted, in the bottom of the middle fridge, Xavier had drizzled olive oil from a squeezy bottle and balsamic vinegar from a paper cone in a delicate zigzag pattern over the surface of the cold soup. It looked easy, but my attempt ends with something that looks like the squiggly mess my printer sometimes makes when the ink cartridge knows I am in a hurry. But the orders keep coming and I place it on the pass. I lick my finger where I had caught the drip of gazpacho from the teapot, and Carlos catches me. He shakes his head and waggles a finger. 'Don't do that, the customers can see,' he hisses.

The foie gras is easy enough, just a slice from a roll of terrine, served with toast; but with other dishes there is an inordinate amount of plate wiping, particularly the tuna carpaccio – thin rounds of tuna prepared by the *poissonier* in the basement and laid out in a circle on the plate. When an order comes in we have to run out to the back kitchen, take a plate from the fridge, remove its plastic wrap and then set about assembling the dish. First, you have to sprinkle the tuna with poppy seeds – but they need to be distributed perfectly or you risked having Carlos huff, shove you aside and take over. You grind some fine ground pink pepper over it; crumble some Szechwan pepper over with your hand; sprinkle finely chopped chives; and then cut some fresh cress and added that to the top. Next, you douse the tuna with basil oil and then, and only then, do you add some sea salt ('If you add the salt too early, it will start to cook the tuna,' Xavier had told me). Oh, and don't forget the few drops of soy sauce, sprinkled from a fork dipped in a pot of soy sauce to finish.

The trouble was that within a minute or so you dousing the tuna with olive oil, it would ooze beyond the perimeter of the tuna and spread over the rest of the plate. It would then have to be meticulously wiped off, which was awkward, messy and time-consuming. I decide to try a different approach, and just douse the centre of the tuna so that, by the time the waiter comes to collect the plate it will have oozed towards the edge of the carpaccio. But Xavier intervenes. '*Non, non*. Not like that, cover all of it.' He takes the bottle from me, and squeezes more oil over the tuna. Within a minute it has flooded the plate and I have to wipe it down two more times before the waiter comes to take it.

About halfway through the lunch service, frazzled and humiliated, I simply stand back, as close to the wall as I can get, wishing myself invisible. I decide to just watch and learn for the rest of service. My eyes soon glaze over and I find myself staring, hypnotised, at the suckling pig turning on its spit in pride of place in the centre of the kitchen. Chef Lecerf spots me and marches over. Carlos sees him coming. 'Stop leaning on the wall!' he hisses.

'Do you want to work in this kitchen, or what?' Lecerf barks. Some of the diners look up, sensing some juicy chef tantrum action. I open and close my mouth searching for something to say, desperate to explain that I would love to help, but no one has actually told me how to do any of this. But he has already stormed back to his station. I try to busy myself wiping down the work surface with a cloth.

At one point, I come within a heartbeat of throwing down my apron and walking out on my very first day. Carlos has barked something in French in his thick Spanish accent at me. I ask him to repeat. He rolls his eyes and sighs. He repeats his command. But I still don't hear. He storms round to my side of the work station and snatches the pepper grinder that I was clutching in my hands and returns to his place on the work station. A few moments later, he yells something else. Again I don't understand. He stares hard at me, his eyes popping, his lips thin with fury. In broken English: 'A whisk, get me a whisk!'

I stammer, '*Oui*, chef!' and flee the front kitchen. Once on the other side of the doors, however, I realise I have no idea where they keep the whisks. Having looked for a good five minutes I feel a rush of air as Carlos barges past me on his way to the patisserie kitchen. He returns brandishing a whisk, for all to see, as if it were the Olympic torch.

By three o'clock the tidal wave of orders has subsided, and by three-thirty it is all over with just a couple of diners scraping the last remnants of their gorgeous desserts from the bowls. We start to tidy up, then wash down the *garde manger* kitchen for the fourth time that day. Suddenly everyone disappears again and I am left alone in the kitchen. After a few minutes they reappear with plates full of chips and burgers and fried eggs. It is three thirty: time to eat.

At four o'clock the staff begin to head for the changing rooms. It seems we are to have a break, the first since eight that morning. Yuri tells me we have an hour. 'Guard your apron,' he says as he sees me untying mine. 'Or someone'll take it.' I leave by the side door and wander away from the restaurant, vaguely trying to find somewhere to sit down for a while. I reach the river, walk down the steps to the quayside, and sit on the bottom step, looking up at the tourists on the Pont Royal above me.

I look down at my hands. My fingertips are already a mesh of tiny scars from the sharp armour of the lobsters I shelled earlier. The index finger of my right hand has two bulging blisters, from where it has rested on my knife. My back aches from its base to my neck. My feet throb. I feel old.

'But wait a second,' I suddenly realise, 'you have just prepared Michelin-star food in the name of the greatest chef of the twentieth century!' In the adrenalin frenzy of the service I hadn't had time to stop and consider the enormity of this. I have achieved my goal. I haul myself up, and return to the restaurant, if not exactly re-energised, then a little more positive.

Back in the restaurant we start to prepare for the evening service, Yuri is hosing down the kitchen floor once again. Suddenly finding himself the senior *stagière*, he has begun to allocate himself the fun jobs and offload the less desirable ones on me. Carlos has given him a ten-litre tub of tomatoes with some hunks of bread and peeled garlic cloves mixed in. Yuri immediately passes it to me.

'Gazpacho,' he says. 'You need to blend it then strain it.' It is a messy, tedious job. At first I over-fill the blender and the gazpacho seeps down the sides of the machine and over work surface. Next, I pummel away like a navvy for almost an hour pushing the blended mix through the *chinois* with a ladle, managing to redecorate both the walls and my uniform. By the end I look like I've taken part in that Spanish festival where everyone gets drunk and throws tomatoes at each other.

Though it is a mess to make, it is instructive to see what goes into a Robuchon gazpacho, or rather, what doesn't go into it. Simplicity is an essential element of his approach to food, his pared down approach is admirable in many ways and very contemporary. But it was almost a let down to learn just how easy it is to assemble his dishes once you knew the formula. Robuchon's gazpacho was reduced to the absolute basics, for instance. Gazpacho nearly always contains cucumber as well as tomato, and it is transformed if you add, say, strawberries. At L'Arpege, a three-star Parisian restaurant renowned for its fruit and vegetable dishes, I tried one with a quenelle of wholegrain mustard ice cream in the centre. Gordon Ramsay puts onion, red pepper, Worcestershire sauce, blanched almonds, Tabasco and lemon juice in his, and then serves it with a tomato sorbet. You could say this is over-gilding the lily, but, personally, part of the reason I love to eat out is to be shown something new, to try something I can't just make at home with half an hour and a blender.

The irony wasn't lost on me as I blended a mountain of marinated tomatoes, that, having gone to all these lengths to escape the tyranny of the TV chef, I had found myself working in a restaurant owned by France's most famous TV chef (host of the long running *Bon Appetit, Bien Sûr*), whose menu – with its Mediterranean ingredients cooked without fuss, or butter, or time-consuming, cream-based sauces – had, dare I say it, a hint of Jamie Oliver about it.

By six it is time for the evening service and the atmosphere changes once again to one of palpable, pre-fight tension. This is a Friday night – along with Saturday, the busiest of the week. The restaurant will usually serve two sittings of forty-two diners. It feels as if we are preparing for a siege as we ready plates with garnishes and lay them out on the shelves in the back kitchen, repeatedly checking and double checking our *mise en place* (the ingredients pre-prepared before the service).

This time I know what to expect, which only serves to heighten my anxiety and, once again, I rapidly find myself confused and helpless. 'Come on, Michel,' Carlos berates me. 'If you are a *stagière* you have to work hard, to prove yourself. Accelerate!' Finally, after an hour or so of burned toast, dropped tomatoes, clumsy saucing and ingredient mix-ups, Carlos, like a referee sensing a punchy boxer, sends me out to the back room to pick chervil leaves from their stalks.

I leave later that night, catch the Metro in completely the wrong direction, and finally get home after midnight.

I had lived the ultimate foodie fantasy for one day but somewhere, not so very deep down, I already knew that a restaurant kitchen – at least this one – was not the place for me.

Chaper 34

Any chef who says he does it for love is a liar.

Marco Pierre White

One of the chefs at Le Cordon Bleu had warned that Robuchon was 'a slave driver', whispering this as if afraid, despite many years having passed since he worked for him, that a Robuchon spy might still overhear. Even so I hadn't expected the atmosphere backstage at L'Atelier to be quite as toxic as it was. This was particularly the case in the *garde manger* where the boss, Carlos, who was in his late twenties and had worked in top hotel kitchens in London, was clearly resentful at being stuck on one of the lower rungs on the kitchen ladder.

I went with him into the *viande* kitchen the next morning, a Saturday, as, following his now customary weary sigh, pause, eye-roll and tut, he showed me for the umpteenth time where to find a sieve. There, his eye rested upon a pile of veal sweetbreads the chef was preparing: 'You're soaking them first, no?' asked Carlos. Guillaume shook his head. 'I always soak them, in milk,' said Carlos, implying Guillaume was wrong (and he *was* wrong, you should soak sweetbreads, preferably in milk, for some hours, before cooking them because it keeps them nice and white and removes some impurities). Carlos clearly felt that he could do better.

So, on the one hand, there was Carlos fed up with his lowly rank, and clearly able to do more. He seemed remote and jaded; long periods of testy silence were broken with the odd eruption at one of the *commis chefs* or *stagières* who neglected to do things precisely according to the Carlos technique. On the other hand was Xavier who, though he had only been in the restaurant for a couple of months and was a *stagière* like me, also thought that he should be working at a higher level in the kitchen, perhaps doing Carlos' job. Over the rest of my first three-day shift, I witnessed several altercations between the two, most of them prompted by Carlos criticising Xavier's work.

The first came halfway through that Saturday morning, and I was caught in the crossfire:

'Those croutons are too thin,' said, Carlos, waving one angrily at Xavier. I told Carlos that I had cut them, not Xavier.

'Yes, but he was responsible,' he said, pointing to Xavier.

'But when you put them in the toaster they get thinner,' replied Xavier, showing Carlos some finished examples. Xavier was right, Carlos could hardly deny the evidence, so just rolled his eyes and stormed off.

Xavier was just one of many *stagières* from various culinary schools in Paris already working at L'Atelier, all in their early twenties. Their superior stamina and drone-like willingness to tackle the most mind-numbing of tasks – picking individual leaves from bushes of chervil; washing salad leaves one by one; squeezing the pips from tomatoes – seriously cramped my prospects of advancing higher in this particular kitchen brigade.

Many of the staff started work at eight in the morning and often didn't finish until two the next morning hence the Atelier 'look', which was baggy eyed, pasty faced, and spotty. By the end of my first three-day shift on Sunday night I was struggling to stay upright and counting the minutes until the end of the last service. We had stopped only for the one hour break at four in the afternoon, which I had passed dozing on a bench in front of a bust of Chateaubriand in the small park on the rue du Bac.

At around eight o'clock in the evening I looked up from my work at the cooks around me. They were the living dead, their bloodshot eyes bulging, backs bowed, shoulders drooping. I was struggling to understand why they were putting themselves through this.

'You make it sound like they're either masochistic psychopaths, or too stupid to work anywhere else,' Lissen had said after I had described my new colleagues to her that night. Of course there were people I had met there who were never going to trouble the Sorbonne, as well as some with an impressive portfolio of personality disorders, but there were others who spoke several languages and who, when they had a spare moment, were friendly and kind. They were also highly skilled of course. I loved watching the Korean *viande* chef, Yon (another Cordon Bleu graduate), sizzling meats on the hot plate in the front kitchen, assessing how well they were cooked with a gentle prod of her spatula, and quickly flipping them with the grace of an expert circus performer. This was hot, uncomfortable work; the meats would spit and hiss at her, as would the *chef de partie* Lecerf, who stood right in front of her. Yon's judgement had to be infallible.

I had already encountered if not his wrath, then at least Lecerf's passive displeasure. At the start of my second three-day shift, he had caught me taking a drink from the water cooler. In most other working environments this would not usually be judged a transgression, and it was my first break of the day at around eleven in the morning. I had paused with the cup in my hand and was staring out of the back door onto the small alleyway, my mind untroubled by thought. Some minutes might have passed, I can't be sure, but I looked up to see Lecerf standing in front of me, glaring with gimlet eyes. '*Bonjour, monsieur,*' he said. This might *sound* like an innocuous greeting, but it is impossible to convey the sense of disdain with which he freighted these two words. I felt as if he had caught me wolfing down the desserts while the patisserie chef's back was turned. I put the cup in the bin and hurried back to the *garde manger*, trying my best to look purposeful.

Worse Lecerf-themed news awaited me back in *garde manger*. Apparently he had complained to Carlos that I was leaving the kitchen at the end of my shifts without asking his permission. This, it turns out, is a grievous faux pas in a professional kitchen: I might just as well have mooned him. So I made a point of approaching Lecerf at the end of that evening to shake hands and say goodbye. Without looking up he grunted and, with an impatient jerk of his head, asked gruffly, 'Have you cleaned up properly back there?' meaning the *garde manger*. I know it was naïve of me to have expected it, but there was no word of thanks at the end of the day, or even an acknowledgement of any kind that I had just worked twelve hours for him, for free. Instead, as happened every day, he made me feel like I was the one who should be grateful for being allowed to work in his kitchen, which I suppose was hard to argue with.

But the punishing hours and the oppressive atmosphere weren't the only challenges of working at L'Atelier. Though there were several women, not to mention several very camp waiters working there, the mood was resolutely masculine. That's fine for some, but I've never really been good at machismo, I don't know the rules and it's not something I am able to fake convincingly. But the kitchen was awash with the stuff, blended with a heady cocktail of adrenalin and testosterone. The clichéd alpha male chef act we have all seen on TV is, perhaps, an inevitable, unavoidable reaction from men who have to wear aprons, fuss over their quenelles and primp chervil all day. Perhaps this is why they feel they have to work absurd hours in hostile conditions, treat each other like apes and bare their knife scars and burns with stoic pride. But is it the environment that informs their behaviour, or do professional kitchens simply attract certain types of people? I don't know. What I did know was that I didn't fit in.

I decided to confront Carlos. The next day, my second Friday at the restaurant, I cornered him in the *garde manger* and told him how unreasonable I thought it was that I had been thrown into the deep end without any training or even explanation of the how the dishes were composed. I felt that the unwritten contract between a restaurant and a *stagière* implied that, though I might chop tomatoes for most of the day, in return the restaurant might take the trouble to give me some training in return. It turned out that he hadn't even known I was a *stagière*. He thought I was a paid *commis chef*. I was secretly flattered by this, but he went on to say that it didn't make much difference as this is how it was, and I would have to deal with it.

'It is the same for everyone,' he said.

'Yes, but, if you'd just explain a few things to me I could help you much better and you wouldn't have to get cross all the time,' I said.

'I'm not cross, it just gets very stressful out there and I don't have the time.'

Kitchens are harsh environments, of course, and as I've said Robuchon's has a reputation to uphold. I suspect that until more women enter the trade that is how it will stay. As it is, each generation of cooks abuses the next, until they themselves take over and reap vengeance on the ones who follow. Marco Pierre White, for instance, recalls in his autobiography that when he began working in a restaurant in Harrogate as a teenager the other chefs never called him by his proper name, they simply yelled 'where's the c**t?' (I got off lightly being called 'Michel'). White perpetuated that abrasive management style and passed it on to Gordon Ramsay who by all accounts is breeding his own new army of angry and short-fused cooks. Chefs frequently employ military terminology to describe what they do – the staff are a 'brigade'; they 'take hits' when orders come in, and so on – BUT IT'S ONLY FOOD! It's *not* life or death, it's a bit of meat or fish cooked over a flame with some boiled vegetables and a sauce. Can't we all be a bit more *civil* about things?

Though things had begun to get easier by my second week, every time I walked through to the front kitchen my stomach would churn with fear. Far from being that little rubber door button was like a brake pedal the accelerator in a car with no brakes: the doors would swing open and I would find myself back in the spotlight. But, like a barefoot man crossing a darkened room strewn with mousetraps, slowly, by painful trial and error, I began to figure out how the dishes were assembled. Lecerf would mumble the orders, and if the others were already busy prepping it would be up to me to respond and, increasingly, I was doing just that: plating dishes, placing them on the pass where they would fall under Lecerf's scrutiny, before being picked up by the waiters and deposited in front of diners.

That Friday afternoon I spent another coupe of hours smashing lobster claws, retrieving the meat in one perfect, claw-shaped piece and removing the thin, plastic-like cartilage from deep within. Next, Xavier showed me how to prepare the lettuces, clipping them like hedges until all of the green leaves were removed and only the sweet, juicy heart remained. Carlos wasn't impressed with the time it took me to fillet some beef for a *tartare* however: 'Come on, Michel. Accelerate. Just because you are a *stagière* doesn't mean you can't work fast!' he yelled. I seethed silently to myself, but then I spotted someone using some mayonnaise – *my* mayonnaise – on a club sandwich, and a gust of achievement filled my sails.

Within three shifts I had worked in *garde manger*, *poisson* and *viande* – all of the kitchen's sections apart from patisserie (for which I was thankful – I asked another *stagière*, a Japanese student who was working in patisserie, what the chef was like. He made the universal 'He's mad' sign). I'd chopped and diced everything there was to chop and dice; I'd helped trim racks of milk-fed lamb and watched over the stock pots alongside Yusuf, the Algerian philosophy student; I had prepared the *palourdes* (clams) with parsley butter; I had made the asparagus cream soup, from scratch, all by myself; and I had filleted a mountain of sardines for the fish chef (an interminable job: as with the heads of the Hydra, the bones of sardines grow back as you are removing them).

Of all the staff at L'Atelier I found Gouki, the Japanese fish chef, the most difficult to understand. His French seemed to emerge, horrifically mangled, from somewhere deep in his bowels. Simple words like *plonge* (chopping board) sounded like the death cry of a samurai.

'Moo! Moo!' he shouted at me, as I sliced some baby fennel for him on a mandolin. 'I'm sorry? Moo, you say?' I asked, confused. 'Moo! Moo!' After some more mooing, a Korean stepped in as a go-between. 'I think he means *moules*,' she said. A little later Gouki pointed towards a crate of live lobsters. 'Santet!' he said. *Sans têtes*. Heads off. He showed me how, ripping the head from the creature while it was still alive, and motioned that I should complete the task. Where was Christine when I needed her? I clenched my teeth and looked away as I dispatched each one, their desperate juices splattering over my uniform. With their dismembered corpses still twitching, the chef instructed me to seal the lobsters' heads in the *sous vide* machine, then put them in the freezer. Anakin Skywalker was turned to the dark side by less.

My proudest moment during my *stage* also came that Sunday afternoon when I was summoned to the front kitchen and told to make the mash potato. As I have mentioned, Robuchon's *purée de pommes de terre* is one of the most famous and controversial side dishes in the restaurant world. It has been called 'the dish that helped make his reputation', and is a heroic riposte to politically correct dietary fads, a gloriously luxurious, unctuous dish with enough calories to fuel a Sumo wrestler for a week. I knew what the ingredients were – every foodie does – his 50:50 potatoes and butter combination is legendary and, again, ridiculously simple, but I had eaten this mash before and there was something otherworldly about it, something that I had found impossible to replicate at home. Now I would discover the secret.

Purée de Pommes de Terre

Ingredients (makes enough for 6 people)

1kg potatoes – most people recommend potatoes that are floury and high in starch like King Edwards although on this occasion I noticed that Robuchon used *rattes* which are smaller and more waxy

Salt

1kg butter – chilled, unsalted, the best quality you can find

100ml full-fat milk

Wash the potatoes well, then cut them into regular chunks. Bring them almost to the boil from cold and simmer gently until well cooked – around twenty-five minutes. (Heston Blumenthal prefers to roast his potatoes in their skins and then scoop out the potato, which really intensifies the potato flavour). Halfway through, add a generous amount of salt. Drain, let them cool a little, and then peel. Now, mill the potatoes using a ricer and after that push the potatoes through a drum sieve with a plastic scraper into a warm pan, stirring to dry out any excess water. Though you may be tempted, do not resort to using a food processor as you will release the starch from the potatoes and end up with glue. Cut the chilled butter into large chunks. Heat the milk in another pan, add the milled potatoes and begin to stir vigorously – ease off on the whisking and the potatoes will catch and burn on the bottom of the pan. Add the butter piece by piece, waiting until the first piece melts before adding the next, and continue to stir as vigorously as you can until either all the butter is incorporated or you have a stroke. Now take a whisk to the mixture. Imagine you are whipping cream; you want the potato mix to be stiff but light. Rivulets will be running down your forehead by this point, but it will be worth the effort. Keep the purée warm in a porcelain mixing bowl over a bain-marie. You can add a little more milk and butter if it dries out before you have a chance to serve it.

Later that night, in the front kitchen Carlos had to fill in for missing personnel on the fish station. Xavier, Ick Yong and I would have to prepare the starters by ourselves. I had really begun to get the hang of things by this point and knew most of the starters well. I knew in which order to layer the vegetable *millefeuille* (drizzle olive oil on the sun-dried tomatoes and mozzarella slices, season them, then layer a fried aubergine slice, mozzarella slice, fried courgette slice on top of each other. Do this twice and top with the sun-dried tomato, bunched up with a basil leaf sticking from the top, and serve with a question mark-shaped dollop of pesto); I knew how to arrange the lobster carpaccio and create the pretty anchovy and red pepper dish that looked the flag of some obscure South American nation (alternating strips of anchovy and steamed red pepper layered over a base of sliced, roasted aubergine). I knew where everything was and how most of it went together.

That night, from the supercharged moment when Lecerf announced the first orders, we danced, Xavier, Ick Yong and I, like swallows swooping for flies in the dusk; circling and reaching, bending, sprinkling, tossing, chopping and squirting. I was finally listening, *understanding* Lecerf's orders and responding without being told what to do. I felt like part of the team. I am sure I was still getting in their way as much as I was helping them but, by the end Xavier was beaming and even Ick Yong allowed herself a modest smile. I was wired on adrenalin but unlike Xavier who was clearly having the time of his life, mine was fear-based – fear of getting it wrong, fear of failing the diners, fear of invoking Lecerf's wrath and the disappointment of my colleagues.

I had survived, but I had my fill of fear.

I am familiar with the redemptive potential of the kitchen narrative, the story of the new arrival's initial struggles, and the hardship conquered by grit and determination leading to mastery of one's chosen métier. But this is not one of those tales. After that night I finished my *stage* and never returned to L'Atelier Joël Robuchon.

A dream of a kind was over, but at least I had been given the chance to discover that my dream was, in reality, some kind of interminable Escher-esque nightmare. Deep within me I knew from my first morning at L'Atelier that my future did not lie in a professional kitchen, but it took a couple of incidents to draw the reality into a sharper focus.

One morning I was standing in the *garde manger* watching Carlos make some foie gras ravioli (using pre-prepared rice pasta sheets from a packet) and awaiting further instructions. 'Don't stand like that,' he scolded. 'You look like a tourist with your arms folded like that.'

What the hell does it matter how I stand when the customers can't see me? I thought to myself. But later, thinking it over, I realised that he was exactly right. I was a tourist.

Earlier that same day I had found out how much Xavier was paid. 'One thousand two hundred euro after tax,' he told me, without looking up from his chopping board. I did a quick calculation – he worked seventeen hours a day, four days a week; that was seventy hours a week – equal to seventeen euro per hour. 'Well, that's not too bad for a week,' I said. I had hardly seen Xavier smile, let alone laugh up, until that point, but he laughed long and loud at this. 'Not a week, that's for a month! Hey Carlos, Michel just asked if we earn one thousand two hundred euro a week! Ha, ha, ha.' He could hardly contain his mirth, but Carlos – who actually earned a little more at one thousand nine hundred – didn't smile.

Earning just over four euro an hour, less than a McDonald's trainee or a parking meter, didn't seem in any way to diminish the enthusiasm with which Xavier approached his work. At the beginning of each service he would clench his fists and hold them out front of his chest to psych himself up and shimmy a little, like a boxer about to enter the ring. 'I love to make the cuisine,' he told me during a rare moment of introspection. 'I love the *rapide* – tak-tak-tak!' I suspect he would have done all this for free – as I was – just for the buzz and the experience of working at L'Atelier.

Even jaded, blasé Carlos still wanted to climb that ladder and cheered up considerably when he was asked to fill in on the fish station. But as for me, I dreaded the service part of the day. I hated the stress, the high-wire act of it all. Seeing the whites of the customers' eyes as they waited hungrily, impatiently, for me to remember whether the chervil or the tarragon leaves went first on the lobster carpaccio made things awfully tense. I also found it frustrating that, in a restaurant, you rarely get to make a whole dish, let alone a whole meal, from start to finish. Restaurants are, for the most part, production lines, L'Atelier in particular. As Yuri said one day as we chopped our way through yet another mountain of tomatoes, 'It's like McDonald's, but with better ingredients.'

The final tipping point came during what turned out to be my last lunch service at the end of my second week. I had just prepared three lobster carpaccios, sprinkling some ground pepper over fine slices of lobster tail, drizzling some lobster dressing, carefully plucking three sprigs of chervil, two of dill and two leaves of tarragon and placing them on top, with a squirt more dressing to finish. I looked up at the faces of the diners sitting around me and, suddenly, finally, everything came into focus: I at last understood the subconscious unease, a nagging feeling that I had been unable to isolate and understand during all those hours working in a professional kitchen.

Looking up at the faces of the diners, I realised why working in a restaurant kitchen was not my destiny. Obviously, I would have rather been on the other side of the counter eating the food, that's a given. But it was more than that. Until I arrived at L'Atelier I had never cooked for strangers before and it didn't feel right. I didn't *know* these people, I had never met or even so much as spoken to them. The chefs I was working with were committed, driven and ambitious, but I could summon no such motivation. I was there out of choice, to see what it was like, and to prove to myself that I could function in that environment, and after a bit of a false start, I discovered that I could. They were there because they had no choice, this was their vocation. I tried. I tried to imagine working my way up through a kitchen over the next five years or so; the seventeen-hour days; the intense pressure of maintaining the highest of standards; the constant fear of mistake and failure; the competition among the *stagières*; and, you know what? I couldn't imagine it. They were younger, fitter, more hungry and prepared to work for peanuts. And there was something else that differentiated me from the other *stagières* and chefs I had been working with: they were fixated on the process, while I was intoxicated by the end result. I never once heard any of the chefs get excited about what they were making, or marvel at the quality of the produce. They didn't seem terribly interested in food, in questioning what they were doing. They were so focused on their own responsibilities that the end result – pleasing the diner – seemed almost irrelevant to them.

All my adult life I had enjoyed making food for people I liked, knew and loved. Like most English males I am not very good at expressing emotions or fondness for people. Making food was my way of showing people I loved them. As trite as that sounds, it is the truth. I remembered something Depardieu had written in the foreword to his book: 'The art of cooking and preparing a meal to share with those you care about is also, for me, a means of communicating that love and friendship without necessarily having to utter a single word.' And I thought about the chemist Hervé This and his research into love as the intangible yet crucial component of good food. The guests at L'Atelier were, I'm sure, lovely people, but they weren't *my* lovely people and, ultimately, it meant nothing to me to cook for them.

Chapter 35

Once you understand the foundations of cooking – whatever kind
you like, whether it's French or Italian or Japanese – you really don't
need a cookbook any more.

Thomas Keller

Am I a quitter? There is no doubt in my mind that, yes, I am. I'm
a quitter, and I'm proud. When the going gets tough, my primal
instinct is to try to find a short cut, and I am not sure there is all
that much shame in that. After all, is not quitting merely an acknowledgement of one's limitations, a survival instinct of sorts? Okay, no.
Quitting is abject failure jazzed up as self-assertion. But what kind
of brainless ninny would repeatedly place himself in a situation that
made him thoroughly miserable, day in, day out, without a penny
payment? I did exactly that for a while of course, but only for as
long as it took me to realise, and properly assure myself, that this
was not to be my future career path and that I was just being a
foolish old fart. I could have kept going, but once you have plumbed
the depths of your folly and realisation has dawned, it is difficult to
maintain the façade and plough on regardless, unless you are a
complete imbecile or a politician.

So, naturally, a few weeks after leaving L'Atelier I began to have
second thoughts about turning my back on restaurant kitchens
forever. I began to positively *yearn* to go back to work in one, just,
you know, to make *sure*. What if L'Atelier was the exception? What
if other restaurants fostered a better team spirit, were nicer and more
interesting to work in? Hadn't I perhaps been a little hasty? Didn't
I still have so much to learn about restaurant cooking?

I talked to friends about doing a *stage* at another restaurant. Henrique and Tessa both recommended Jacques Cagna, a well-established classical French restaurant in Saint-Germain, much more my kind of thing they said. Lissen and I had lunch there in its sombre, lavish dining room surrounded by nineteenth-century oil paintings and attended by a black-aproned sommelier. It was a heavy, complex, satisfying kind of menu – Jacques Cagna is known for its fish and shellfish but it also featured meaty heavyweights like pig's feet stuffed with truffles, roasted wild duck with celery purée and crème de cassis, snails, terrines, foie gras in various forms, and so on – exactly the kind of food I had come to Paris to eat and cook. Afterwards I asked the manager about the possibility of doing a *stage*, mentioning that I knew Tessa and Henrique, who had both worked there. She called for the chef, who came up to the dining room and introduced himself. I explained that I had graduated from Le Cordon Bleu and had been working at L'Atelier but wanted to work in a more traditional haute cuisine kitchen. Yes, said the chef, a short, dark stocky man in his mid-thirties, I was welcome to come and work in the kitchen, I could start the following Monday.

I arrived at nine thirty and walked into the small, ground-floor kitchen, which was almost entirely taken up with an ancient red and gold Molteni stove. On one side worked the *viande* chefs – two friendly, quiet Japanese men, to whom the chef introduced me. I was to work on the other side of the stove with the *poissonier*, a Sri Lankan named Bala. The *garde manger* chef and his *stagière* assistant worked in the corner of the kitchen beside the *plongeur,* while the chef played a kind of roaming midfielder role during prep time, stationing himself by the dumb waiter during service where he would assemble and dress the plates on a piece of patterned carpet, which he would unroll from beside one of the ovens and cover with a fresh, white linen table cloth.

Bala was kindly, patient and polite; he was also faintly amused that I wanted to work in the kitchen in the first place, but eager for me to become a fully integrated member of the brigade as soon as possible. Because of my age, I suspect he thought me to be more experienced than I was and within minutes of me arriving he slapped the largest turbot I had ever seen on the chopping board in front of me. 'You know how to fillet this?' I nodded. I love filleting fish and, even if I say it myself, I was by that stage really quite good at it. I set to work and did a fine job. 'I think you know a little about cuisine, no?' Bala said approvingly. My heart swelled.

My next task, simply to accept a bag of macaroni being passed across the stove – already crammed with bubbling pots of stock and water – did not go so well. I hadn't realised that the bag was open and the macaroni went everywhere. The chef witnessed this and I braced myself for a tirade, but instead of exploding as Carlos might have, he smiled and shrugged. '*Ce n'est pas grave,*' he said, and helped me pick them up.

Jacques Cagna is the antithesis of fashionable Paris eateries like L'Atelier and, perhaps because of this, its kitchen was relaxed and easy going. Delivery men, waiting staff, *voituriers* (the valet parking guys) and friends and family of the chef would wander in and out throughout the day. People – the chef included – smoked; downstairs in the cramped basement the pastry chef listened to Metallica on his tiny stereo; there were jokes and friendly jibes and not a hint of pretentiousness or ego. Even at the height of our busiest service hour, there was neither tension nor stress. Despite the chilled vibe, the food was superb. It is true the decor was looking a little jaded and the menu was perhaps in need of freshening up, but to judge by the care the chef lavished on his plates and the lengths the *viande* chefs took to prepare their stocks and meats (I saw them take an entire week to make a hare terrine, for instance) it looked like they were actively seeking – and deserved – a second Michelin star. And, anyway, the restaurant still has two Eiffel Towers in the Lebey Paris restaurant guide – which is a more useful reference if it is good food, rather than all the frills and fripperies of classic Michelin service, you are after.

In stark contrast to my time at L'Atelier, I began each day at

Jacques Cagna excited and keen to work and learn, and learn I did. Bala always took the time to explain how each dish was made and let me work alongside him during service right from the start. He trusted me to fry the cod steaks (reminding me that, to get a nice crispy skin, you should heat the pan, *then* add the oil, then the fish, moving it around at the start of cooking to ensure it doesn't stick), and to prepare lobsters, then cook them too. I was cooking things! Over actual flames! Leaping, scary flames! Medieval flames – for this was, truly, a medieval, flame-fired kitchen (Hervé This would have been appalled). It would become intolerably hot during service, my chef's whites would stick to my back within a quarter of an hour of arriving, but I loved it. I loved working properly with a team, creating gorgeous food and fulfilling my potential as a cook.

During the service orders would be taken upstairs by the waiters on small slips of paper, stuffed into short metal tubes and sent down from the first-floor dining room via a see-though plastic pipe into a small bucket (an old mustard tub) in the kitchen below. It was a Heath Robinson-style set up – the pipe was tied to the wall with string and a small metal plate had been placed in the bottom of the bucket so that the chef would be alerted to each new order. As each order landed it would make a loud clank, the rate of clanks-per-minute increasing during as service continued. In the middle of an unusually busy lunch service one day, with the orders ricocheting like the bullets from Ned Kelly's helmet, I rushed down into the basement to retrieve some more pigeon carcasses from the fridge (full of carefully preserved poultry carcasses – a reminder of how precious bones are to the French kitchen). As I turned the corner at the bottom of the narrow, spiral staircase I walked straight into the clenched fist of the *plongeur*, a gigantic African on the scale of Michael Clarke Duncan in *The Green Mile*. It was an accident and, fortunately, my stomach preceded me and took the full force of the blow, but I buckled up, winded. He looked mortified, picked me up and gave me a great big hug. He kept on hugging for at least a minute until I was able to persuade him that I was okay and he released me from his crushing, but well-intended squeeze.

At around eleven in the morning all the staff would convene for the staff meal in the downstairs dining room and sit, mostly in silence, slurping down great platefuls of pasta and meat sauce. Afterwards we usually had a few minutes to get some air. I treasured these moments wandering in the street outside – the rue des Grands-Augustins where Picasso had painted *Guernica* – dressed in my chef's whites, nodding to chefs from other restaurants as they too took their breaks.

One day during my break I popped into Ze Kitchen Galerie, a cool fusion restaurant a few doors down from Jacques Cagna. I had tried several times to make a reservation over the phone but, as one of the city's trendier venues, it had proved impossible. In person, dressed in my chef's whites, however, it was no problem at all. Of course they had a table: when for?

When Lissen and I and two friends turned up for the reservation the next evening, I was treated like an old friend by the maître d' and given four complimentary glasses of champagne. I felt as if I had joined, if only for a brief part of my life, some secret brotherhood of Parisian chefs.

But it was to be brief, I was sure of that. Ultimately, though my stint at Jacques Cagna had been so much more enjoyable and rewarding than the one at L'Atelier, it had still been a relief to learn that this world of heat and toil, of endless mind-numbing days and frantic nights, was not for me. Kitchen life, at least full-time, long-term kitchen life, is hardly compatible with having a young family. To enter a restaurant kitchen is to say goodbye to your own kin, and to join a new kitchen family. I have spoken to several chefs, including a couple at Le Cordon Bleu, and their stories are all the same as far as their family lives were concerned – they were all divorced, they had seen little of their children growing up, their families were strangers, distant, unfathomable. One told me he had three children. 'That must be great at Christmas,' I said. 'Not really, we are so different, I don't really know them and they don't really respect me,' he said with a shrug.

I know many people join the catering trade precisely because they want to get away from their families, or in some cases because they have no families; their familial bonds are welded in the heat of a thousand lunch and dinner services. But I quite like the family I have and, most of the time, they are charitable enough to give the impression of quite liking me. Though it had been necessary for me to try it to make sure, the life of a professional chef had probably never really an option. I was just too dumb to realise it beforehand.

I had at least picked up a few closely guarded restaurant secrets. I knew, of course, that some of the food that ends up on your plate has been prepared way in advance – it has to be – but I was taken aback by how much of the menu is prepared and sometimes cooked hours, even days before. In both of the kitchens I worked in every fridge was filled with countless Tupperware boxes and clingfilm parcels squirreled away ready for the call from the waiters that they had been selected for consumption. A reheat on the stove top, a vigorous stir or a blast with the immersion blender and some plating magic and no one was any the wiser, and nor need they be. I saw little that caused me any concern about hygiene and though, of course, food made *à la minute* will always taste better than a reheat, with dishes of this quality it doesn't matter quite as much that the food wasn't entirely fresh and, besides, part of the job of front of house is to add value to the food with service and theatre. That, and the huge amounts of salt and butter, is why food just tastes better in restaurants.

I had also learned about the secret materials and tools of the professional kitchen. They use vast quantities of kitchen towels; tea towels; pure alcohol for cleaning; metal bowls; cigarettes; coffee; plastic wrap; and ice cubes, ice being just as vital as fire for, among other things, stopping vegetables from overcooking when they are removed from boiling water. And, of course, good stocks are an essential, and the stockpot rightly remains the focal point of all French restaurant kitchens.

To announce my retirement from the restaurant business, shortly after I finished at Jacques Cagna I held a dinner party. I invited all those who had been present at the book burning back in England, plus some of the new friends I had made during the last year – there were fourteen of us in all.

Earlier in the day I visited the market and bought whatever had caught my eye – a pumpkin straight from *Halloween* central casting; some small, fresh goat's cheese *crottins*; a kilo of end-of-season wild mushrooms; a rack of lamb; and a punnet of fresh raspberries.

That afternoon, I made a pumpkin soup, adding some honey at the end (the secret ingredient of the pumpkin soup *amuse bouche* I had made at Jacques Cagna), and served it with a dollop of sour cream with chopped chives in the middle. I served the goat's cheese cooked in a puff pastry case with a thyme and onion confit; I served the lamb chops sandwiched between a pistachio and chicken mousse 'stuffing' and wrapped in a crispy *warka* dough with the bone sticking out and tied with blanched parsley stalks, on a white bean purée, with sautéed mushrooms and some fresh and crunchy *haricots verts* from Joël Thibault. For dessert I made an eggtastic raspberry clafoutis with pistachio crème anglais; and with coffee I served some salty chocolate *ganaches* that I had made with *sel de guèrande*.

I am not a chef, nor will I ever be, but I am proud to say I did it all without using a single recipe.

Maybe, in a few years, I'll be able to get away with calling myself a cook.

Epilogue

What the French know about cooking

Looking back over this book, correcting all the mistakes my editor had pointed out and reigning in the adjectives, it occurred to me that if you cut away all the stuff about me and what I thought about things, this book has at its heart a few points which, cobbled together, add up to some kind of manifesto, a cooking creed if you like.

The main points are as follows, (you're going to kick yourself for not skipping straight to this):

* Don't keep it simple, try complicated once in a while. I know simplicity in cooking is fashionable right now, but it won't always be so. I hope we return to complexity, to more mucking about with food, but in a good way. I don't mean that we should be wrapping things in caul fat and cabbage every night (once a lifetime is probably enough), and I don't mean fussy food for fussy's sake, but a good stock will, for instance, make a great sauce which will lift a good piece of meat or fish that has been cooked simply and gently to restaurant standards. And a great potato purée, fine and silky, is a joy for ever. Let's be clear about this: good food doesn't happen in a trice, most of the time it isn't easy or straightforward. If it is on the table in ten minutes, I'll wager it's either crap or salad, and not a very good salad at that. Good food requires effort, but the plate should appear effortless; a chef should be a swan, paddling furiously beneath the water, while all above remains serene.

* Molecular gastronomy is wonderful, dazzling, funny and clever but you've got to know the rules of cooking in order to break them without anyone getting hurt/having to eat broccoli ice cream. And, if we are being pedantic, isn't all cooking 'molecular'? Doesn't all cooking rearrange molecules?

* Brownings in the pan are not just a by-product, or something that makes washing up more of a chore. They are one of the greatest flavour enhancers in the world. A crusty pan should be your goal every time you set out to make a great sauce.

* And don't forget, you don't want non-stick pans, you want 'stick' pans. Teflon is the work of the Devil.

* Olive oil is for dressings. Use peanut oil to fry in, with a bit of butter if you dare. It will taste better and will reach the necessary temperature. Keep it away from the mayonnaise too.

* Listen to your pans. If they are sizzling they are trying to tell you something.

* In terms of knives, all you need is one really big, sharp knife; one really sharp, small knife; and a potato peeler. Nothing else. None of our chefs used the special, bendy-bladed fish knives for filleting fish, for instance. They all made do with normal, rigid-bladed kitchen knives, which work better.

* In terms of other equipment you might not find in a normal kitchen, you will need a fine sieve or chinois; perhaps a drum sieve if you are a bit neurotic about your purées; a ricer; meat and oven thermometers; a good blender and a mandolin. That's about it.

* Observing the season's bounty is all very well if you live near a good farmer's market, or in France, but for everyone else it is not so straightforward. Even if you do live near a good market, you will still find January to March awfully bleak if you adhere to this

philosophy. So, yes, if you can it is great to buy locally grown stuff fresh from the soil or tree, but if you work a little harder at transforming what ingredients are available, you can achieve miracles.

* Don't worry, it's not you. Recipes don't work.

* In my opinion, chefs spend a disproportionate amount of time fussing with chervil, a herb whose sole purpose in life is to make ladies go 'ah' when the plate is placed in front of them. Meanwhile I still have yet to fully understand why we go through all that trouble with artichokes. Are they really worth it?

* Taste what you are cooking at every stage of the process, right up until you serve it. Brian Clough used to say that it only took a second to score a goal, similarly, it only takes a second for a sauce to ruin.

* Rest roasted meat for half the time you cook it. It has been through a lot.

* If you are designing your own kitchen, the first thing you should add is a shelf above the stove, preferably one made from slatted steel to let the air circulate. It is the perfect resting place for meat.

* Leaving a sauce unthickened takes great courage. Even if your guests look confused by the lack of body, maintain your composure. You will have taken the higher ground and, given time, they will come to regard you as a pioneer.

* Few things can make you feel as smug as having a supply of clarified butter in the fridge.

* Shellfish can't feel pain. If you know different, please don't write in.

* The two best things you can do to streamline your food preparation are to put some wet kitchen paper under your chopping board and have a rubbish bowl on the worktop.

* Children really only need sugar and fat to function properly. Tea cakes ought to do it, but if they begin to look peaky, a burger or two should do the trick. They'll come round to vegetables eventually, when they are so constipated they can hardly walk and their skin is so bad they look like they have leprosy.

* If you are spending more time matching your Kitchenaid to your kettle to your cupboards than you are cooking, something is very wrong.

* If anyone can figure out a way to sell flour in bags that don't leak – which, to be frank, we really ought to have mastered by now, what with having landed on the moon and invented the microprocessor – they will be set for life.

* Unless you plan, it is remarkably easy to eat badly in Paris.

* Some food really is worth the price of a second-hand car.

* There are worse things in the world than chocolate-covered strawberries.

Acknowledgements

The chefs of Le Cordon Bleu may feel they have created a monster, nevertheless I would like to express my deepest gratitude to them for all they have taught me. I might have disagreed with their methods from time to time – not to mention their use of pre-grated cheese – but their knowledge and experience would humble all but the greatest of French chefs. (And, just in case you are wondering, I should make it clear that no one at the school – not the chefs, the school administration or even my fellow students – knew I would write a book about my experience and I paid my own way just like everyone else.)

To my family, Lissen, Asger and Emil, I thank you from my heart for supporting me throughout this extraordinary year. I know it wasn't always easy and I apologise in advance for any health issues that may arise in the future as a result of the vast quantities of cream and red meat you were required to eat during the course of my education, but I could not have done it – and would not have wanted to do it – without you.

Without my fellow students – Sarah, Tessa, Christine, Hayden, Andy, Dingbang, Henrique and Jamie among them – to share my time with at Le Cordon Bleu, the experience would not have been remotely as enjoyable as it turned out to be.

Thanks to my publisher Dan Franklin for his continued faith in my hare-brained schemes; to my agent, Camilla Hornby, for helping make said schemes seem slightly less hare-brained; and to my editor, Ellah Allfrey, for preventing me from making even more of a fool of myself than I might otherwise have done.

I would also like to thank Mahie and Niels Oluf Kyed for their local knowledge and incredible generosity while in Provence, as well, of course, as the kitchen staff of Jacques Cagna and L'Atelier Joël Robuchon who were, in truth, far more patient with me than I ever deserved.

Finally thanks, too, to my mother, for planting the seed of my love of food and cooking. The more I cook, the more I realise how much you taught me.

Michael Booth
Paris, 2007

Index